See the WIDER picture

Red roofs of Dubrovnik, Croatia

Dubrovnik's old town area has many houses and buildings with bright red roofs, strong city walls and beautiful palaces and churches. In 1667 a huge earthquake almost destroyed the whole town and killed more than 5000 people. Today, Dubrovnik is one of the most popular places for tourists in the Mediterranean Sea.

What are the most beautiful cities and towns in your country?

Course Map

Your Student's Book comes with access to:

▶ The Student's eBook

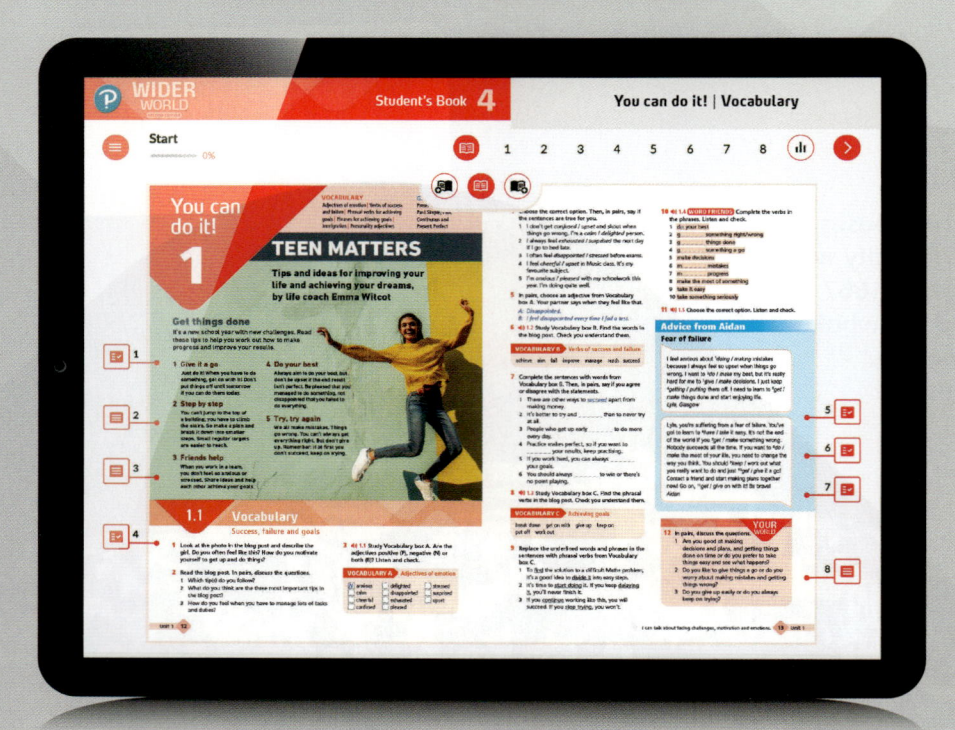

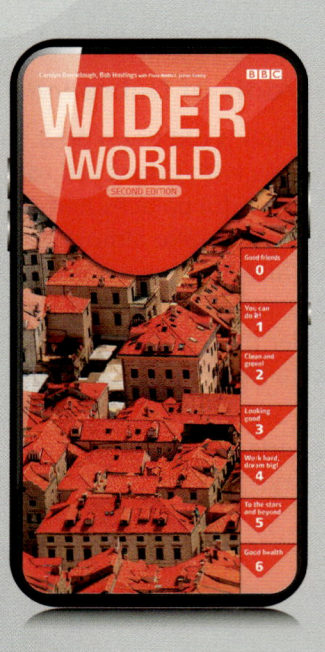

Audio, video and interactive activities with instant marking bring the content of the Student's Book to life in the eBook. It includes everything you need to participate in online lessons.

Wider World Second Edition is fully accessible on your computer, tablet and mobile phone. You can enjoy the full functionality of your course wherever you are.

You can access your digital components through the Pearson English Portal. See the inside front cover for access details.

Classroom Lessons

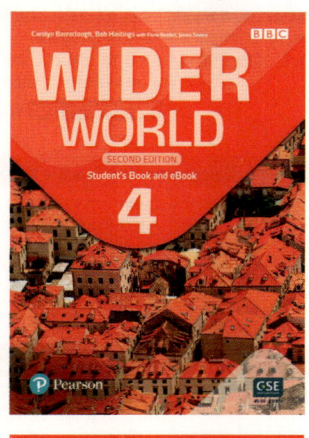

Student's Book

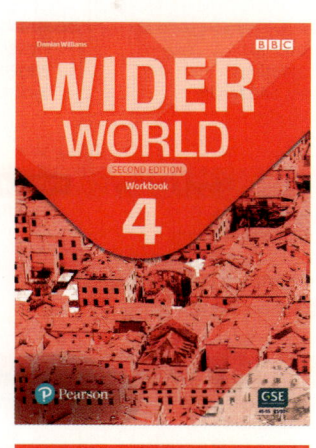

Workbook

Online Lessons

eBook

Homework

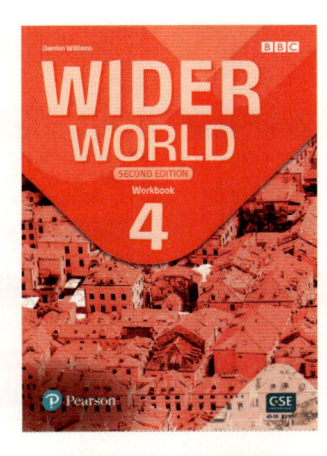

Workbook

Contents

Unit				
Good friends 0	**0.1 Catching up with Bea** Relationships | Present Simple | Adverbs of frequency | Wh- questions | School | Comparatives and superlatives pp. 6–7		**0.2 Catching up with Eren** Present Continuous | Using everyday technology p. 8	
	Vocabulary	**Grammar**	**Reading and Vocabulary**	**Grammar**
You can do it! 1	Success, failure and goals: • Adjectives of emotion • Verbs of success and failure • Achieving goals pp. 12–13	• Present tenses (Present Simple, Present Continuous, state and dynamic verbs) p. 14	*New beginnings* An article about starting a new life in Canada BBC VIDEO Wider World p. 15	• Past Simple, Past Continuous and Present Perfect BBC VIDEO Wider World p. 16
	BBC CULTURE *Tough journeys*	VIDEO *An almost impossible journey*		Visible thinking: Why do you say that?
Clean and green! 2	Protecting the environment • Talking about the environment • Compound nouns: the environment • Protecting and damaging the environment BBC VIDEO Wider World pp. 24–25	• Past Perfect p. 26	*Leave no trace* A story about a hike in the countryside p. 27	• *Used to* and Past Simple p. 28
	SET FOR LIFE Self-management Develop a growth mindset *Open your mind* pp. 34–35			
Looking good 3	Clothes and appearance • Clothes and accessories • Describing clothes and accessories • Appearance pp. 36–37	• Present Perfect Continuous p. 38	*Fresh trends* An article about trends in fashion p. 39	• Present Perfect Simple and Continuous BBC VIDEO Wider World p. 40
	BBC CULTURE *A closer look at fashion*	VIDEO *The price of fashion*		Visible thinking: Think, Pair, Share
Work hard, dream big! 4	Work and jobs • Jobs, work • Working conditions BBC VIDEO Wider World pp. 50–51	• Talking about the future (*will, be going to*, Present Continuous, Present Simple) p. 52	*Training for work with virtual reality* An article about virtual reality training p. 53	• Future Continuous BBC VIDEO Wider World p. 54
	SET FOR LIFE Communication Make a good first impression *A job interview* pp. 60–61			
To the stars and beyond 5	Space • Space • Dimensions and distance • Large numbers pp. 62–63	• Zero, First and Second Conditionals BBC VIDEO Wider World p. 64	*Stars in their eyes* An article about space tourism p. 65	• Third Conditional BBC VIDEO Wider World p. 66
	BBC CULTURE *Pushing the limits*	VIDEO *Exploring the unknown*		Visible thinking: Consider different viewpoints
Good health 6	Sickness and health • Health problems • First aid kit • Word building: health and illness BBC VIDEO Wider World pp. 74–75	• Reported statements and questions p. 76	*Healthy and happy?* An article about health apps p. 77	• Reported commands and requests p. 78
	SET FOR LIFE Social responsibility Make a difference *Take action!* pp. 84–85			
Beyond words 7	Communication and body language • Effective communication and body language • Word building: communication BBC VIDEO Wider World pp. 88–89	• The passive p. 90	*April Fool's Day in the media* An article about April Fool's jokes p. 91	• The passive with *will* p. 92
	BBC CULTURE *How languages evolve*	VIDEO *Keeping languages alive*		Visible thinking: Connect, Extend, Challenge
Experience art 8	Art and literature • Visual arts • Describing art • Literature and books BBC VIDEO Wider World pp. 100–101	• Modal verbs for ability (*can, could, be able to, manage to*) p. 102	*Express yourself!* An article about a young artist p. 103	• Modal verbs for obligation and prohibition (*must, have to, can't, mustn't, not be allowed to*) p. 104
	SET FOR LIFE Critical thinking Think critically *Good thinking!* pp. 110–111			
Party time! 9	Celebrations • Celebrations and special occasions • Types of celebration BBC VIDEO Wider World pp. 112–113	• Defining and non-defining relative clauses p. 114	*Ideas for celebrating turning eighteen* Short texts about birthdays BBC VIDEO Wider World p. 115	• Direct and indirect questions p. 116
	BBC CULTURE *Festivals for Generation Z*	VIDEO *Two different festivals*		Visible thinking: See, Think, Wonder

GRAMMAR TIME pp. 126–134   **IRREGULAR VERBS** p. 135   **STUDENT ACTIVITIES** pp. 136–137, 142

0.3 Catching up with Carla Holidays and travel | Past Simple | Transport p. 9	**0.4 Catching up with Abe** Hobbies and free time activities | Present Perfect | *For* and *since* p. 10	**0.5 Revision** p. 11		

Listening and Vocabulary	Speaking	Writing	Revision	Progress Check
A conversation about projection mapping p. 17	VIDEO *Do you need a hand?* Asking for and offering help SET FOR LIFE Self-management p. 18	A blog post describing a personal challenge • Verbs that express emotion p. 19	Vocabulary Activator p. 20 Revision p. 21	**1–3 pp. 48–49** • Vocabulary and Grammar: multiple choice, open cloze, transformations • Speaking: role play • Listening: note completion • Reading: gapped text • Writing: an email
Project: a digital poster about a desert pp. 22–23				
Conversations about elections, campaigns and the environment p. 29	VIDEO *You've got a point!* Agreeing and disagreeing BBC VIDEO Wider World SET FOR LIFE Social responsibility p. 30	A survey report • Quantifiers p. 31	Vocabulary Activator p. 32 Revision p. 33	
A conversation about the National Museum of Fashion BBC VIDEO Wider World p. 41	VIDEO *What a cool hat!* Giving and responding to compliments SET FOR LIFE Communication p. 42	An email describing appearance • Opinion adjectives p. 43	Vocabulary Activator p. 44 Revision p. 45	
Project: An infographic about fast fashion pp. 46–47				
A conversation between young entrepreneurs p. 55	VIDEO *Bea's news bulletin* Warnings, recommendations and prohibition SET FOR LIFE Self-management p. 56	A job application letter • Formal style p. 57	Vocabulary Activator p. 58 Revision p. 59	**1–6 pp. 86–87** • Vocabulary and Grammar: multiple choice, open cloze, word formation • Speaking: role play • Listening: text completion • Reading: multiple choice • Writing: a for and against essay
A radio programme about a record-breaking adventure p. 67	VIDEO *I hope it works* Instructions SET FOR LIFE Self-management p. 68	A for and against essay • Linkers of addition p. 69	Vocabulary Activator p. 70 Revision p. 71	
Project: An online advert for a day trip pp. 72–73				
A talk about extreme sports BBC VIDEO Wider World p. 79	VIDEO *I wish I could help!* Asking for and giving advice SET FOR LIFE Creativity p. 80	A forum post about an experience • Reporting verbs p. 81	Vocabulary Activator p. 82 Revision p. 83	
Conversations about advertising, promotion and marketing BBC VIDEO Wider World p. 93	VIDEO *What do you mean?* • Clarifying and rephrasing • Question tags SET FOR LIFE Communication p. 94	A review • Prepositional phrases p. 95	Vocabulary Activator p. 96 Revision p. 97	**1–9 pp. 124–125** • Vocabulary and Grammar: multiple choice, transformations, open cloze • Speaking: collaborative task • Listening: multiple choice • Reading: gapped text • Writing: an email
Project: A digital presentation about an endangered language pp. 98–99				
A conversation about a day as a newspaper journalist p. 105	VIDEO *This one is the best!* Comparing ideas and expressing opinions BBC VIDEO Wider World SET FOR LIFE Self-management p. 106	A comparison • Linkers of contrast p. 107	Vocabulary Activator p. 108 Revision p. 109	
A radio interview about fireworks p. 117	VIDEO *Sorry to bother you* Being polite SET FOR LIFE Communication p. 118	An informal invitation • Informal writing p. 119	Vocabulary Activator p. 120 Revision p. 121	
Project: A digital leaflet for a festival pp. 122–123				

CLIL ENVIRONMENT p. 138   ART AND DESIGN p. 139   SCIENCE p. 140   HISTORY p. 141

Good friends

0

VOCABULARY
Relationships | School | Using everyday technology | Holidays and travel | Transport | Hobbies and free time activities

GRAMMAR
Present Simple | Adverbs of frequency | *Wh-* questions | Comparatives and superlatives | Present Continuous | Past Simple | Present Perfect | *For* and *since*

Bea Baxter is sixteen. Bea and her cousin Abe Kerr live in New Park, near London. They usually get on really well and spend a lot of time together.

Abe's good at photography and his new hobby is baking. He likes hiking and cycling. His friend Eren King loves tennis and enjoys cycling with Abe although he sometimes has problems with his bike.

Bea and her best friend Carla Silva are classmates. They aren't neighbours, but Carla lives in the next street, so they often see each other. Carla likes acting and art. She has First Aid classes every week too. Bea doesn't do First Aid classes – she prefers to do gardening and programming in her free time.

Bea and Carla sometimes play frisbee with Abe and Eren in a local park. They usually have fun. The park's a great place to relax and they all like hanging out there.

0.1 Catching up with Bea

Relationships | Present Simple | Adverbs of frequency | *Wh-* questions | School | Comparatives and superlatives

1 ▶ 1 ◄) 0.1 Watch or listen. What hobbies and interests do Bea and her friends have? Do you share any of the same interests?

2 Read the text again and decide if the sentences are true (T) or false (F).
1. ☐ Bea and her cousin live in the same town.
2. ☐ Abe and Bea often argue.
3. ☐ Eren and Abe don't enjoy any of the same things.
4. ☐ Carla lives near Bea.
5. ☐ Carla and Bea have similar interests.
6. ☐ All the friends enjoy spending time in the park.

3 ◄) 0.2 Study Vocabulary box A. Which of the words can you find in the text?

VOCABULARY A — Relationships

aunt   best friend   classmate   cousin   grandmother
great-grandfather   half-sister   neighbour   parents
relative   stepbrother   stepfather

4 **I KNOW!** In pairs, add more words to Vocabulary box A. You have three minutes! Then compare your answers with another pair.

5 Study Grammar box A. Find more examples of the Present Simple in the text.

GRAMMAR A — Present Simple, adverbs of frequency, wh- questions

Present Simple
I live in London.
I don't like doing sports.
Do you live near your cousins?
Does she go to your school?
She likes acting.
She doesn't do First Aid classes.
Yes, I do./No, I don't.
Yes, she does./No, she doesn't.

Adverbs of frequency
always, never, usually, often, rarely, sometimes

Wh- questions
Where do you live?
When do you see friends?
Who do you hang out with?
Which school do you go to?
Why do you like your home?
What sports do you play?
How often do you visit your relatives?

6 Complete the questions with the Present Simple form of the verbs in brackets. Then write answers that are true for you.
1 *Where do you relax* (where/you/relax)?
2 _____ (what/you/usually/do) in your free time?
3 _____ (you/think) it's better to live in a city or a small town?
4 _____ (who/you/often/meet) at the weekend?
5 _____ (you/spend) a lot of time online?
6 _____ (you/see) your neighbours every day?

7 🔊 0.3 Read the dialogue. What subjects and classes do Abe and Bea like/dislike?
Abe: Have you got your timetable for this term yet?
Bea: Yes, I'm actually looking forward to Monday mornings! I have Biology first and then Information Technology.
Abe: Why do you like Biology so much? It's the worst science subject!
Bea: Biology's fun – and it's easy. I have to say IT is the best, though. I'd love to do some more programming. I might do a science discovery project this year too.
Abe: Sometimes I just don't understand you!
Bea: Well, that's because you're really good at Art and creative subjects.
Abe: True. Hey, do you want to try some after-school classes?
Bea: Yeah, why not? Let's have a look at the list.
Abe: What about First Aid?
Bea: You're joking! I need to do something more relaxing after school.
Abe: We can join Drama Club.
Bea: Hmm … I guess it's better than chess or football.

8 🔊 0.4 **I KNOW!** Study Vocabulary box B. In pairs, add more words to each group. You have three minutes! Then compare your answers with another pair.

VOCABULARY B — School

School subjects
History   Information Technology (IT)   Physics

Places at school
canteen   library

Types of assessment
practical exam   project

Verbs
learn   revise   take exams

9 Study Grammar box B. Find examples of comparative and superlative forms in the dialogue in Exercise 7.

GRAMMAR B — Comparatives and superlatives

Comparatives
The new library is bigger than the old one.
Art is more interesting than Science.
Practical exams are better/worse than written exams.

Superlatives
The classrooms have the latest technology.
The first day back at school is the most difficult.
It's the best/worst school in the area.

10 Complete the sentences with the comparative or superlative form of the adjectives in brackets.
1 Abe thinks their school is *the friendliest* (friendly) in the area.
2 Bea is _____ (excited) about her timetable than Abe.
3 New Park Secondary is _____ (big) school in the area.
4 This year's after-school classes are _____ (interesting) than last year's classes.
5 Abe is _____ (good) at creative subjects than science subjects.
6 Bea thinks Biology is _____ (easy) than other subjects.

YOUR WORLD

11 In pairs, compare different schools, school subjects and after-school classes.
History is more boring than Science.

Unit 0

0.2 Catching up with Eren
Present Continuous | Using everyday technology

My mum and I are having an amazing time in Istanbul this month. We're visiting my grandparents in the city centre. We're being tourists as well and exploring the city. We're by the Bosphorus today. We're sitting in a café at the moment. I'm writing my blog and uploading some photos, and Mum's watching boats go by.

My mum is originally from Turkey, so she's visiting some of her old school friends here in Istanbul. I'm spending a lot of time with my cousins because they live near my grandparents. I don't understand much Turkish, so I'm glad my cousins speak good English. I'm trying to use some basic Turkish phrases, but I'm not learning very fast!

We aren't staying in Istanbul much longer. School term starts next week, so we have to fly home at the weekend. I'm looking forward to catching up with my friends when I get back to New Park. I message them every day. I hope they're missing me!

1 🔊 0.5 Look at the photo. Where do you think Eren is? What do you think he's there for? Read the text and check.

2 Read the text again and answer the questions.
  1 What language does Eren speak with his cousins?
  2 Can he speak Turkish?
  3 When does he have to leave Turkey? Why?

3 Study the Grammar box. Find more examples of the Present Continuous in the text.

> **GRAMMAR** ▸ **Present Continuous**
>
> He**'s studying** Turkish this year.
> I**'m not learning** very fast.
> **Are** you **exploring** the city?   Yes, I **am**./No, I**'m not**.
>
> **Time expressions**
> at the moment, now, right now, this month, this year, today

4 Complete the dialogues with the Present Continuous form of the verbs in brackets.
  1 A: What *are you doing* (you/do) on the laptop?
     B: I _____ (look for) information about London for my English homework.
  2 A: Why _____ (he/read) a German book?
     B: Because he _____ (study) German Literature at school this year.
  3 A: _____ (you/enjoy) that book?
     B: Yes, it's great! Everyone _____ (talk) about it!

5 🔊 0.6 **WORD FRIENDS** Study the phrases and find examples in the text.

chat online   send links
chat with people   send videos
download apps   share links
download songs   share videos
film a video   text someone
go online   upload pictures
make a video   upload videos
message someone   write a blog
post on social media

6 🔊 0.7 Complete the text with words from Exercise 5. Listen and check.

> I'm trying to learn Turkish. I'm not having lessons at school – I [1] *go* online to learn basic grammar and vocabulary. When I'm not on holiday with my family in Turkey, I often chat [2] _____ my grandparents on the phone. I also [3] _____ songs in Turkish to my phone so I can listen and learn the words. I have two Turkish cousins and we often [4] _____ links to music videos. I sometimes [5] _____ them in Turkish and they like to upload [6] _____ and videos of my grandparents.

YOUR WORLD

7 In pairs, talk about a language you are learning. Say what you are learning about now and how you use technology to help you.

0.3 Catching up with Carla
Holidays and travel | Past Simple | Transport

This is Carla Silva. Her dad, Pedro, is from Brazil. He came to England many years ago to study, but he found a job, so he decided to stay. He met Carla's mum, Alicia, when they were at college in London. Alicia was born in Spain, but her parents moved to the UK when she was a baby.

Last summer Carla and her parents had a great holiday. They spent a month in Brazil. They flew from London to São Paulo, hired a car and drove all over the country. They did lots of wonderful things. They sailed on the Amazon River, went horse-riding, saw some amazing animals, sunbathed on some beautiful beaches and stayed in some great hotels and campsites. They also visited Pedro's family, so Carla got to know lots of relatives. She spoke Portuguese with them. Carla didn't want the holiday to end.

1 🔊 0.8 Study the Vocabulary box. Write the words below in the correct categories. Listen and check.

> B&B   campsite   city break   coach   ferry   hiking   sightseeing

VOCABULARY — Holidays and travel

Means of transport: boat   plane   train
Types of holiday: activity camp   beach holiday
Accommodation: hostel   hotel
Activities: horse-riding   sailing   sunbathing

2 **I KNOW!** How many more words related to holidays and travel can you think of in one minute?

3 🔊 0.9 Read the text. Name three facts about Carla's parents and three things they did on holiday this summer.

4 Study the Grammar box. Find more examples of the Past Simple in the text. Which verbs are regular and which are irregular?

GRAMMAR — Past Simple

They **stayed** in a hotel. (regular verb)
We **had** a great holiday. (irregular verb)
They **didn't stay** in a campsite.
Did you **hire** a car?   Yes, I did./No, I didn't.
When did he **come** here?

Time expressions
earlier this morning, in 2020, last summer, over a year ago, the day before yesterday, yesterday, when she was …

5 Make questions in the Past Simple. Then, in pairs, ask and answer the questions.
 1 Pedro / come / to England / last week / ?
   Did Pedro come to England last week?
 2 Carla's parents / meet / in Madrid / ?
 3 they / spend / a year in Brazil / ?
 4 Carla / visit / her mother's family / ?
 5 Carla / speak / Spanish / during the holiday / ?

6 🔊 0.10 In pairs, listen and answer the questions.

7 🔊 0.11 **WORD FRIENDS** Study the phrases. Check you understand them.

catch a bus/a ferry/a train   **sail** a boat/a yacht
drive a car   **take** a bus/a train
fly a helicopter   **travel** abroad/by bus
ride a bicycle/a horse

8 Choose the correct option.
 1 When was the last time you *took / rode* a train?
 2 Do you know anyone who can *fly / drive* a helicopter?
 3 When did you learn to *ride / drive* a bike?
 4 Did you *travel / catch* a bus to get to school today?
 5 Would you like to learn to *drive / sail* a boat?

9 In pairs, ask and answer the questions in Exercise 8.

YOUR WORLD

10 In pairs, talk about an enjoyable trip or holiday you went on. Talk about where you went, how you travelled and what you did.

0.4 Catching up with Abe

Hobbies and free time activities | Present Perfect | *For* and *since*

This is Abe Kerr. His mum is American and his dad is English. Before, they lived in the US, but then they moved to New Park. Abe and his dad have been here for a year now. His mum hasn't been here for so long – only since April.

At first, Abe found England boring compared to the US and he didn't think much of the food. But since then, he's discovered some amazing new places and met some lovely people, and now he thinks it's a cool place to live.

Abe has done a lot of exciting things this year. He's taken some awesome photos and recently he's taken up a new hobby: film-making. He's already directed a film. He's also run a 5K race, but he hasn't taken part in any longer races yet.

Since he arrived, he's spent a lot of time hanging out with his cousin Bea and he's made some great new friends, especially Eren and Carla. They've had a lot of fun together.

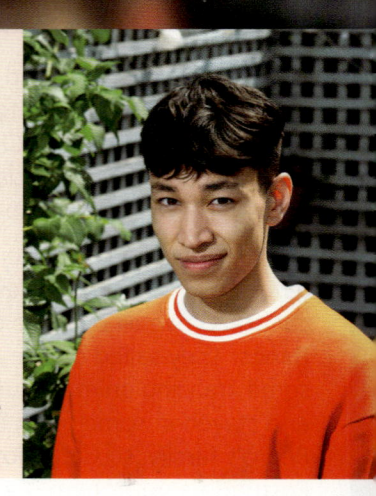

1 🔊 0.12 Read the text and mark the sentences T (true) or F (false).
1. ☐ Abe's dad is English.
2. ☐ Abe doesn't like England.
3. ☐ He's into photography and film-making.
4. ☐ He's not into sport.
5. ☐ His cousin's name is Carla.

2 🔊 0.13 **WORD FRIENDS** Study the phrases. Check you understand them. Can you add more phrases for hobbies and free time activities?

direct a film
discover new places
hang out with friends
run a race
take a photo
take part in a marathon
take up a hobby

3 In pairs, ask and answer questions using the phrases in Exercise 2.
Would you like to take part in a marathon?

4 Study the Grammar box. Find more examples of the Present Perfect in the text.

GRAMMAR Present Perfect

Affirmative
He *has* (just/already) *directed* a film.
They *have moved* to England.

Negative
I *haven't* (ever)/I *have* never *lived* in the US.
He *hasn't taken* part in a marathon (yet).

Questions
Have you (ever) *visited* the US?   Yes, I *have*./No, I *haven't*.
Has she (ever) *run* a 5K race?   Yes, she *has*./No, she *hasn't*.

For and *since*
They've lived in England *for* a year. (a period of time)
She's been here *since* April. (a point in time)

5 Complete the sentences with the Present Perfect form of the verbs in brackets.
1. We *haven't lived* (not live) here very long.
2. The film _____ (not start/yet).
3. _____ (you/ever/have) a pet dog?
4. Oscar _____ (not eat) lunch today.
5. Ella _____ (always/like) Art.
6. I _____ (not see) Jo since May.
7. Ali _____ (be) my friend for years.

6 Make questions in the Present Perfect. Then, in pairs, ask and answer the questions.
1. how long / Abe and his dad / live / in New Park / ?
   How long have Abe and his dad lived in New Park?
2. Abe's mum / be / in England / for a year / ?
3. why / Abe / change / his opinion of England / ?
4. what hobby / he / recently / take up / ?
5. Abe / ever / run / a marathon / ?
6. who / Abe / spend / a lot of time with since / he / arrive / ?
7. he / make / any friends / ?

YOUR WORLD

7 Complete the sentences so they are true for you.
1. My family has lived here since …
2. I've been at this school for …
3. My best friend has never …
4. Our English teacher has just …
5. I've liked [band/singer] for …

8 In pairs, ask and answer questions to find out your partner's answers in Exercise 7.
How long has your family lived here?

0.5 Revision

1 Look at the photo and answer the questions.
  1 What are the four friends doing?
  2 Who do you think said these things?
    a 'I'm in the park with my friends, Mum.'
    b 'Wow! You did well to catch that one!'
    c 'Hey, guys. Sorry I'm late.'

2 🔊 0.14 Listen to a phone conversation between Carla and her mum and answer the questions.
  1 What did Carla do before going to the park?
  2 Where are Carla's parents?
  3 What are they doing?
  4 What have they bought?
  5 What's the weather like now?
  6 What does Carla want her mum to do?

3 Look at the quiz below. Complete the questions with one word in each gap.

4 In groups, do the quiz. Use the texts in Lessons 0.1–0.4 to help you.

YOUR WORLD

5 In pairs, write two similar quiz questions about you and/or your classmates. Give your teacher the questions and have a class quiz with two teams.

How old is Agata?
What does Marco like doing in his free time?

How much can you remember?

1 _____ old is Bea?
2 _____ Bea and Carla go to the same school?
3 What _____ Bea like doing in her free time?
4 _____ do Eren's mother's parents live?
5 _____ languages does Eren speak when he's in Turkey?
6 _____ did Eren and his mum travel to Turkey: by train, boat or plane?
7 When _____ Carla's dad come to England?
8 Where _____ Carla's mum born?
9 _____ did Carla sail on a boat last summer?
10 Who _____ taken up film-making?
11 _____ did Abe not like England at first?
12 How long _____ Eren and Carla known Abe?

You can do it! 1

VOCABULARY
Adjectives of emotion | Verbs of success and failure | Phrasal verbs for achieving goals | Phrases for achieving goals | Immigration | Personality adjectives

GRAMMAR
Present tenses | Past Simple, Past Continuous and Present Perfect

TEEN MATTERS

Tips and ideas for improving your life and achieving your dreams, by life coach Emma Witcot

Get things done

It's a new school year with new challenges. Read these tips to help you work out how to make progress and improve your results.

1 Give it a go
Just do it! When you have to do something, get on with it! Don't put things off until tomorrow if you can do them today.

2 Step by step
You can't jump to the top of a building; you have to climb the stairs. So make a plan and break it down into smaller steps. Small regular targets are easier to reach.

3 Friends help
When you work in a team, you don't feel so anxious or stressed. Share ideas and help each other achieve your goals.

4 Do your best
Always aim to do your best, but don't be upset if the end result isn't perfect. Be pleased that you managed to do something, not disappointed that you failed to do everything.

5 Try, try again
We all make mistakes. Things go wrong. You can't always get everything right. But don't give up. Remember: if at first you don't succeed, keep on trying.

1.1 Vocabulary

Success, failure and goals

1 Look at the photo in the blog post and describe the girl. Do you often feel like this? How do you motivate yourself to get up and do things?

2 Read the blog post. In pairs, discuss the questions.
  1 Which tip(s) do you follow?
  2 What do you think are the three most important tips in the blog post?
  3 How do you feel when you have to manage lots of tasks and duties?

3 🔊 1.1 Study Vocabulary box A. Are the adjectives positive (P), negative (N) or both (B)? Listen and check.

VOCABULARY A — Adjectives of emotion

- [N] anxious
- [ ] calm
- [ ] cheerful
- [ ] confused
- [ ] delighted
- [ ] disappointed
- [ ] exhausted
- [ ] pleased
- [ ] stressed
- [ ] surprised
- [ ] upset

4 Choose the correct option. Then, in pairs, say if the sentences are true for you.
1. I don't get *confused / upset* and shout when things go wrong. I'm a *calm / delighted* person.
2. I always feel *exhausted / surprised* the next day if I go to bed late.
3. I often feel *disappointed / stressed* before exams.
4. I feel *cheerful / upset* in Music class. It's my favourite subject.
5. I'm *anxious / pleased* with my schoolwork this year. I'm doing quite well.

5 In pairs, choose an adjective from Vocabulary box A. Your partner says when they feel like that.
A: *Disappointed.*
B: *I feel disappointed every time I fail a test.*

6 🔊 1.2 Study Vocabulary box B. Find the words in the blog post. Check you understand them.

VOCABULARY B — Verbs of success and failure
achieve   aim   fail   improve   manage   reach   succeed

7 Complete the sentences with words from Vocabulary box B. Then, in pairs, say if you agree or disagree with the statements.
1. There are other ways to <u>succeed</u> apart from making money.
2. It's better to try and _____ than to never try at all.
3. People who get up early _____ to do more every day.
4. Practice makes perfect, so if you want to _____ your results, keep practising.
5. If you work hard, you can always _____ your goals.
6. You should always _____ to win or there's no point playing.

8 🔊 1.3 Study Vocabulary box C. Find the phrasal verbs in the blog post. Check you understand them.

VOCABULARY C — Achieving goals
break down   get on with   give up   keep on   put off   work out

9 Replace the underlined words and phrases in the sentences with phrasal verbs from Vocabulary box C.
1. To <u>find</u> the solution to a difficult Maths problem, it's a good idea to <u>divide it</u> into easy steps.
2. It's time to <u>start doing</u> it. If you keep <u>delaying it</u>, you'll never finish it.
3. If you <u>continue</u> working like this, you will succeed. If you <u>stop trying</u>, you won't.

10 🔊 1.4 **WORD FRIENDS** Complete the verbs in the phrases. Listen and check.
1. d<u>o</u> your best
2. g_____ something right/wrong
3. g_____ things done
4. g_____ something a go
5. make decisions
6. m_____ mistakes
7. m_____ progress
8. make the most of something
9. take it easy
10. take something seriously

11 🔊 1.5 Choose the correct option. Listen and check.

Advice from Aidan
Fear of failure

I feel anxious about ¹*doing / making* mistakes because I always feel so upset when things go wrong. I want to ²*do / make* my best, but it's really hard for me to ³*give / make* decisions. I just keep ⁴*getting / putting* them off. I need to learn to ⁵*get / make* things done and start enjoying life.
Lyle, Glasgow

Lyle, you're suffering from a fear of failure. You've got to learn to ⁶*have / take* it easy. It's not the end of the world if you ⁷*get / make* something wrong. Nobody succeeds all the time. If you want to ⁸*do / make* the most of your life, you need to change the way you think. You should ⁹*keep / work* out what you really want to do and just ¹⁰*get / give* it a go! Contact a friend and start making plans together now! Go on, ¹¹*get / give* on with it! Be brave!
Aidan

YOUR WORLD

12 In pairs, discuss the questions.
1. Are you good at making decisions and plans, and getting things done on time or do you prefer to take things easy and see what happens?
2. Do you like to give things a go or do you worry about making mistakes and getting things wrong?
3. Do you give up easily or do you always keep on trying?

I can talk about facing challenges, motivation and emotions.

1.2 Grammar
Present tenses

1 Are you a morning person or do you like to stay in bed late?

2 🔊 1.6 Read the introduction to a podcast. What problem does Mel have in the morning? What is the podcast going to be about?

TALK TIME with Mel and Zac

GET THE MOST OUT OF YOUR MORNINGS!

I don't find it easy to get out of bed and get ready in the morning. When I'm feeling sleepy, I don't want to get up. All the statements below are true for me. I think I need help!

- I always press 'Snooze' when my alarm goes off at 7 a.m.
- I love to stay in bed as long as possible.
- I spend ages in the shower because I always listen to my favourite playlist.
- It's often hard to find my clothes because they're in a pile on a chair … or on the floor.
- I don't always have time for breakfast, so I have a snack instead.

Which statements are true for you? Be honest!

Are you looking for ideas to improve your morning routine? Zac's not a morning person either, but he's making progress this term. Today Zac and I have our friend Joe with us. We're sharing some fresh ideas on how we can get the most out of our mornings on school days.

3 🔊 1.7 Listen to the podcast. What ideas do Zac and Joe have that can help people get ready in the mornings? Do you use any of these ideas?

4 Study the Grammar box. Complete the sentences under the box with the correct form of the verbs in brackets.

GRAMMAR Present tenses

Present Simple
I always *press* 'Snooze' when my alarm goes off. (routine)
I *don't find* it easy to get up. (permanent situation)

Present Continuous
Lots of people *are listening* to this podcast right now. (present action)
This term I*'m trying* to change my routine. (temporary situation)
He*'s making* progress this term. (changing situation)

State verbs
belong, know, prefer, etc.
I *know* you're always at school early. NOT ~~I'm knowing~~

State and dynamic verbs
I *think* I need help! (state verb: opinion)
What *are* you *thinking* about? (dynamic verb: mental process)

GRAMMAR TIME > PAGE 126

1 <u>Are you having</u> (you/have) lunch now?
2 When I _____ (listen) to my playlist, I never _____ (feel) stressed.
3 _____ (you/have) any advice to help us?
4 I _____ (live) near the school, so I _____ (usually/not get up) early.
5 My marks at school _____ (get) better all the time!

5 🔊 1.8 Choose the correct option. Listen and check.

I ¹*think / 'm thinking* I waste a lot of time in the morning, so I ²*try / 'm trying* to change my routine this term. First of all, I make the most of my time on the bus journey to school. I sometimes revise for tests, but I ³*prefer / 'm preferring* to listen to Spanish podcasts because they're more interesting. I ⁴*learn / 'm learning* lots of new words and phrases with this routine. I think my Spanish ⁵*improves / is improving* and I'm doing well in class now. I ⁶*know / am knowing* my accent is getting better too!

YOUR WORLD

6 In pairs, describe your morning routine. Are you trying to change something in it? Tell the class about your partner's routine.

Unit 1   14   I can use different tenses to talk about the present.

1.3 Reading and Vocabulary
A new life in Canada

New beginnings

Changing schools is always a challenge, but what happens if your new school is on the other side of the world? We asked two young people who are starting a new life in Canada.

Arjun Patel grew up in Mumbai, India, more than 12,000 miles from his new home in Toronto, Canada. However, his parents think that a fresh start is good for their family. And they're not alone. Each year over 80,000 new arrivals in Canada come from India.

In fact, over twenty percent of Canada's population are immigrants. Why are so many people moving here? There's a lot of support for migrants and their families. Arjun is finding that Canadians are very welcoming. He's already made a few friends. 'The best way to make friends quickly is to join a club or take up a new sport.' Arjun is doing just that. He's learning to play ice hockey because it's very popular in Canada.

Arjun is enjoying his new life, but he's facing some challenges. 'I don't like certain stereotypes. For example, people often think that my parents work in an Indian restaurant. It's annoying.' In fact, both his parents are doctors. Some things make his life in Toronto easier, though. 'Five students in my class are from other countries and one girl is from Mumbai!'

Arjun's classmate Martina Castro, from Brazil, is also discovering a new life in Canada. Unlike Arjun, Martina is finding things hard. Her parents don't speak much English. They can read and write basic English, but they don't like it when people speak fast. 'I sometimes go with my mum to the shops so I can translate. It's a lot of responsibility. I feel like the parent!'

What does Martina miss about Brazil? 'Right now, everything! My grandparents are so far away. I miss my cousins, friends … even teachers! I miss Brazilian food, sunshine and beaches. Toronto is on a beautiful lake, but I prefer sandy beaches.' The Canadian climate is much colder than in Brazil, so that's a challenge too. Martina's family are exploring the area at the moment. 'Our trip to Niagara Falls was pretty awesome. We're trying to stay positive, but I need some new friends!'

1 Would you like to move to another country? Where would you like to go? Why?

2 🔊 1.9 Read the article. Where are Arjun and Martina from? What do they like and dislike about their new lives?

3 Read the article again and complete the sentences. Write no more than three words in each gap.
1 The distance between Mumbai and Toronto is about _____ .
2 People who move to Canada can find a lot of help and _____ .
3 Arjun recommends joining a club or starting _____ .
4 Arjun likes living in Canada, but he dislikes some _____ .
5 Martina feels like her mother's parent when she has to _____ .
6 Martina and her family are trying to keep a _____ attitude to the challenges.

4 Look at the highlighted immigration words in the article. Sort them into verbs and nouns. Then check you understand them.

5 In pairs, discuss the questions.
1 What did you learn about Canada?
2 What did you learn about life as an immigrant?
3 What would you find difficult about life in Canada?

VIDEO — WIDER WORLD

6 ▶ 2 Watch two people talking about problems that immigrants face. Which of these things do they mention?

culture food jobs language stereotypes

7 What would you miss if you moved to another country? What would be helpful for newcomers to feel at home?

I can understand an article about immigrants and the problems they face.

15 Unit 1

1.4 Grammar
Past Simple, Past Continuous and Present Perfect

1 Think about a challenge you have faced recently. In pairs, describe it and say how it made you feel.
Last month I cycled fifty kilometres to make money for charity. It was hard, but I enjoyed it.

2 🔊 1.10 Look at the photo and read the article quickly. What was Poorna's challenge?

REACHING THE TOP

In 2014 thirteen-year-old Indian Poorna Malavath became the youngest girl to climb Mount Everest.

One day some government officials came to Poorna's village. They were looking for children from poor backgrounds to send on an expedition to Mount Everest. They wanted to show there are no limits for anyone. From 100 children, they chose just two: Poorna and an older boy. They went on an eight-month training programme in the mountains. While they were training, the temperature often fell as low as −35°C and they ate packaged food, which didn't taste very good. The climb to the top of Mount Everest lasted fifty-two days. It was dangerous, but Poorna didn't give up. When she reached the top of the world's highest mountain, she felt happy and proud.

Since then Poorna has become famous. They have even made a film about her life: *Poorna: Courage Has No Limit*. She hasn't stopped climbing. So far, she has climbed the highest mountains on six continents. In 2019 she reached the highest peaks in South America, Oceania and Antarctica. She hasn't climbed Mount Denali, the highest mountain in North America, yet, but that's her next target. For Poorna, climbing has become her life.

3 Study the Grammar box. Find more examples of the Past Simple, Past Continuous and Present Perfect in the article.

GRAMMAR | Past Simple, Past Continuous and Present Perfect

Past Simple
In 2014 she *reached* the top of Mount Everest. (finished action)
The temperature often *fell* as low as −35°C. (repeated action)

Past Continuous
It *was raining* on Sunday afternoon. (background description)
At three o'clock we *were watching* a film about Poorna Malavath. (action in progress)

Past Simple and Past Continuous
The teacher *was speaking* when some officials *came* into the classroom. (a longer action interrupted by a shorter one)

Present Perfect
She *has become* famous. (result in the present)
She *has climbed* Mount Aconcagua. (experience)

Present Perfect and Past Simple
Poorna *has climbed* many mountains. She *climbed* Mount Everest in 2014.

GRAMMAR TIME > PAGE 126

4 Choose the correct option.
1 Many women *climbed / have climbed* Mount Everest, but Poorna was the youngest.
2 She sometimes felt scared while she *was climbing / has climbed* the mountain.
3 On 27 July 2017 Poorna *reached / has reached* the top of Mount Elbrus.
4 The film about Poorna *got / was getting* good reviews when it first came out.
5 Someone *has written / was writing* a book about Poorna's life.

5 Complete the questions with the Past Simple, Past Continuous or Present Perfect form of the verbs in brackets. Then, in pairs, ask and answer the questions.
1 What <u>were you doing</u> (you/do) at 8 p.m. last night?
2 How many mountains _____ (you/climb)?
3 _____ (you/ever/eat) packaged food?
4 Where _____ (you/go) last weekend?
5 _____ (it/rain) when _____ (you/get up) this morning?

VIDEO ▶ WIDER WORLD

6 ▶3 Watch six people talking about being away from home. Where did they go? What did they think of the places?

7 In pairs, talk about a time when you were away from home. Think about the questions in Exercise 6.

I can use different tenses to talk about past events and experiences.

1.5 Listening and Vocabulary
Projection mapping

1 Do you like trying new things? Why?/ Why not?

2 🔊 1.11 Study the Vocabulary box. Can you add more words?

> **VOCABULARY** | **Personality adjectives**
>
> active   competitive   creative   curious   generous
> gentle   organised   patient   reliable   sensible

3 Complete the sentences with words from the Vocabulary box.
1. Someone who always has new ideas is _creative_ .
2. Someone you can trust is _____ .
3. Someone who is always moving and doing things is _____ .
4. Someone who wants to know and learn new things is _____ .
5. Someone who always wants to win is _____ .

4 Write definitions for the other five words in the Vocabulary box.

5 In pairs, take it in turns to describe a person you know. Use words from the Vocabulary box.
My best friend is always confident and reliable.

6 Look at the photo showing an example of projection mapping. Have you ever seen projection mapping before? What was it like?

7 🔊 1.12 Listen to Alex telling Mia about a workshop. Choose the correct answer.
a Mia has seen the information, but wasn't interested at first.
b Mia has bought tickets for her and Alex to go to the workshop.

8 🔊 1.12 Listen again. Complete the information with a word or phrase in each gap.

> ### PROJECTION MAPPING WORKSHOP
> ### New, easy and great fun!
>
> **Location:** ¹_Science_ Museum
> **Address:** ²_____ Road
> **Title of workshop:** *Bringing the* ³_____
> **For:** fourteen- to ⁴_____-year-olds
> **Time:** ⁵_____ a.m. to 4 p.m.
> **Please bring:** ⁶_____ and a drink
> **Cost per person for this special event:** ⁷£_____

9 🔊 1.12 Listen again and answer the questions.
1. What did Mia think the workshop was about?
2. Where do you create the videos in a projection mapping workshop?
3. Where did Mia see an example of projection mapping?
4. Is Alex creative or curious?
5. Why can't Mia go to the workshop on her own?
6. Why does Mia have to go to Alex's house on Saturday?

10 **YOUR WORLD** In pairs, talk about the classes and workshops below. What type of person are they right for? Are they right for you? Why?/Why not?

> chess   cooking   climbing   creative writing
> gardening   photography   sewing   singing

You have to be organised if you do the cooking class because you plan recipes and shopping lists. I'm not very organised, so I don't think this is the right class for me.

I can understand a conversation about projection mapping.

1.6 Speaking
Asking for and offering help

VIDEO ▶ **DO YOU NEED A HAND?**

Eren: Hi, Abe. What are you doing? Are you making chocolate cookies?
Abe: I'm making a chocolate brownie for my dad. It's his birthday today. I've never baked a cake before, so it's quite a challenge.
Eren: I'm impressed! Do you need a hand?
Abe: I don't know. Maybe. OK, so can you pass me the flour, please?
Eren: Sure. Here you go. Hey, your T-shirt is getting dirty with the flour. Why don't you wear this apron?
Abe: Cool, thanks … Oh! The food mixer isn't working.
Eren: Can I help you with it?
Abe: That would be great, thanks.
Eren: You didn't switch it on at the wall.
Abe: Oh, OK, thanks. Would you mind getting some nuts from the cabinet over there?
Later …
Abe: Look, a complete failure! I baked it for too long, I guess.
Eren: Hmm … it looks more like a giant chocolate cookie. Hmm, it's crispy and it tastes fabulous. Admit it: you needed me!
Abe: All right, I admit it. All great chefs need assistants.
Eren: So true!

SOUNDS GOOD! I'm impressed! • A complete failure! • I admit it. • So true!

1 Have you ever cooked something? What was it? Was it a success?
I made pasta with tomato sauce once. It was delicious.

2 ▶ 4 🔊 1.13 Watch or listen and answer the questions.
1 What is Abe making?
2 What does Eren think of the brownie after he tastes it?
3 What mistake does Abe make?

3 Why did Abe need Eren's help?

SET FOR LIFE
4 Why is it important to plan all tasks and stages of work carefully? What can happen if you don't? Discuss in pairs.

5 Study the Speaking box. Find examples of the phrases in the dialogue.

SPEAKING **Asking for and offering help**

Asking for help
Can/Could you help me?
Would you mind (helping me)?
Can/Could you give me a hand (with …)?

Replying
Of course.   Sure!
Sorry, I can't.   Of course not.
I'll be with you in a minute.

Offering help
Do you need any help/anything else?
Can I get you anything?
Can/May I help you?
Do you need/Can I give you a hand?
What can I do for you?

Replying
That would be great, thanks.
That's really nice of you, thanks.
Thanks for helping/your help.
No, I'm fine, but thanks anyway.

6 🔊 1.14 Complete the dialogue with one word in each gap. Listen and check. Then, in pairs, practise the dialogue.

A: Can you ¹*give* me a hand? I don't know how to install this programme.
B: ² _____ . Just click there.
A: Ah, thanks for your ³ _____ .
B: Do you ⁴ _____ anything else?
A: No, I'm ⁵ _____ , but thanks anyway. Oh! Yes, would you ⁶ _____ getting me some water?
B: Of ⁷ _____ not. Here you are.

YOUR WORLD
7 In pairs, go to page 136 and role play the situations.

I can ask for and offer help.

1.7 Writing
A blog post describing a personal challenge

MOMENTS WITH MARCO

My personal challenge

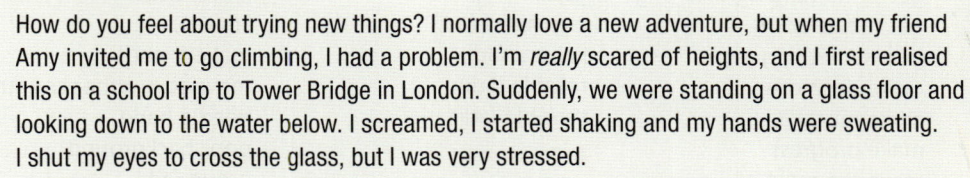

1. How do you feel about trying new things? I normally love a new adventure, but when my friend Amy invited me to go climbing, I had a problem. I'm *really* scared of heights, and I first realised this on a school trip to Tower Bridge in London. Suddenly, we were standing on a glass floor and looking down to the water below. I screamed, I started shaking and my hands were sweating. I shut my eyes to cross the glass, but I was very stressed.

2. So, when Amy told me about the climbing class, I was nervous, but I decided to give it a go. When I arrived and saw the climbing wall, I shivered with nerves. It was quite high, but the instructor helped me and showed me how to climb slowly and safely. At the beginning it was quite difficult, but gradually, I felt less anxious, although I had to concentrate very hard.

3. The experience has made me more confident. That day I made the most of the lesson and I couldn't stop smiling. Now I climb regularly and I'm never scared.

1 Read Marco's blog post. Which paragraph describes:
   1 a challenge that helped Marco?
   2 how the experience changed Marco?
   3 a bad experience in the past?

2 Study the Writing box. Find examples of the phrases in Marco's blog post.

> **WRITING** — A blog post describing a personal challenge
>
> **1 Reason for the challenge**
> I normally love …   I often dream about …
> The problem is/was, I …
> I first realised this when/at/on …
>
> **2 Description of the challenge**
> When I heard/my friend told me about …
> I decided to give it a go.
> When I arrived at/started/saw … , I shivered/screamed.
> At the beginning it was quite difficult, but gradually, I …
> In the end, I …
>
> **3 After the challenge**
> The experience has made me …
> That day I …   Now I … regularly.
> Now I'm not afraid of/to …   I'm thinking of becoming a …

3 Study the Language box. Find examples of the verbs in Marco's blog post. Then, in pairs, discuss how Marco felt before, during and after the challenge.

> **LANGUAGE** — Verbs that express emotion
>
> cry   scream   shake   shiver   shout   sweat

4 In pairs, take it in turns to use verbs from the Language box in a sentence.
The film was so sad that it made me cry.

5 In pairs, choose one of the challenges below. Why is it difficult? How would you feel before, during and after it?

> joining a new sports team
> performing in front of your schoolmates
> staying with a family in another country

WRITING TIME

6 Write a blog post with a description of a personal challenge.

1 Find ideas
Make notes for your blog post. Think about:
• why you wanted to do the challenge.
• what the challenge was like.
• how you felt after the experience.

2 Plan
Organise your ideas into paragraphs. Use Marco's blog post to help you.

3 Write and share
• Write a draft of your blog post. Use the Language box and the Writing box to help you.
• Share your blog post with another student for feedback.
• Write the final version of your blog post.

4 Check
• Check language: have you used verbs that express emotion?
• Check grammar: have you used a variety of past tenses?

I can write a description of a personal challenge.

Vocabulary Activator

WORDLIST 🔊 1.15

Adjectives of emotion
anxious (adj)
calm (adj)
cheerful (adj)
confused (adj)
delighted (adj)
disappointed (adj)
exhausted (adj)
pleased (adj)
stressed (adj)
surprised (adj)
upset (adj)

Verbs of success and failure
achieve (v)
aim (v)
fail (v)
improve (v)
manage (v)
reach (v)
succeed (v)

Achieving goals
break down (v)
get on with (v)
give up (v)
keep on (v)
put off (v)
work out (v)

Word friends (achieving goals)
do your best
get something right/wrong
get things done
give something a go
make decisions
make mistakes
make progress
make the most of something
take it easy
take something seriously

Immigration
arrival (n)
explore (v)
face challenges
immigrant (n)
migrant (n)
miss (v)
population (n)
stereotype (n)
support (v)
translate (v)

Personality adjectives
active (adj)
competitive (adj)
creative (adj)
curious (adj)
generous (adj)
gentle (adj)
organised (adj)
patient (adj)
reliable (adj)
sensible (adj)

Extra words
accent (n)
adventure (n)
advice (n)
basic English
brave (adj)
confident (adj)
courage (n)
cry (v)
culture (n)
discover (v)
experience (n)
fear of failure
find things hard
fresh ideas (n)
fresh start (n)
get better/worse at something
goal (n)
gradually (adv)
impossible (adj)
in a rush
join a club
limit (n)
make friends
move to another country
need a hand
poor background
proud (adj)
responsibility (n)
result (n)
routine (n)
scared of heights
scream (v)
set my alarm
shake (v)
share (v)
shiver (v)
shout (v)
solution (n)
stay positive
step by step
suffer (from) (v)
sweat (v)
take something up (v)
target (n)
workshop (n)

---

1 Complete the words in the school report comments. Then, in pairs, say which ones describe you.
1 'An a*ctive* student; g_____ things done.'
2 'An o_____ student – always plans her work and takes it s_____ , making great p_____ .'
3 'Always does his b_____ , but should remember that it's OK to get things w_____ sometimes.'
4 'Really makes the m_____ of lessons, is c_____ and asks questions, and g_____ on with the work.'

2 Complete the questions with verbs from the wordlist. Then, in pairs, discuss the questions.
1 When did you last _____ a difficult challenge?
2 When did you last _____ off something you needed to do and then had a problem?
3 When were you last the only one who could _____ out the answer to a puzzle?
4 How did you relax the last time you _____ it easy?

3 Find the negative word in each group. Then, in pairs, choose one of the negative words and say how it can also be positive sometimes.
1 explore   miss   support   succeed
2 succeed   achieve   fail   reach
3 generous   stressed   gentle   sensible

4 Answer the questions with words from the wordlist. Then write a similar question. In pairs, answer your partner's question. What do you call:
1 the number of people in a city or country?
2 a person who likes to be the best at something?
3 a person who goes to live in another country?
4 the way you feel when you wanted something but didn't get it?
5 a person you can trust to help you?

5 🔊 1.16 **PRONUNCIATION** Listen to how we pronounce the underlined vowels and decide which sound you hear. Write the words in the correct column.

act*i*ve compet*i*tive del*i*ghted d*i*sappointed
m*i*grant m*i*ss organ*i*sed rel*i*able surpr*i*sed

/ɪ/	/aɪ/
active	

6 🔊 1.17 **PRONUNCIATION** Listen, check and repeat.

Unit 1   20

Revision

Vocabulary

1 Choose the correct answer.
1. I was ___ by the instructions, so I didn't know what to do.
   a disappointed   b confused   c delighted
2. Our Science teacher says we should be ___ about everything and ask questions.
   a anxious   b reliable   c curious
3. This school ___ to help every student get the best possible results.
   a reaches   b aims   c improves
4. I was so ___ after the school trip that I fell asleep on the sofa when I got home.
   a exhausted   b sensible   c surprised
5. Mr Evans is a very ___ teacher – he stays calm when he has to explain things again.
   a generous   b patient   c cheerful

2 Complete the text with the words below.

best   down   go   mistakes   on   out   progress   right   ~~seriously~~   up

After I watched the film series *The Queen's Gambit*, I started playing chess again, but not just for fun. I joined a club because I wanted to take it ¹*seriously* and become a good player. But I lost most of my games because I often made ² _____ . To win, it wasn't enough just to do my ³ _____ . Part of me wanted to give ⁴ _____ chess, but I kept ⁵ _____ trying. I tried to work ⁶ _____ the reasons why I lost by looking at my games. I broke them ⁷ _____ into three parts: opening, middle game and endgame. I learned how to play the openings because you have to get that ⁸ _____ or you lose right away! I made ⁹ _____ and started to think about playing in hard competitions. I gave it a ¹⁰ _____ and beat some good players!

Grammar

3 Complete the dialogues with the correct form of the verbs in brackets. Then, in pairs, practise the dialogues.
1. A: What*'s your mum doing* (your mum/do) at the moment?
   B: I think she's at work.
2. A: Where were you when it was time to come to class?
   B: I _____ (talk) to my friends.
3. A: I'm hungry. I _____ (not eat) very much today.
   B: Would you like a sandwich?
4. A: My dog _____ (not like) to be alone. Can I bring him when I come to your house?
   B: Of course!
5. A: _____ (you/watch) anything interesting last night?
   B: Yes! A spy film with Bradley Cooper.
6. A: What's so funny? Why _____ (you/laugh)?
   B: You've got chocolate all over your face!

4 Choose the correct option.

✉

Hi Tom,

¹*I'm writing / I write* this email from my new bedroom in our new flat! It's a nice flat and ²*I'm preferring / I prefer* it to the old one, but everything is a bit crazy right now! We ³*were only moving in / only moved in* yesterday. Dad can't do much to help because he hurt his leg while he ⁴*was painting / painted* the kitchen. ⁵*He waits / He's waiting* for it to improve so he can get back to work. Mum ⁶*organised / has organised* the living room, so at least we can go there to relax.

Julia

Speaking

5 In pairs, do the speaking task. Student A, go to page 136. Student B, go to page 142. Role play both situations.

Dictation

6 🔊 1.18 Listen. Then listen again and write down what you hear during each pause.

BBC CULTURE

Tough journeys

ENDURANCE TESTS
The most challenging races

You're stressed and anxious, and you have problems sleeping. What you need is a challenge. There has never been a better time, but which one to go for? Marathons and triathlons are still popular, but there have been a few changes to the traditional kind: newer events have appeared. Participants race in tough natural landscapes like mountains or deserts, which represent a greater challenge to them. These races are popular in the USA and are very competitive.

The first long-distance triathlon was the Ironman. It started in the 1970s in Hawaii, on Waikiki Beach, and there are now forty countries across the world which hold Ironman events. An Ironman is the hardest one-day endurance test in the world. Participants must complete a 3.86-km swim, a 180-km bike ride and run a whole marathon – no stopping is allowed! The world championships are held in Hawaii every year.

Other tough races include the TransRockies in Canada. It is a seven-day, 400-km mountain bike race. Participants cycle up and down the Rocky Mountains in all kinds of weather, but they enjoy some fantastic views at the same time. Don't try it if you're scared of heights. Alternatively, head for New Mexico, where there is a ride that lasts three days through the desert – just try cycling through sand dunes!

As for the traditional marathon, you can still take part in the world's biggest, in New York. However, if you want to push yourself even more, try the World Marathon Challenge. This is seven marathons, in seven days, on seven different continents. It's called the World Marathon Challenge for a reason! For many people, this is the challenge of a lifetime. Participants have to run 295 km and spend up to sixty-eight hours in the air – all at their own risk!

endurance (n) the ability to keep going
landscape (n) a type of area in a country
participant (n) a person who takes part in something
sand dune (n) a hill made of sand
tough (adj) difficult to do

---

1 In pairs, discuss the questions.
1. What is a triathlon? What three sports does it typically include?
2. Which triathlon challenge do you think is the most difficult? Why?
3. Would you like to take challenges like this?
4. Are there races or challenges like this in your country? If so, what are they?

2 🔊 1.19 Read the article and mark the sentences T (true) or F (false).
1. ☐ New events in modern triathlon marathons are more difficult than the traditional ones.
2. ☐ Long-distance triathlons started in ancient Greece.
3. ☐ There are no breaks for Ironman participants.
4. ☐ People who suffer from fear of heights shouldn't enter the TransRockies race.
5. ☐ The bicycle races only take place in mountain landscapes.
6. ☐ The World Marathon Challenge is more challenging than the New York marathon.
7. ☐ Organisers of the World Marathon Challenge are responsible for participants' safety.

3 Read the article again. In pairs, discuss the questions.
1. Why do you think people take part in these types of events?
2. How do you think people prepare for them?

BBC ▶ An almost impossible journey

4 Look at the photos and discuss the questions.
1 What kind of landscape can you see in the photos? Where do you think it is?
2 What are the two men doing?
3 What problems do you think they will have in the desert?

5 ▶ 5 Watch Part 1 of a TV programme about two desert travellers and check your answers to Exercise 4.

6 ▶ 5 Watch the video again and choose the correct option.
1 The Empty Quarter is the *highest / largest* sand desert in the world.
2 Ben and James are travelling in the same way as *British / American* explorer Wilfred Thesiger.
3 The goal of their journey was to *have an adventure / repair a friendship*.

7 ▶ 6 Watch Part 2 of the video and answer the questions.
1 What other places have Ben and James travelled to?
2 Which country do they travel through on this trip?
3 Why did the trip take them longer than planned?

8 (VISIBLE THINKING) In pairs, follow these steps.
WHY DO YOU SAY THAT?
1 Study the discussion question and decide on your own opinion.
Can friendships become stronger when friends face difficult situations together?
2 Match the sentence halves. Then think about how each one could support your opinion.
1 ☐ The two men planned this trip
2 ☐ The desert trip was really tough
3 ☐ They congratulated each other
a when they finished the trip.
b because they wanted to be friends again.
c so the two men had fights.
3 In pairs, decide on three pieces of advice on how to stay friends when you face difficult problems together.

PROJECT TIME

9 In groups of four, prepare a digital poster about a desert. Follow these steps.

1 In your group, choose which desert your poster will be about. Decide who will find answers to these questions.
- Where is the desert located? What is its climate?
- Are there any animals and/or plants there?
- Do any people live there? What can you say about their lifestyle?
- What dangers are there?

2 Individually, prepare your part of the poster.
- Find answers to your question(s) and write a short text.
- Find photos to illustrate the information.

3 In your group, create your poster. You can use an online poster maker.
- Put all the texts and photos together.
- Decide on a layout.
- Think of a title for the poster.
- Check and edit the poster.

4 Share your poster with the class.
- Answer other students' questions.
- Ask questions and comment on the other posters.

Clean and green!

2

VOCABULARY
Talking about the environment | Compound nouns: the environment | Protecting and damaging the environment | Environmental issues | Elections and campaigns

GRAMMAR
Past Perfect | *Used to* and Past Simple

GLOBAL WARMING
PROBLEMS AND SOLUTIONS

Global warming is definitely one of the biggest problems facing the world today. It began many, many years ago, and it is mainly due to human activity. Different things we do cause different problems, which all have one thing in common: they make global warming worse. But there are things we can do to help. Today we're looking at some of them.

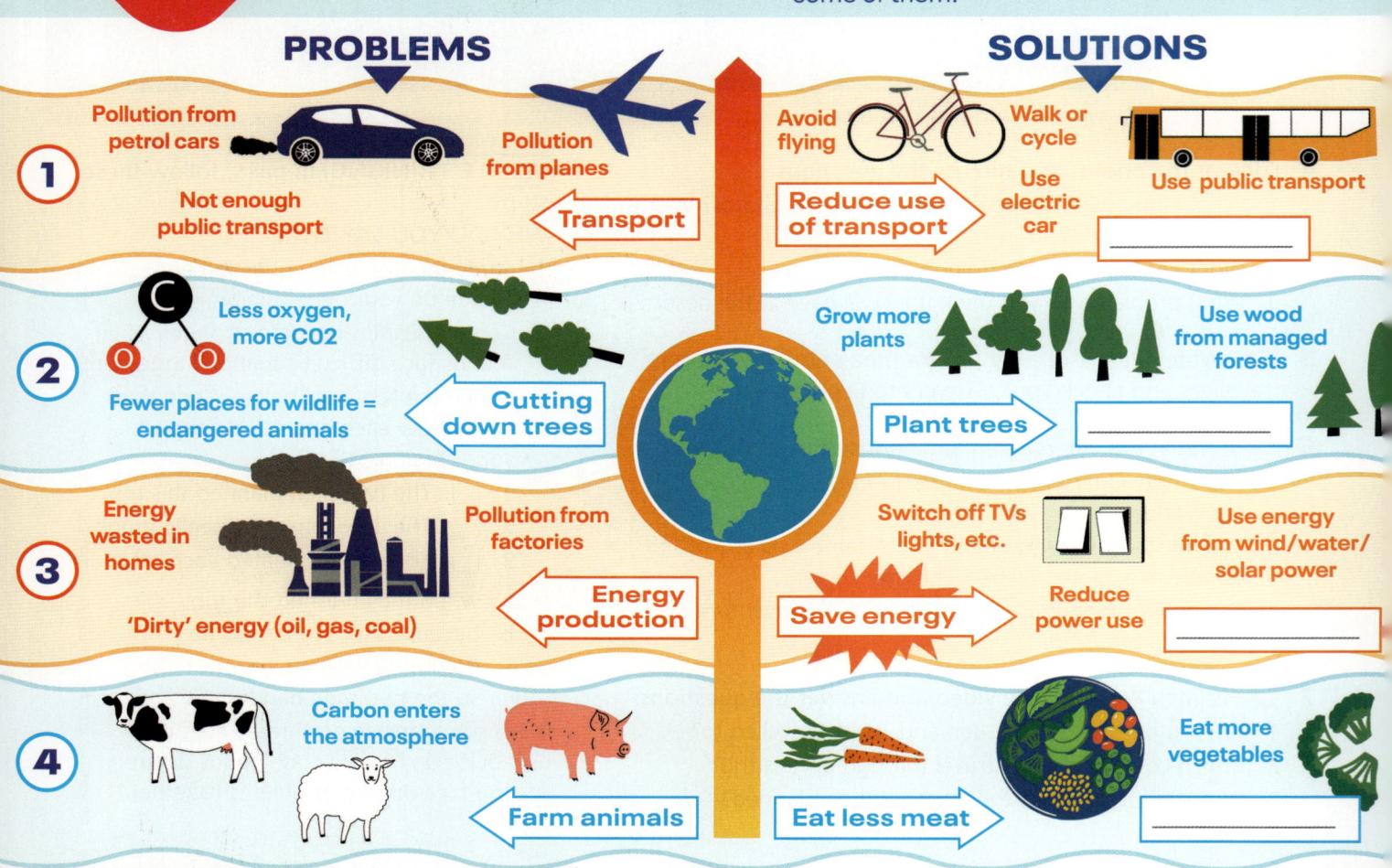

PROBLEMS

1
- Pollution from petrol cars
- Pollution from planes
- Not enough public transport
- → Transport

2
- Less oxygen, more CO2
- Fewer places for wildlife = endangered animals
- ← Cutting down trees

3
- Energy wasted in homes
- Pollution from factories
- 'Dirty' energy (oil, gas, coal)
- ← Energy production

4
- Carbon enters the atmosphere
- ← Farm animals

SOLUTIONS

- Avoid flying
- Walk or cycle
- Reduce use of transport →
- Use electric car
- Use public transport
- _____

- Grow more plants
- Use wood from managed forests
- Plant trees →
- _____

- Switch off TVs lights, etc.
- Use energy from wind/water/solar power
- Save energy → Reduce power use
- _____

- Eat more vegetables
- Eat less meat →
- _____

2.1 Vocabulary

Protecting the environment

1 Look at the diagram. Which environmental problem do you think is the most serious? Why?

2 🔊 2.1 Complete the gaps in the diagram with the solutions below. Listen and check.

> Dry washing outside   Recycle more paper and cardboard
> Share cars and car journeys
> Try some non-meat products

3 🔊 2.2 Study Vocabulary box A. Which words can you find in the diagram?

VOCABULARY A	Talking about the environment

atmosphere   endangered animal   factory
food waste   oil   oxygen   petrol   pollution
solar power   wind power

Unit 2 24

4 Complete the sentences with the correct form of words from Vocabulary box A.

1. One large tree can provide enough <u>oxygen</u> for 3–4 people.
2. Many creatures live in forests, so cutting down trees leads to more _____ .
3. Sunny areas like the Sahara Desert may be good places for _____ 'farms'.
4. Using _____ in cars and other vehicles is very bad for the atmosphere.
5. A lot of _____ in the sea and rivers comes from plastic.
6. _____ creates energy from the movement of air.

5 🔊 2.3 Match the words below with the words in Vocabulary box B to make compound nouns. Listen and check.

> car   centre   change   ~~dioxide~~   energy
> source   warming

VOCABULARY B — Compound nouns: the environment

carbon <u>dioxide</u>   global _____
climate _____   recycling _____
electric _____   renewable _____
energy _____

6 Complete the quiz questions with the correct form of compound nouns from Vocabulary box B.

The environment quiz

1. You can take almost anything to a _____ . But which of these things is the easiest to recycle?
   crisp packets / toothpaste tubes / aluminium cans
2. We're seeing more _____ on our roads. But how long does it usually take to fully recharge an empty car battery?
   30 minutes / about 8 hours / about 12 hours
3. It's very important to use _____ such as solar power. What percentage of Iceland's energy comes from hot water under the ground?
   70% / 80% / 90%
4. You can help to fight _____ by checking how much energy you use. Which of these things uses the most energy in five minutes?
   an electric shower / a games console / a smartphone
5. All humans breathe in oxygen. Then they breathe out _____ . Plants take this in and release oxygen into the air. Which plants do this the best?
   vegetables / trees / flowers

7 In pairs, do the quiz in Exercise 6. Go to page 136 and check your answers.

8 🔊 2.4 **WORD FRIENDS** Complete the phrases with the verbs below. Listen and check.

> clean up   protect   reduce   save   ~~throw away~~

1. recycle/reuse/<u>throw away</u> — plastic bags/rubbish/aluminium cans
2. _____/damage — the planet/the environment/our health
3. _____/waste — water/electricity/money/energy
4. pollute/_____ — the air/the ocean/rivers/beaches
5. _____/increase — pollution/food waste

9 🔊 2.5 Choose the correct option. Listen and check.

THE FOOD WASTE CHALLENGE

Although food waste is a natural product, it ¹*damages / protects* the environment because it creates dangerous gases which harm the atmosphere. Unfortunately, we ²*clean up / throw away* too much food – we waste about one third of all the food we produce! It's possible to ³*increase / recycle* this food waste to use it as compost in the garden.

Another thing we can all do is to ⁴*save / protect* any extra food that is left at the end of a meal and put it in the fridge, not throw it in the bin. Then we can ⁵*waste / reuse* that food to make another meal – for example, a soup or an omelette. If we are all more careful about the food we eat, we can ⁶*reduce / pollute* food waste and help the environment.

VIDEO ▶

WIDER WORLD

10 ▶7 Watch four people talking about being green. What do they do to help the environment?

11 How green are you? Are your town and school green? Discuss in groups.

I can talk about pollution and the environment.

2.2 Grammar
Past Perfect

1 Which of the items below produce energy?

jellyfish   milk   natural gas   sugar   sun   wind

2 🔊 2.6 Read the blog post quickly and answer the questions.
1. How much do elephants eat?
2. How can animal waste help the zoo?

Super zoo power!

Did you know that you can heat a building with animal waste? At school, I heard about a local zoo that had tried it, so I went to see for myself. When I got there, the zoo-keeper had just fed the elephants. He told us that they've got huge appetites and can eat 100 kg of fruit and vegetables every day! Over the previous week he had collected a container of waste from all the plant-eating animals in the zoo. I hadn't realised what a mountain of animal waste looked like!

How do they use the animal waste? They mix it with water, food waste and old straw from the animals' beds, and they produce a 'biogas'. This goes into an engine that produces electricity. So, had this idea really helped the zoo? Absolutely! Before they started using the waste, the zoo had found it difficult to control how much they spent on electricity. Now they can keep the animals warm and save money too!

3 Study the Grammar box. Find more examples of the Past Perfect in the blog post.

GRAMMAR — Past Perfect

Past Perfect
He **had collected** a container of waste.
I **hadn't realised** what it looked like.
Had this idea **helped**?   Yes, it **had**./No, it **hadn't**.

Past Perfect and Past Simple
When I **got** there, the zoo-keeper **had just fed** them.
He**'d already mixed** the waste with water **before** I **arrived**.
I **left** the zoo after we**'d had** lunch.

Time expressions
when, before, after, just, already, by the time

GRAMMAR TIME > PAGE 127

4 Read the sentences. Underline the action that happened first.
1. The lions were thirsty because nobody had given them water.
2. The workers had left the factory before the fire started.
3. After the party had finished, we cleaned up the garden.
4. Once I'd seen that documentary, I began recycling seriously.
5. I couldn't cycle to work because someone had stolen my bike.
6. The penguins had just finished eating when we arrived.
7. I wanted to recycle the empty cans, but Sam had thrown them away.

5 Complete the sentences with the Past Perfect form of the verbs in brackets.
1. The monkeys were sick because a visitor *had given* (give) them the wrong food.
2. Maria showed me some photos she _____ (take) at the zoo.
3. We _____ (not realise) how useful animal waste was until we read that article.
4. They _____ (already/feed) the animals when I got there.
5. _____ (you/hear) about biogas before you visited the zoo?

YOUR WORLD

6 Complete the sentences so they are true for you. Use the Past Simple and the Past Perfect. Then, in pairs, compare your sentences.
1. I had never … before …
2. I had just … when …
3. I had already … , but then …

I can use the Past Perfect to talk about past events.

2.3 Reading and Vocabulary
A hike in the countryside

1 How often do you go to the countryside? What do you enjoy about it?

2 🔊 2.7 Read the story quickly. Did Evan agree or disagree with his friend? How do you know?

3 Read the story again and choose the correct answer.
1 What problem did Evan and his friends find on their trip?
   a a traffic jam on the way to the country
   b rubbish in a lovely place
   c a large group of unfriendly walkers
   d an illegal waste dump
2 Who suggested clearing up the litter?
   a Evan
   b everyone in the group
   c Amy
   d the members of Leave No Trace
3 What is the objective of Leave No Trace?
   a to remove rubbish from the countryside
   b to persuade people not to go camping
   c to encourage people to visit beautiful places
   d to take care of the countryside
4 What did Evan and Amy disagree about?
   a banning cyclists from hiking paths
   b reducing the number of visitors to the countryside
   c stopping people from climbing Mount Everest
   d protecting the Grand Canyon
5 What is the main purpose of the story?
   a to advertise the Brecon Beacons National Park
   b to show how hiking can help you make friends
   c to compare hiking in Wales with hiking on Mount Everest
   d to raise a serious environmental issue

4 In groups, write a leaflet advising people how to behave in the countryside. Use the highlighted words and phrases for environmental issues in the story.

YOUR WORLD

5 In pairs, discuss the questions.
1 How serious is the problem of littering in beauty spots near where you live?
2 How can we solve the problems of littering and overcrowding in the countryside?

LEAVE NO TRACE

Last weekend the weather was great, so I went hiking with friends in the Brecon Beacons National Park. Unfortunately, there was a problem: lots of people had had the same idea. We had to queue to get out of the car park and onto the path!

After a few hours we stopped for a picnic next to a beautiful mountain stream. Then we noticed the mess. Some other walkers had left all sorts of litter on the ground and in the water. There was paper, food, cans, plastic, even a broken walking pole! It was like a waste dump.

We all felt angry and started talking about the problem. But then one of my friends, Amy, took some plastic rubbish bags out of her backpack and handed them around. 'There's no point complaining,' she said. 'Let's do something about it!' Everyone started picking up rubbish and before long, the place was beautiful again.

Once we'd finished, Amy told me about an environmental organisation she'd heard of called Leave No Trace. Their aim is to protect the environment – to encourage people to respect the countryside and to leave no trace – that is, make sure it's as clean and beautiful when you leave as it was when you arrived. They advise you to keep to paths, use proper campsites, take your rubbish away with you, be careful with campfires and respect wildlife and other people.

Just then, a group of mountain bikers rode past. 'Isn't *that* the problem?' I asked, pointing at the cyclists. 'There are too many people. Maybe we need to limit the numbers allowed to come to beautiful places like this.' Amy laughed. 'How could you control that?' 'Well, not everywhere, obviously, but certain places like national parks should be protected. Did you see that photo of the queue of people waiting to get to the top of Mount Everest?' Amy nodded. 'OK, maybe we need to limit access to a few places like Everest and the Grand Canyon, but not everywhere. It's impossible.'

We agreed to disagree.

I can understand a story about the environment.

2.4 Grammar
Used to and Past Simple

1 Do you think it's important for a town or city to have parks and open spaces? Why?/Why not?

2 🔊 2.8 Read the blog post. What are the main changes in Bruno's street? How are things better?

GREEN STREETS
by Sofia Morales

My cousin Bruno used to live in a noisy street in Barcelona, Spain. Now he lives in a quiet street with lots of trees and benches, but he hasn't moved! What happened? I spoke to him yesterday to find out more.

Your street looks fantastic in this photo. Did you use to play here when you were young?
No way! Our street used to be full of traffic all day. It wasn't safe for kids, so we used to play on our balconies.

What happened?
A few years ago architects designed a plan to move traffic to certain streets. They created more green spaces.

What do other people think?
My friends are all happy. We didn't use to go outside much. Now it's safer to use our bikes or walk. We can hang out in the street and it feels much friendlier.

3 Study the Grammar box. Find more examples of *used to* in the blog post.

GRAMMAR — Used to and Past Simple

Used to and Past Simple
Our street *used to be* full of traffic. (past state/situation)
Our street *was* full of traffic.
We *didn't use to go* outside much. (past habit/regular action)
We *didn't go* outside much.
Did you *use to play* here? Yes, I *did*./No, I *didn't*.
Where *did* he *use to play*?

Past Simple
I *spoke* to him yesterday. (single action in the past)

GRAMMAR TIME > PAGE 127

4 Complete the sentences with the correct form of *used to* and the verbs in brackets.
1 I *used to love* (love) walking, but I prefer cycling now.
2 We _____ (not recycle) our rubbish, but we do now.
3 My mum _____ (drive) to work, but now she gets the bus.
4 He _____ (leave) all the lights on, but now he switches them off.
5 When my dad was little, he _____ (not waste) food.
6 My cousins _____ (not go) outside much when they were my age.

5 Complete the questions with the correct form of *used to* and the verbs in brackets. Then, in pairs, ask and answer the questions.
1 *Did you use to live* (you/live) near a park when you were little?
2 _____ (you/go) swimming often?
3 _____ (you/travel) by bus or car?
4 Where _____ (your friends/meet)?
5 How often _____ (you/play) outside?
6 _____ (your neighbourhood/look) very different?

6 🔊 2.9 Complete the text with the correct form of *used to* and the verbs in brackets. Use the Past Simple if *used to* is not possible. Listen and check.

My gran ¹*used to live* (live) in London, but she ²_____ (move) to Manchester last year. London was very different sixty years ago. The roads are busy now, but there ³_____ (not be) much traffic back then. Gran and her friend ⁴_____ (take) the bus to school when they were young – it was exciting for them. Every day they ⁵_____ (run) upstairs to get the front seat, but one day Gran ⁶_____ (fall) down the stairs! She ⁷_____ (not enjoy) the bus ride after that.

YOUR WORLD

7 In pairs, compare your present habits with your past habits. Think about your home, school, friends and hobbies.

I do a lot of exercise now, but I didn't use to do much exercise a few years ago. I used to spend all day in front of the computer.

Unit 2 — I can use *used to* and the Past Simple to talk about past habits and states.

2.5 Listening and Vocabulary
Elections, campaigns and the environment

1 In pairs, discuss the questions.
1. Is it a good idea for students to meet with teachers to discuss important things about their school? Why?/Why not?
2. What kind of things should they discuss?

2 🔊 **2.10** Listen to a dialogue and answer the questions.
1. Where are the people?
2. What are they doing?
3. Who wins the election?
4. What does the new student council president want to do?

3 🔊 **2.11** **WORD FRIENDS**
Complete the sentences with the phrases below. Listen and check.

> become a member of
> hold an election   join a campaign
> organise an event   sign a petition
> vote for a candidate

1. I'm going to *join a campaign* to get more people in my area to recycle rubbish.
2. David and Martina have decided to _____ a group that protects local wildlife.
3. Yes, of course I'll _____ to help clean the local park. Have you got a pen?
4. Let's _____ in which people make things from rubbish. We could call it Trash to Treasure.
5. You shouldn't _____ just because he or she is your friend or someone you know.
6. Every year we _____ at our school to choose new student councillors.

4 🔊 **2.12** Listen to four dialogues. Choose the correct answer.
1. What is the date of the student election?
   A OCTOBER 10   B OCTOBER 11   C OCTOBER 12
2. What is the boy going to do?
   A   B   C
3. What did Mark's dad use to recycle when he was a boy?
   A PAPER   B GLASS   C PLASTIC
4. What kind of campaign has Sarah joined?
   A   B   C

YOUR WORLD

5 In pairs, write an election leaflet explaining why people should vote for you as student councillors. Present your leaflet to the class. Vote for the best candidates.

As student councillors, we would plant more flowers around the school. We would also … In addition, we would …

I can understand conversations about elections and campaigns.

2.6 Speaking
Agreeing and disagreeing

VIDEO ▶ YOU'VE GOT A POINT!

Abe: Hi, Eren! Are you ready?
Eren: Hi, Abe! Look, there's no way I can go cycling today.
Abe: Why not? Your bike looks OK to me.
Eren: Well, the tyres are soft, for a start.
Abe: So what? You can pump them up.
Eren: I suppose so.
Abe: In the US, I cycled a lot. It's a great way to get around.
Eren: Yes, I agree.
Abe: Why don't we cycle to school tomorrow?
Eren: Well, I don't think we should do that.
Abe: Why not? I think it's a great idea.
Eren: I disagree. It's quicker by bus and my brakes don't work properly either!
Abe: Hmm … they just need adjusting. It might actually be quicker by bike. And it's better for your health. And for the environment.
Eren: True, but it is dangerous.
Abe: You've got a point, but we'll be fine if we stay on the bike lanes.
Eren: Maybe you're right.
Abe: So, I'll meet you here at 8.00 tomorrow. Be ready on time. We don't want to be late.
Eren: OK then.

The next morning …
Eren: Abe, we're way too early.
Abe: See? You can sleep for seven minutes longer tomorrow.
Eren: Absolutely!

SOUNDS GOOD! So what? • We're way too early. • See?

1 Do you usually have the same opinions as your friends and family? What kinds of things do you disagree about?

2 ▶ 8 ◀)) 2.13 Watch or listen and answer the questions.
1 What do Abe and Eren disagree about?
2 What reasons do they give to justify their opinions?
3 Who wins the argument?

3 Which of Abe's and Eren's arguments about cycling do you agree with? Why?

5 Study the Speaking box. Find examples of the phrases in the dialogue.

SPEAKING Agreeing and disagreeing

Agreeing
I think that's a good/great idea.
I think so too.
Absolutely! I (totally) agree.
You can say that again!

Partially agreeing
Maybe you're right, but …
You've got a point, but …
True, but …
I suppose/guess so/not.

Disagreeing
I don't agree.
I don't think we should …
I'm not sure about that.
I (totally) disagree.
I don't think so.
That's not always true.

6 ◀)) 2.14 Listen and respond to each statement with a phrase from the Speaking box.

VIDEO ▶ WIDER WORLD

7 ▶ 9 Watch four people talking about protecting animals and public transport. Do they agree with these statements? What reasons do they give?
1 People spend too much money on protecting animals. They should spend it on helping people instead.
2 Everyone should use public transport.

8 In pairs, discuss one of the statements in Exercise 7.

SET FOR LIFE
4 What would encourage people to use bikes more often? Discuss in pairs. Use these ideas to help you.
- more and safer bike lanes
- an inexpensive public bike hiring system
- secure on-street bicycle parking

2.7 Writing
A survey report

1 Read the survey report. Do you find anything surprising about the results?

ARE YOU ENVIRONMENTALLY FRIENDLY?

Objective

The aim of the survey was to find out if students in our class were environmentally friendly. We asked ten questions. Thirty students took part.

Survey results by question

1 **Do you think you can do anything to help protect the environment?** All students think they can do something to protect the environment.
2 **Have your habits changed to protect the environment?** Half of the class say that their habits have changed. Some students recycle rubbish.
3 **Do you switch off lights when you don't need them?** Only thirty percent turn off lights when they leave a room.
4 **Do you waste electricity by leaving chargers plugged in?** Most students don't leave chargers plugged into the socket.
5 **Do you ride a bike to school?** None of the students ride a bike to school. Some ride a bike to see friends or at the weekend.
6 **Do you eat meat every day?** Almost all of the class eat meat every day.
7 **Do you think eating less meat can help the environment?** Only two people think eating less meat can help the environment.
8 **Do you make an effort to save water?** About three quarters of the class try to save water.
9 **Do you recycle plastic bags or plastic bottles?** Most of the class recycle plastic bags and about sixty-five percent recycle plastic bottles.
10 **Do you buy second-hand clothes?** Surprisingly, none of the students buy second-hand clothes.

Summary conclusions

To sum up, we found that most students thought that they could protect the environment. They all said that their habits had changed. Students made an effort to save water, but only a few made an effort to save energy. Most students recycled plastic bags and bottles. Surprisingly, most students didn't know that eating less meat and buying second-hand clothes could help the environment.

In conclusion, the students in our class could be more environmentally friendly.

2 Study the Writing box. Find similar phrases in the survey report.

WRITING A survey report

1 **The objective**
The objective of the survey was to …
The aim of this report is to …

2 **Report findings by question**
Thirty percent of the students think …
None of the/Only a few students ride a bike …
Half of the class buy …

3 **Summary conclusions**
In conclusion, we found that all of the class thought …
Surprisingly, only a few students ate …

3 Study the Language box. Find examples of quantifiers in the survey report.

LANGUAGE Quantifiers

We use quantifiers in reports: *all, almost all, many/most, three quarters, half, some, a few, not many, none.*
We can also use percentages: *thirty percent/30%.*

4 In groups, create your own questionnaire for an environmental survey and carry it out. Record the results.

WRITING TIME

5 Write a survey report using the information you have collected from your survey.

1 **Find ideas**
Make notes for your survey report. Think about your objective, your findings and your summary conclusions.

2 **Plan**
Organise your ideas into three sections. Use the report in Exercise 1 to help you.

3 **Write and share**
- Write a draft of your report. Use the Language box and the Writing box to help you.
- Share your report with another student for feedback.
- Write the final version of your report.

4 **Check**
- Check language: have you used quantifiers and percentages?
- Check grammar: have you used the correct tense for each section?

I can write a report with an objective, results and conclusions.

Vocabulary Activator

WORDLIST 🔊 2.15

Talking about the environment
atmosphere (n)
endangered animal (n)
factory (n)
food waste (n)
oil (n)
oxygen (n)
petrol (n)
pollution (n)
solar power (n)
wind power (n)

Compound nouns: the environment
carbon dioxide (n)
climate change (n)
electric car (n)
energy source (n)
global warming (n)
recycling centre (n)
renewable energy (n)

Word friends
(protecting and damaging the environment)
clean up rivers
damage the planet
increase pollution
pollute the air
protect the environment
recycle plastic bags
reduce food waste
reuse aluminium cans
save energy
throw away rubbish
waste water

Environmental issues
environmental organisation (n)
leave no trace
mess (n)
national park (n)
respect the countryside
respect wildlife
waste dump (n)

Word friends
(elections and campaigns)
become a member of
hold an election
join a campaign
organise an event
sign a petition
vote for a candidate

Extra words
bike lane (n)
bin (n)
biogas (n)
breathe (v)
campfire (n)
campsite (n)
cardboard (n)
careful (about/with) (adj)
charge a battery
coal (n)
compost (n)
countryside (n)
create green spaces
creature (n)
crisp packet (n)
cut down trees
cyclist (n)
design a plan
dryer (n)
encourage (v)
environmentally friendly (adj)
farm animal (n)
in a terrible state
keep the air clean
leave lights on

litter (n)
local council (n)
non-meat product (n)
organise a clean-up
overcrowding (n)
path (n)
pick up rubbish
plant trees
plastic (n)
produce (v)
public transport (n)
release (v)
rubbish bag (n)
share cars
source (n)
stream (n)
survey (n)
switch off lights
toothpaste tube (n)
traffic (n)
trash (n)
turn into (v)
turn off lights
wasteful (adj)
wildlife (n)
zoo-keeper (n)

1 Choose the word which does not fit the phrases.
1 pollute *the air / rivers / your health / beaches*
2 recycle *plastic / the environment / cans / rubbish*
3 *wind / electric / energy / solar* power
4 protect *electricity / the planet / your health / the environment*
5 waste *atmosphere / water / energy / money*
6 leave a *mess / no trace / an event / petition*

2 Use the wordlist to find these things.
1 two gases *oxygen, …*
2 one word with the same pronunciation as 'sauce'
3 two verbs which say what you can do with money
4 three places
5 two things we should reduce
6 four things we should respect

3 Choose the correct option.
1 I've never visited a national *source / park*.
2 Did you vote in the *campaign / election*?
3 We always leave no *limit / trace* after we have a picnic.
4 I always switch lights off to *reuse / reduce* our electricity bill.
5 We need to clean *out / up* our local river.

4 PRONUNCIATION Study the table and phonemes. Then say the words below.

Vowels				Consonants	
/æ/	cat /kæt/	/aɪ/	high /haɪ/	/dʒ/	age /eɪdʒ/
/uː/	blue /bluː/	/eɪ/	day /deɪ/	/w/	when /wen/
/ɔː/	more /mɔː/	/əʊ/	no /nəʊ/	/j/	yes /jes/

1 /ɪnˈdeɪndʒəd ˈænɪməlz/
2 /rɪˈnjuːəbəl ˈenədʒi/
3 /ˈɡləʊbəl ˈwɔːmɪŋ/
4 /ɪnˌvaɪrənˈmentl ˈdæmɪdʒ/

5 🔊 2.16 **PRONUNCIATION** Listen and check. Then listen again and repeat.

Revision

Vocabulary

1 Complete the words in the sentences.
1. We create food w<u>a s t e</u> from the food we don't eat.
2. F_____ produce useful things, but some also produce harmful waste.
3. O__ is a thick dark liquid from under the ground.
4. Nearly all animals need o_____ to breathe.
5. The gases around the Earth are our a_____ .
6. When people v____ , they choose the best candidate in an election.

2 Choose the correct answer.
1. You can ____ a plastic bottle by cutting it in half and growing a plant in it.
   a reuse   b reduce   c respect
2. We're organising a social ____ to bring together as many people as possible.
   a event   b member   c election
3. ____ change causes some unusual weather patterns that we see today.
   a Global   b Climate   c Atmosphere
4. I think ____ cars are a great idea for using cleaner energy.
   a petrol   b electric   c renewable
5. Mother animals always ____ their children from possible danger.
   a increase   b hold   c protect

3 Complete the quiz questions with the words below. Then, in pairs, do the quiz.

> campaign   clean   endangered   global   ~~recycling~~
> renewable

Are you environmentally friendly?

If you can answer 'yes' to most of these questions, you certainly are!

1. Do you often go to your nearest <u>recycling</u> centre to throw away your glass and plastic rubbish?
2. Do you know the other main type of _____ energy, besides solar power?
3. Can you name a gas which makes _____ warming worse?
4. Have you ever joined a _____ to help _____ animals or the environment?
5. Would you give your free time to help _____ up your area?

Grammar

4 Choose the correct option.
1. When we arrived at the cinema, the film *had already started / already started*.
2. The shop *just closed / had just closed* when we got there to buy crisps.
3. When my friend finished reading the book, she *lent / had lent* it to me.
4. My new alarm clock didn't have batteries, so I *had bought / bought* some.
5. The cat wasn't hungry because somebody *fed / had fed* her.
6. I went to collect the post, but the birthday cards from my family in Canada *didn't arrive / hadn't arrived*.

5 Complete the sentences with the correct form of *used to* and the verbs in brackets.
1. I <u>didn't use to like</u> (not like) <u>tomatoes</u> when I was younger.
2. I _____ (collect) <u>superhero action figures</u> when I was younger.
3. My <u>grandparents</u> _____ (take) me to school.
4. I _____ (not visit) <u>art galleries</u> when I was a child.
5. I _____ (play) with <u>toy cars</u> as a child.
6. I _____ (be) afraid of <u>the dark</u>.

6 Change the underlined parts of the sentences in Exercise 5 to make them true for you.

7 Complete the text with the correct form of *used to* and the verbs in brackets. Use the Past Simple if *used to* is not possible.

We ¹<u>moved</u> (move) to the city six years ago. Before that we ² _____ (live) in a country house next to a farm. I ³ _____ (help) with the animals on the farm. One summer my cousins ⁴ _____ (come) to stay with us. They really ⁵ _____ (like) life in the country too! After that they ⁶ _____ (visit) us at our country house every summer.

Speaking

8 In pairs, do the speaking task. Student A, go to page 136. Student B, go to page 142.

Dictation

9 🔊 2.17 Listen. Then listen again and write down what you hear during each pause.

Unit 2

SET FOR LIFE

Open your mind!

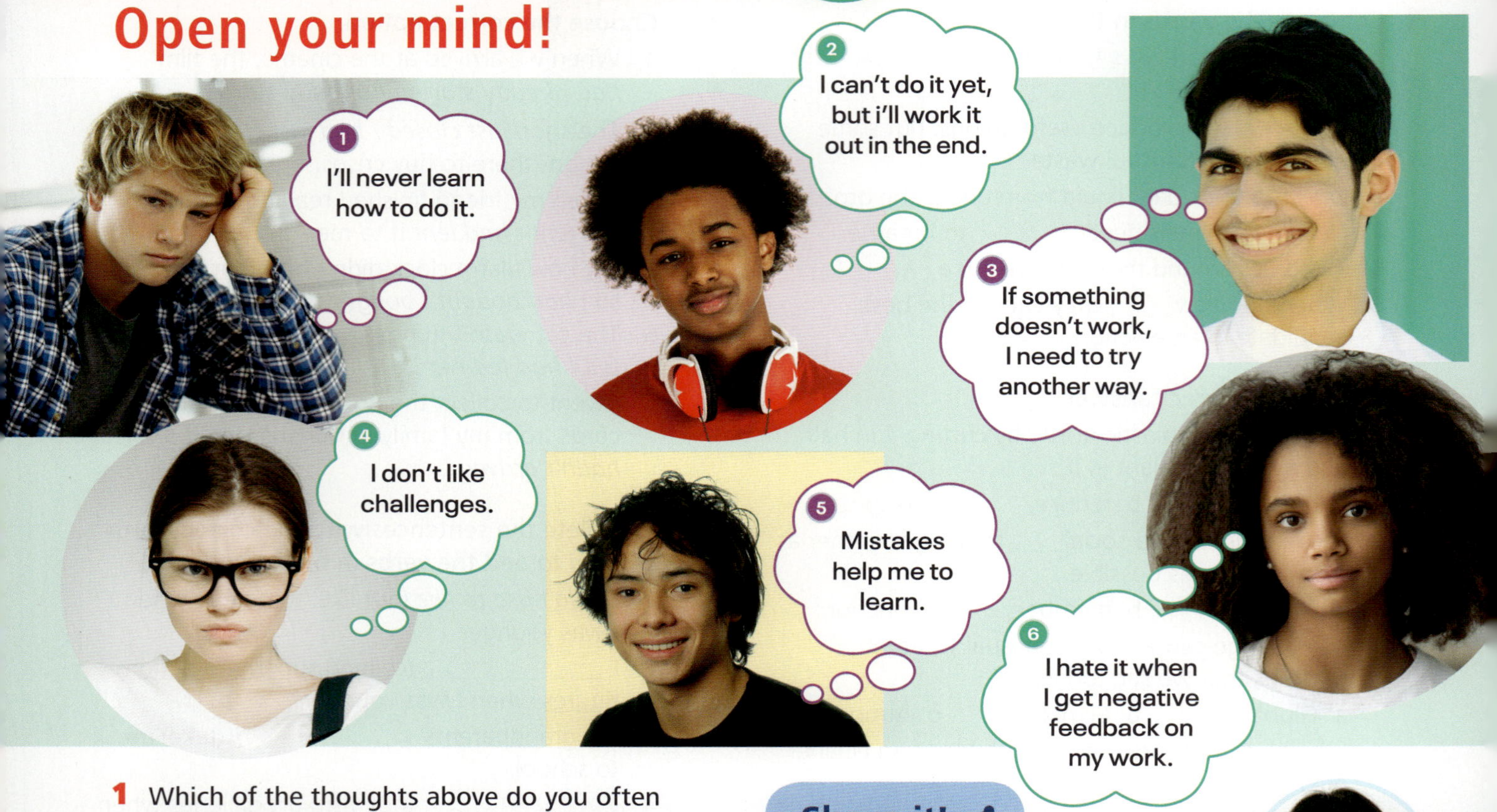

1. I'll never learn how to do it.
2. I can't do it yet, but I'll work it out in the end.
3. If something doesn't work, I need to try another way.
4. I don't like challenges.
5. Mistakes help me to learn.
6. I hate it when I get negative feedback on my work.

1 Which of the thoughts above do you often have? Which thoughts do you think are the most helpful?

2 🔊 2.18 Listen to Josh's conversation with his teacher. Which of the thoughts above does he have?

3 🔊 2.18 Choose the correct option. Then listen again and check.
1. With easier work, Josh can learn *more / less*.
2. The connections between different parts of your brain get *weaker / stronger* if you use them a lot.
3. People with a *growth / fixed* mindset believe that their brain can change.
4. People with a *growth / fixed* mindset usually don't try as hard as they can.
5. If you can't do something, you should try again in *the same / a different* way.

4 Look again at the thoughts above. Which show a growth mindset? Which show a fixed mindset?

5 Read about Mia's problem and the advice she got from other teenagers. In pairs, decide which tip shows a growth mindset. Which do you think is the best tip?

Share it!

Mia_MT
I used to be the best tennis player in my town and I loved playing. But now lots of people are better than me. It isn't much fun anymore. Do you think I should give up tennis and try a new sport?

LizAlto:
Some people stop improving as they get older – there's nothing that you can do about that. Don't continue with something that isn't fun. Try something new!

StarMan:
You were the best player in your town, so you clearly have lots of ability. But maybe the other players are working harder than you when they train. Think about how you can train differently.

Mark21:
I know it can be difficult in sport, but stop comparing yourself with other people. Think about your tennis level now, and how you can improve it. Find your fun from getting better than you were before.

6 Read about three other teenagers' problems. In pairs, discuss the situations and the advice that you might give them. Use the expressions from the Useful phrases box.

1 I've always been very messy and it's really starting to annoy me. I keep losing things in my room and forgetting to do things because I can't find my timetable. I'd love to be really organised like some of my friends, but that's just not my personality.

2 It's my dream to be a politician, but I think I'm too shy to talk in public. Is it time to find a new dream?

3 I'm terrible at Science. I try really hard, but I always get bad grades. Should I stop trying in my Science homework so I have more time for the subjects that I'm good at, like foreign languages and History?

7 Read the Useful tips. In pairs, discuss the questions.
1 Have you been in any situations in the past where you didn't have a growth mindset? What happened?
2 Imagine you are giving advice to your past self. What might you say?
You can't do it yet, but you'll work it out. Don't stop trying!

SET FOR LIFE

8 In pairs, role play a conversation about having a growth mindset. Follow the instructions.

1 Choose one of the problems in Exercise 6 or use your own idea.

2 Write a dialogue. Use expressions from the Useful phrases box.
Student A: You are the person with the problem.
Student B: You are Student A's friend. Give him/her advice and explain about growth mindset.

3 Practise your dialogue. Use your body language and voice to show how you feel.

4 Act out your dialogue to the class or record it on your phone.

Develop a growth mindset

USEFUL TIPS

A growth mindset helps you to be the best that you can be in school and in other areas of your life.

- Keep challenging yourself.
- Learn from mistakes and feedback, but don't feel bad about them.
- Never think that you can't do something. Think that you can't do it *yet*.
- When you're not succeeding, ask yourself, 'What can I do differently?'
- Remember that with hard work you can change your brain.

USEFUL PHRASES

Suggesting a new way to do something
Why don't you … ?
Try doing it a different way.
It'll help you to improve.

Encouraging a growth mindset
You can become (more intelligent/better at …ing).
Hard work brings results.
You can change!

Asking for advice
What should I do?
If I still can't do it, then what?

Looking good

3

VOCABULARY
Clothes and accessories | Adjectives to describe clothes and accessories | Appearance | Fashion | Parts of clothes and shoes

GRAMMAR
Present Perfect Continuous | Present Perfect Simple and Continuous

J.K.'S GAMING BLOG

Online gaming characters used to look boring, so I was really happy when new character creation games came along because now players can control the look of characters. I've just designed a 'skin' for a character in my favourite game. You choose a basic character and then you change the appearance, so things like eyes, hair and skin colour. In my favourite game, if you want to become a character yourself, you can also upload a picture of your face.

You can choose the clothes and accessories, and change the colour and design if you want to. I'm calling my character Zoraya. She's got dark skin and long dark hair. She has her hair tied up on top of her head. Her eyes are yellow, like a tiger's, and she's got huge gold earrings. Zoraya's wearing a black top and some bracelets, and she's got cool, loose gold trousers with big pockets, a huge gold belt and gold sandals. She's definitely got terrific style, so now she's ready to enter the game.

3.1 Vocabulary

Clothes and appearance

1 In pairs, take it in turns to describe your favourite character in a video game, cartoon, film or book to your partner.

2 Read J.K.'s blog. Which character from the picture is she describing?

3 🔊 3.1 Study Vocabulary box A. Which items can you see in the picture?

VOCABULARY A Clothes and accessories

ankle boots   bracelet   cap   chain
elbow/knee/shoulder pads   leggings   mask
ring   sandals   suit   tights

4 🔊 **3.2** Listen and match the names with four of the characters in the picture on page 36.
1. ☐ Titan
2. ☐ Jazz
3. ☐ Firefly
4. ☐ Argon

5 🔊 **3.3** Study Vocabulary box B. Write the adjectives in the correct group below. Listen and check.

VOCABULARY B	Adjectives to describe clothes and accessories
casual checked colourful cotton denim fashionable flowery gold leather linen loose neat old-fashioned ordinary plain scruffy silver smart striped terrific tight	

General appearance	_casual_ , _____ , _____ , _____
Opinion	_fashionable_ , _____ , _____ , _____
Size/Fit	_____ , _____
Colour	_____ , _____ , _____
Pattern	_____ , _____ , _____
Material	_____ , _____ , _____ , _____

⚠️ **WATCH OUT!**
We use adjectives in this order:
opinion/general – size/fit – colour – pattern – material.
She loves her **fashionable, plain, leather** jacket.
He's wearing a **casual, red, checked, cotton** shirt.

6 In pairs, take it in turns to describe different clothing items in the picture on page 36. Use two or three adjectives in the correct order. You partner guesses the character.

A: This character has got a terrific, orange and black, striped mask.
B: Is it Titan?

7 🔊 **3.4** **WORD FRIENDS** Complete the phrases with the adjectives below. Listen and check.

average   ~~dark~~   painted   pierced   slim   straight

1. **have** pale/_dark_ skin, _____ nails, _____ ears, freckles, dyed/curly/_____ hair
2. **be** good-looking, in your thirties, _____, well-built, _____ size/height
3. **wear** a costume, jewellery

8 **I KNOW!** Can you add more words to each group in Exercise 7?
have brown eyes, be tall, wear a hat, …

9 Complete the descriptions of Marvel film characters with verbs from Exercise 7. Do you know who they are?

He's big and strong, so he ¹_is_ really well-built. He ² _____ short, dark hair. He usually ³ _____ scruffy, purple shorts and a belt. He often looks angry, so he ⁴ _____ (not) good-looking. He ⁵ _____ green skin too.

She's strong and she ⁶ _____ quite slim. She ⁷ _____ straight, blonde hair. She ⁸ _____ a tight, red and blue suit with a gold star on it. She often ⁹ _____ red gloves, a red belt and red boots too.

10 Describe the appearance and clothes of a famous film or TV character. Your classmates guess the character.
He's … He has … He often wears …

11 🔊 **3.5** Complete the words in the text. Listen and check.

The best item of clothing ever!

My favourite item of clothing is an ¹o r _d_ _i_ _n_ _a_ _r_ _y_ denim jacket and I love it because it goes with everything. It's just a normal, ²p _ _ _ blue jacket with ³s _ _ _ _ _ _ buttons down the front. It was my older brother's, but he doesn't ⁴w _ _ _ it anymore. He isn't very ⁵s _ _ _ these days, so it doesn't fit him anymore. It's too ⁶t _ _ _ _ _ for him.

12 **YOUR WORLD** In pairs, take it in turns to describe your favourite item(s) of clothing.

I can describe clothes, accessories and appearance.

3.2 Grammar
Present Perfect Continuous

1 Do you think online adverts are annoying? Do you ever click on them to buy things? Why?/Why not?
I don't mind online adverts because …

2 🔊 3.6 Read the introduction to a podcast. What do influencers do?

TALK TIME with Mel

LABELS AND LOGOS
ARE INFLUENCERS HONEST?

Have you noticed all the adverts on social media? No? Well, maybe that's because some of them don't really look like adverts. I've been using a new social media platform since last summer and I've been seeing a lot more posts from influencers. Recently they've been sharing video reviews of products like clothes, shoes or make-up. These influencers are often normal people just like you and me, but they receive 'payment' for their reviews in free products from fashion companies. Is that OK?

I wanted to understand a bit more about influencers, so my friend Nina has been helping me for a few days. She's taught me a lot.

3 🔊 3.7 Listen to the podcast and answer the questions.
1. What kind of company is Nina an influencer for?
2. What two things does Nina do to make it clear she's an influencer?

4 Study the Grammar box. Find more examples of the Present Perfect Continuous in the text in Exercise 2.

GRAMMAR — Present Perfect Continuous

I've been seeing a lot more posts from influencers.
I haven't been working for money.
How long have you been working for this company?

Time expressions
recently, lately, all day/night
Recently they've been sharing video reviews.
since last Friday/October/Saturday/I woke up
I've been using a new social media platform since last summer.
for two hours/three years/a long time/ages
Nina has been helping me for a few days.

GRAMMAR TIME > PAGE 128

5 Complete the sentences with one word in each gap. Use the Grammar box to help you.
1. She *has* been working as an influencer for ages.
2. I've been doing this _____ about a year.
3. I haven't _____ following any influencers for long.
4. You've been sharing some videos with me _____ .

6 Complete the advert with the Present Perfect Continuous form of the verbs in brackets.

AWESOME INFLUENCERS WANTED!

¹*Have you been looking* (you/look) for a job as an influencer? Here at Awesome Fashion, our designers ² _____ (create) a fantastic range of accessories. We ³ _____ (work) hard and now we need YOU to help us. So, if you ⁴ _____ (think) about becoming an influencer, send us a short video about yourself. Our sales ⁵ _____ (grow) quickly for the past year and with your help, we're going to be huge!

7 Complete the sentences with *for* or *since*.
1. Have you been following these influencers *for* a long time?
2. Kate's been saving up _____ ages to buy some expensive jeans.
3. Tom has been practising for the show _____ May.
4. We haven't been shopping _____ weeks. Let's go tomorrow.
5. Al hasn't been taking any selfies _____ his mum cut his hair!

YOUR WORLD

8 In pairs, discuss the questions.
1. What kind of clothes and accessories have you been wearing recently?
2. Who influences your choice of clothes? Your parents or friends? Your favourite pop stars or sports heroes? Someone else?

3.3 Reading and Vocabulary
Trends in fashion

Fresh trends

What's been happening in the world of fashion? The way we make and buy clothes is changing. Here are some of the key trends.

A Slow fashion

'Fast fashion' used to be really important. When a celebrity wore a new outfit, a copy could be in the shops within days. Some of the biggest high street stores made their money this way. Factories made clothes quickly and cheaply. ^{1}____ Slow fashion, on the other hand, encourages us to be kind to the planet. Recently more people have been following this trend to choose clothing carefully and to keep it for longer.

B DIY fashion

One trend linked to slow fashion is DIY (Do It Yourself) fashion. This often involves working with second-hand clothes. Many young designers have been making old clothes into different ones, so, for example, jeans might become shorts or a jacket. They often mix and match materials or add new features such as belts, chains or different fabrics. ^{2}____ It's also a great way of creating an individual look.

C Rental

For people who love wearing lots of different clothes, clothing rental is becoming more popular. You can rent clothes from special companies or designers. There are different ways to pay – for example, you could borrow one outfit for a few days. ^{3}____ Sharing clothes like this is good for the planet.

D 3D printing

For a new look, you could try some futuristic 3D printed clothes like some of the costumes in the *Black Panther* films. The good thing about 3D printing is that there is very little waste. Each item is made to fit the person who buys it. ^{4}____

E Ethical materials

Do you think animal-friendly clothing is important? Designers in Mexico have been working on a special kind of 'leather' made from cactus plants. ^{5}____ Plant materials are much kinder to the planet than plastic or leather from cow skins.

We're lucky to have so many new, planet-friendly options. Fashion has always been about expressing your identity, but it's good to know that we can do this without damaging the environment.

1 Are you interested in fashion? Do you follow fashion trends?

2 Look at the title and headings in the article. Are you familiar with any of the trends?

3 🔊 3.8 Read the article. For each gap (1–5), choose the correct sentence (a–h). There are three extra sentences. Listen and check.
   a Reusing clothes like this means we don't throw things away.
   b The designers created fantastic patterns on the material.
   c However, the machines are expensive and it's easier to make shoes than clothes.
   d People didn't use to enjoy working there.
   e People wore these items for a short time and then threw them away.
   f Others have made plant leather from pineapples and mushrooms.
   g Keep your old clothes or give them to a charity shop.
   h Alternatively, you can rent a few clothes every month.

4 Match the statements to fashion trends A–E in the article. Which opinion is closest to your own?
   1 ☐ I'm a vegetarian. I avoid using animal products.
   2 ☐ I'm quite creative and have lots of old clothes in my wardrobe. I don't wear them all, but I don't want to throw them away. I like to have my own personal style.
   3 ☐ I'm trying to be more environmentally friendly, so I've stopped buying fast fashion.
   4 ☐ I love fashion and I get bored wearing the same clothes all the time. I like trying new things, but I don't want to buy lots of new clothes – I haven't got any space in my wardrobe!
   5 ☐ I'm interested in how technology can help design.

5 Look at the highlighted fashion words in the article and check you understand them.

YOUR WORLD
6 Would you like to follow any of the trends in the article? Why?/Why not? Discuss in pairs.

I can understand an article about new trends in fashion.

3.4 Grammar
Present Perfect Simple and Continuous

ARIA'S BLOG

Everyone wants one!

Last month it was my best friend Amy's birthday and I made her a case for her tablet. I've been very busy since Amy's birthday because lots of people have been asking me to make one for them! I've been creating lots of new designs and have made tablet cases for eight people in my class at school. I think people like them because they're different. They like the fact that you can't buy them in the shops. I've been taking photos of all the cases I've made. I've uploaded some photos here so you can tell me what you think.

Jess
I've been looking for a cool case for my tablet for ages and I haven't found anything I like. These are awesome! I'm going to try making one. Thanks, Aria!

Nat
I've been reading your blog since you started it and I've found it really useful. Your ideas are great, and my friends love them.

1 Have you ever made your own clothes or accessories? What are the advantages and disadvantages of making your own things? Think of design, time and quality.

2 🔊 3.9 Read the blog post and the comments. What does Aria make? Why do her friends want them?

3 Study the Grammar box. Find more examples of the Present Perfect Simple and Continuous in the blog post and comments.

> **GRAMMAR** — **Present Perfect Simple and Continuous**
>
> **Present Perfect Simple**
> I've made tablet cases for eight people. (focus on the result)
> I haven't found anything I like. (focus on the result)
>
> **Present Perfect Continuous**
> She's been looking for a present for weeks. (focus on the activity)
> I've been taking photos of all the cases. (focus on the ongoing action)
>
> **For and since**
> I've been looking for a cool case for my tablet for ages.
> I've been very busy since Amy's birthday.
>
> **Note:** with state verbs (know, understand, etc.), we only use the Present Perfect Simple.

GRAMMAR TIME > PAGE 128

4 Choose the correct option.
1. Here you are. *I've made / I've been making* you a necklace. Do you like it?
2. *I've been / I've been being* interested in fashion since I was about twelve.
3. I'm really tired. *I've shopped / I've been shopping* all morning.
4. *I've tried / I've been trying* on five different dresses and I don't like any of them!
5. *I've worn / I've been wearing* these shoes all evening and my feet really hurt!

5 Make questions in the Present Perfect Simple or Continuous. Then, in pairs, ask and answer them.
1. how long / you / have / your mobile phone / ?
2. how long / you / learn / English / ?
3. how long / you / know / your best friend / ?
4. how long / your favourite shop / be / open / ?

VIDEO — **WIDER WORLD**

6 ▶ 10 Watch two people talking about their family members. Who are they? What are they good at making? How long have they been making these things?

7 Do you know anybody who is good at making things? What do they make, how long have they been doing this and what have they made? Discuss in pairs.

Unit 3 — I can understand the difference between the Present Perfect Simple and Continuous.

3.5 Listening and Vocabulary
The National Museum of Fashion

1 What are some of the strangest fashions you have seen? What fashions were popular in the past and are popular again?

2 🔊 3.10 Study the Vocabulary box and label the photos. Listen and check.

> **VOCABULARY** Parts of clothes and shoes
>
> button   collar   heel   hood   laces   pocket   sleeve
> sole   zip

1 _____   4 _____   7 _____
2 _____   5 _____   8 _____
3 _____   6 _____   9 _____

3 Choose the correct option.
  1 I left my money in my coat *pocket / collar*.
  2 There's a hole in the *sole / button* of my shoe. When it rains, my toes get wet!
  3 This *zip / collar* is really uncomfortable. It's too tight around my neck.
  4 I can't walk in these shoes. The *heel / hood* is broken.
  5 Oh no! I can't take my jeans off. The *zip / sole* is stuck!
  6 I always leave the top *heel / button* open on my shirt.
  7 It takes a long time to put my new boots on. They have long *laces / sleeves*.
  8 In the spring and summer I usually wear short *laces / sleeves*.

4 What do you think these objects are?

5 🔊 3.11 Listen to a conversation about the National Museum of Fashion. Number the photos in Exercise 4 in the order you hear about them.

6 🔊 3.11 Listen again and choose the correct answer.
  1 Sylvia says the museum
    a is mostly about modern fashion.
    b shows only clothes from the past.
    c has both old and modern clothes.
  2 'Chopines' were
    a fifteen centimetres high.
    b only popular in Venice.
    c in fashion between the fifteenth and seventeenth centuries.
  3 Who wore very tall chopines?
    a both men and women
    b women who loved fashion
    c women who wanted to show their social status
  4 A 'ruff' is a type of collar that was popular
    a before the fourteenth century.
    b in the sixteenth and seventeenth centuries.
    c for men but not for women.
  5 Napoleon's soldiers had buttons on their sleeves
    a to help keep their uniforms cleaner.
    b to make the soldiers look more fashionable.
    c to make the uniforms more comfortable.

VIDEO ▶ **WIDER WORLD**

7 ▶ 11 Watch five people talking about unusual items of clothing. List the items they mention.

8 In pairs, take it in turns to talk about the most unusual item of clothing you have ever seen. Think about these questions.
  1 What was it and where did you see it?
  2 What did it look like?
  3 Did you like it? Why?/Why not?

I can understand a conversation about unusual clothes.

3.6 Speaking
Giving and responding to compliments

VIDEO ▶ **WHAT A COOL HAT!**

Bea: It's only one week until the fancy-dress party and I still haven't found a costume. Have you?
Abe: No, I haven't. I think I'll skip it.
Bea: Really? I know: let's go to the garage. There are some of Mum's old Art class boxes there. And Granny's stuff too. I'm sure we'll find something there to use.

Two minutes later …

Bea: Right, why don't we look in these boxes? Hey, look at these baby shoes.
Abe: Yes, they're so cute.
Bea: Wow, what a cool hat! I love it!
Abe: You look great in that. Why don't you wear it?
Bea: Really? Cheers. I'm glad you like it. What's in your box?
Abe: Hmm … lots of different masks. What about this?
Bea: It's cool. It really suits you.
Abe: Thanks.
Bea: Hang on. This will be amazing!
Abe: Hmm … yeah! I like it!
Bea: Have you got a bright green shirt too?
Abe: No, but I've got a green sweater.
Bea: I think you'll be the best-dressed fruit at the party!

SOUNDS GOOD! • I'll skip it. • Hang on.

1 ▶ 12 ◀)) 3.12 Watch or listen. What are Bea and Abe looking for? Why?

2 What costume would you like to wear at a fancy-dress party? Go to page 142 to check Abe's costume.

3 How do Bea and Abe compliment each other?

SET FOR LIFE

4 In pairs, discuss the questions in pairs.
1 Is it easier to compliment people on their actions or their looks? Why?
2 Should we be completely honest when we comment on appearance? Or is it important to say something nice, even if it's not exactly true?

5 Study the Speaking box. Find examples of the phrases in the dialogue.

SPEAKING Giving and responding to compliments

Giving compliments
You look good/great in that (outfit/colour).
It's/You're so cute/nice/friendly/kind!
Your clothes are great.   That cap's awesome.
You've got amazing hair/a nice smile.
I (really) like/love your style.   It (really) suits you.
What a cool hat!
You've got great taste in clothes.
That's really helpful/thoughtful.

Responding to compliments
Thanks.   Cheers.
You've made my day.
That's really nice of you.
Really?   Do you think so?
I'm glad you like it.

6 ◀)) 3.13 Put the dialogues in the correct order. Listen and check. Then, in pairs, practise the dialogues.
1 ☐ Yes, it suits you.
  ☐ You look good in blue.
  ☐ Yes, I got it yesterday, but I'm not sure about the colour.
  [1] That jacket is awesome. Is it new?
  ☐ Do you think so?
2 ☐ Thank you. I'm glad you like it.
  ☐ You look really smart. Have you had a haircut?
  ☐ Honestly, I really like the style. It's cool.
  ☐ Yes, I went to the hairdresser's at the weekend.

YOUR WORLD

7 In pairs, take it in turns to compliment your partner. Your partner responds.

I can give and respond to compliments.

3.7 Writing

An email describing appearance

1 Have you ever worn a costume for an event? Describe the event and your outfit.

2 Read Nick's email. What event is he describing? What costumes are he and Miranda wearing?

> ✉
>
> SUBJECT: School show
>
> Dear Gran and Grandad,
>
> **[1]** I've got some brilliant news! Our school show this year is the musical *Oliver!* and I'm playing the part of a poor boy. We've been rehearsing for weeks and the show starts next weekend, so I hope you can come.
>
> **[2]** You might not recognise me in my costume, so I'll describe it. All the poor boys wear baggy trousers. We have scruffy hair and dirty faces. We also have accessories like strange hats and coloured scarves. My scarf is dark blue and I have a flat cap and a checked shirt, so look out for me!
>
> **[3]** By the way, Miranda is in the show too. She thinks it's fantastic. She's playing the part of a boy. Her outfit is similar to mine, but she's taller than me, so she's easy to see. Miranda's hair is tied up under a hat, so you can't see it. Like most of the 'boys', she's got a plain white shirt, but she's the only person with a red scarf.
>
> The stage looks stunning and it's an incredible show. Please let me know if you can make it. Thanks.
>
> Hope to see you there!
>
> **[4]** Lots of love,
>
> Nick

3 Study the Writing box. Find examples of the phrases in Nick's email.

WRITING An email describing appearance

1 Start your email
- Thanks for your message.
- Guess what? I've been busy because …
- I've got some brilliant news!

2 Describe clothes and appearance
- We have accessories like strange hats …
- Her outfit is similar to/different from mine, but …
- She/He/It looks stunning/cool/attractive.

3 Give more information
- By the way, …
- I also wanted to tell you that/about …

4 End your email
- Hope to see you there/soon.
- I'm looking forward to seeing you.
- Cheers, Bye for now, Lots of love, Speak soon,

4 Study the Language box. Find examples of opinion adjectives in Nick's email. Can you add any other opinion adjectives? Compare your ideas with the class.

LANGUAGE Opinion adjectives

Opinion adjectives make your writing more interesting and personal.

attractive   average   brilliant   fantastic   horrible
impressive   incredible   original   strange   stunning

5 Choose the correct option.
1. I really enjoyed my sister's school show. It was *strange / fantastic*.
2. It's my favourite song. It's *incredible / average*.
3. I don't like that T-shirt because the design is *strange / brilliant*.
4. This film is popular because all the actors are really *horrible / attractive*!

WRITING TIME

6 Write an email to a relative or friend about your outfit/costume for an event. Use one of the ideas below or think of your own event.

> a fancy-dress party   a festival   a play or show
> a special family event

1 Find ideas
Make notes for your email. Think about:
- what event you want to write about.
- whether it is set in the past or in the future.
- your outfit and your opinion of it.

2 Plan
Organise your ideas into paragraphs. Use Nick's email to help you.

3 Write and share
- Write a draft of your email. Use the Language box and the Writing box to help you.
- Share your email with another student for feedback.
- Write the final version of your email.

4 Check
- Check language: have you used opinion adjectives to make your writing more personal?
- Check grammar: have you used the correct tenses for past or future events?

I can write an email describing people's clothes and appearance.

Vocabulary Activator

WORDLIST 🔊 3.14

Clothes and accessories
ankle boots (n)
bracelet (n)
cap (n)
chain (n)
elbow pads (n)
knee pads (n)
leggings (n)
mask (n)
ring (n)
sandals (n)
shoulder pads (n)
suit (n)
tights (n)

Adjectives to describe clothes and accessories
casual (adj)
checked (adj)
colourful (adj)
cotton (adj)
denim (adj)
fashionable (adj)
flowery (adj)
gold (adj)
leather (adj)
linen (adj)
loose (adj)
neat (adj)
old-fashioned (adj)
ordinary (adj)
plain (adj)
scruffy (adj)
silver (adj)
smart (adj)
striped (adj)
terrific (adj)
tight (adj)

Word friends (appearance)
be average height
be average size
be good-looking
be in your thirties
be slim
be well-built
have curly hair
have dark skin
have dyed hair
have freckles
have painted nails
have pale skin
have pierced ears
have straight hair
wear a costume
wear jewellery

Fashion
clothing rental (n)
ethical materials (n)
high street store (n)
individual look (n)
key trend (n)
new feature (n)
new outfit (n)
second-hand clothes (n)
slow fashion (n)
young designer (n)

Parts of clothes and shoes
button (n)
collar (n)
heel (n)
hood (n)
laces (n)
pocket (n)
sleeve (n)
sole (n)
zip (n)

Extra words
3D printed clothes (n)
attractive (adj)
average (adj)
awesome (adj)
awful (adj)
bright (adj)
brilliant (adj)
charity shop (n)
create (v)
design (v)
express your identity
fantastic (adj)
fashion choice (n)
fit (v)
go with (v)
helmet (n)
horrible (adj)
impressive (adj)
incredible (adj)
influencer (n)
item of clothing (n)
look (n)
original (adj)
pattern (n)
popular (adj)
scarf (n)
strange (adj)
stunning (adj)
style (n)
suit (v)
taste (n)
uncomfortable (adj)
uniform (n)

---

1 Find the opposites of these adjectives in the wordlist.
1 colourful/*plain* shirt
2 pale/_____ skin
3 smart/_____ look
4 straight/_____ hair
5 tight/_____ clothes

2 Write the correct word for each definition.
1 You pull it up and down to close and open clothes. *zip*
2 Clothes with this pattern have lines. _____
3 The part of a shirt around your neck. _____
4 These clothes are cheap to buy because someone has worn them before. _____
5 A young person who creates new kinds of clothes. _____
6 You wear these on your feet in summer. _____
7 You wear this on your finger. _____
8 You wear this on your neck. _____
9 If a piece of clothing has this, you can put things in it. _____
10 If a piece of clothing has this, you can cover your head with it. _____

3 Complete the descriptions of computer game avatars with words from the wordlist. Then write your own description.
1 I wear a purple o*utfit* with wide shoulder p_____ . I have straight h_____ and painted n_____ .
2 My clothes are old-f_____ – from the twentieth century – and made from ethical m_____ . I wear a m_____ , so people can't see my face.

4 🔊 3.15 **PRONUNCIATION** Listen to how we pronounce the underlined sounds in words 1–4.
1 cost<u>u</u>me, j<u>e</u>wellery , _____ , _____
2 sl<u>ee</u>ve, _____ , _____ , _____
3 str<u>i</u>ped, _____ , _____ , _____
4 pl<u>ai</u>n, _____ , _____ , _____

5 🔊 3.16 Match the words below with the words in Exercise 4 with the same sound. Listen and check. Then listen again and repeat.

chain   dyed   heel   height   ~~jewellery~~   knee
laces   loose   nails   neat   new   tight

Unit 3   44

Revision

Vocabulary

1 Choose the correct option. Then, in pairs, discuss the questions.
1. Do you prefer to wear T-shirts with a *collar / sole* or without?
2. Do you play any sports that need knee *leggings / pads*?
3. Do you enjoy wearing *freckles / sandals* in the summer?
4. Do you think a *chain / bracelet* on a neck for men is a good look?
5. Do you think *painted / pierced* ears look good?
6. Do you follow a key *trend / ring*?

2 Complete the words in the sentences.
1. When you have d*yed* hair, your hair is not a natural colour.
2. S_____ clothes are old, and they might have holes or be dirty.
3. I can't wear this shirt – it's missing some b_____ .
4. A c_____ pattern has squares of two different colours, like a chess board.
5. Dancers wear t_____ on their legs because they can move easily in them.
6. People wear a s_____ with a matching jacket and trousers for formal occasions.
7. If you are not tall or short, you are probably a_____ height.
8. He buys all his clothes from high s_____ stores.

3 Complete the dialogue with the words below. Then draw a quick sketch of the party item.

> boots   ~~costume~~   ethical   heels   laces   leather   ordinary

A: What ¹ *costume* are you wearing for the 'crazy' fancy-dress party?
B: So far, I only know what I'm wearing on my feet: these ankle ² _____ – look!
A: Cool! Are they made of ³ _____ ?
B: No, I don't wear animal products. They're made of ⁴ _____ materials. Do you like the blue ⁵ _____ ?
A: Yes, but it will take you ages to tie them. And the ⁶ _____ look very high. Won't you fall over?
B: No, they feel fine. But do you think they look too ⁷ _____ ?
A: No way! They're unusual!

Grammar

4 Complete the sentences with *for*, *since* or *recently*. Then change the sentences to make them true for you.
1. I've been at my school *for* four years.
2. I've been listening to some new music _____ .
3. I haven't eaten anything _____ eight o'clock this morning.
4. I've been learning English _____ five years.
5. _____ we've been getting a bit too much homework at school.
6. We've lived in this house _____ I was eight years old.
7. I've had my mobile phone _____ four months.
8. No one has given me a present _____ my birthday.

5 Complete the questions with the Present Perfect Simple or Continuous form of the verbs in brackets. Then, in pairs, ask and answer the questions.
1. Which capital cities *have you visited* (you/visit)?
2. How long _____ (you/know) your English teacher?
3. How long _____ (you and your classmates/come) to this school?
4. What kind of food _____ (you/eat) at home recently?
5. What new TV shows _____ (you/see) this year?
6. How long _____ (you/learn) English?
7. What kind of clothes _____ (your best friend/wear) lately?
8. How long _____ (you/have) your phone and/or your computer?

Speaking

6 In groups of three, follow the instructions.
1. Sit facing each other.
2. Choose something to compliment each of the other students in your group on. Use the ideas below or your own.

> drawing ability   handwriting   pencil case
> school bag   shoes   smile

3. Think of something nice to say about each thing.
4. Take it in turns to say someone's name in the group and compliment them.
5. Respond to the other students' compliments.

Dictation

7 🔊 3.17 Listen. Then listen again and write down what you hear during each pause.

BBC CULTURE
A closer look at fashion

The QUEEN'S FASHION
A model for others

It's hard to imagine that the royal look could be a fashion icon in the UK, but that's exactly what it has become in recent years.

The Queen's headscarf, Burberry check or tartan skirt might seem old-fashioned, but when they are reinvented by famous designers such as Dolce & Gabbana, these country clothes take on a very trendy look. Changing the shape of a sleeve or a pocket can give them a modern touch. The royal tartan check was even used in punk fashion as a statement of rebellion. Yes, rock stars wore kilts!

But the Queen's Barbour jacket is perhaps the most distinctive of all her garments. Dating from the 1890s, Barbours were originally made for country people and sailors who needed hard-wearing, waterproof clothes. But now they are equally popular with farmers, 'fashionistas' and film stars – both male and female. One of the latest stars to wear one was actor Daniel Craig in the James Bond films. Helen Mirren also wore one in her role as – yes, you guessed it – the Queen!

But what is so special about Barbour jackets? Well, they look good. But they also last a long time. Some people have had their Barbour jacket for decades and the company itself provides its own waxing and repair service for customers. These practices belong to a way of thinking about clothes called slow fashion. They help the environment because they support the idea of looking after what we already have instead of getting more. In fast fashion, clothes companies are producing clothes so fast that it's damaging the planet.

Thankfully, people are waking up to the problems. The Queen, Daniel Craig and Helen Mirren can take some comfort from the fact that their fashion choice is not only slower, but more thoughtful. It's better to make helpful choices and have good clothes than to always have new fashions.

---

distinctive (adj) easy to recognise because it is different or special
garment (n) a piece of clothing
hard-wearing (adj) lasting a long time and looking good even if used a lot
kilt (n) a Scottish skirt for men
wax (v) put wax on something to make it waterproof
waterproof (adj) stopping water going through

---

1 In pairs, discuss the questions.
  1 Who can you see in the photo?
  2 How would you describe her clothes?

2 🔊 3.18 Read the article and choose the correct option.
  1 The writer believes it's *strange / normal* that the Queen is a fashion icon.
  2 The Queen's look is often *transformed / copied exactly*.
  3 In the past the Barbour jacket was only used as a *working garment / fashion item*.
  4 Barbour jackets are worn by *men only / both sexes*.
  5 Barbour jackets last a *long / short* time.
  6 The Queen's clothes are examples of *slow / fast* fashion.
  7 Following slow fashion means buying *more / fewer* clothes.
  8 The writer says that people are learning *more / nothing* about the problems of fast fashion.

3 **VISIBLE THINKING** Follow these steps.
  THINK
  1 Do you think celebrities should encourage positive habits with their fashion choices? Why?/Why not?
  PAIR
  2 In pairs, tell each other what you think and why.
  SHARE
  3 Share your opinions with the class and listen to other students' ideas. Are they similar to yours?

BBC ▶ The price of fashion

4 Look at the photos and discuss the questions.
1. What can you see in the photos?
2. How can you connect the photos?
3. What problems could the fashion industry and clothes production cause?

5 ▶ 13 Watch Part 1 of a TV programme about the fashion industry and check your answers to Exercise 4.

6 ▶ 14 Watch Part 2 of the video and mark the sentences T (true) or F (false).
1. ☐ People have started producing cotton very recently.
2. ☐ People are generally aware how much water is needed to produce clothes.
3. ☐ The Aral Sea is in Asia.
4. ☐ The Aral Sea was important for the fishing and tourist industry.

7 How does the documentary suggest we should change the way we think about clothes? Do you agree?

PROJECT TIME

8 In groups of four, create an infographic about fast fashion, its effect on the environment and possible solutions. Follow these steps.

1 In your group, think about fast fashion and people in your school. Decide who will find answers to these questions.
- What are your classmates' shopping habits?
- How does clothes production affect the environment?
- What can individual shoppers do to help?
- What are some alternatives to fast fashion which might be less harmful to the environment?

2 Individually, create your part of the infographic.
- Find answers to your question(s) and write a short text.
- Find photos to illustrate the information.

3 In your group, create your infographic. You can use an infographic template.
- Put all the texts and photos together.
- Decide on a layout.
- Check and edit your infographic.
- Practise presenting your infographic.

4 Share your infographic with the class.
- Answer other students' questions.
- Ask questions and comment on the other infographics.

Progress Check Units 1–3

Vocabulary and Grammar

1 Choose the correct answer.
1. Of course you'll win! Just ___ your best!
   a make   b do   c give
2. We ___ Mark since 2020.
   a know   b 've known   c 've been knowing
3. I'm not tall or short. I'm average ___ .
   a height   b size   c built
4. Thomas has ___ excellent results in judo this year!
   a reached   b succeeded   c achieved
5. You wear ___ on your legs like trousers. They are tight but comfortable.
   a ankle boots   b leggings   c sandals

2 Complete the email with one word in each gap.

Hi, Hatty!
It ¹*was* great to hear from you yesterday! I'm delighted that you've joined a ²_____ to clean up our local area. I've been waiting ³_____ ages for something like this. I hate the way some people just ⁴_____ away rubbish without thinking.

I'm afraid I can't help this weekend because my teacher ⁵_____ given us a lot of homework. It's for Monday, so I can't ⁶_____ it off. I need to ⁷_____ it done. But can I join you later next week. I ⁸_____ the environment seriously too, and I would like to help! Let me know.

Love,
Amy

3 Complete the second sentence with the word in bold so that it means the same as the first one. Use no more than four words.
1. I was on the phone to my parents when the door bell rang. **TALKING**
   My parents *were talking to me* on the phone when the doorbell rang.
2. My cousins have stopped watching so much television. **USED**
   My cousins _____ more television than they do now.
3. My new jacket has been my favourite outfit recently. **WEARING**
   I _____ my new jacket a lot recently.
4. I think Louis is aged somewhere between thirty and forty. **THIRTIES**
   Louis _____ , I think.
5. This is now my fifth year in Gdansk. **LIVED**
   I've _____ five years now.

Speaking

4 Complete B's responses with the words below. There are three extra words.

> anyway   are   ~~glad~~   have
> much   so   that's   this

1. A: You look great in that outfit.
   B: Thanks, I'm *glad* you like it.
2. A: May I help you?
   B: No, I'm fine, but thanks _____ .
3. A: Does this hat suit me?
   B: Hmm … I don't think _____ . The colour isn't right.
4. A: You've got great taste in clothes.
   B: Thanks, _____ really nice of you.
5. A: I think this shirt looks great on me.
   B: Maybe you _____ right, but I think the other one looks better.

5 Imagine you are in a shop which sells clothes and accessories. In pairs, follow the steps below. Then change roles.

Step 1
Student A: Choose one of the items in the photos below and mime trying it on.
Student B: Compliment Student A on how they look.
B: You look great in those sunglasses!

Step 2
Student A: Thank Student B, but say you can't decide if you should buy it.
Student B: Offer to help Student A.
A: Really? Do you think so? I can't decide what to get!
B: Can I help you?

Step 3
Student A: Accept the help, then give your opinion about a different item.
Student B: Agree or disagree.
A: That would be great, thanks. What about this cap? I think it looks cool!
B: I'm not sure about that.

48

Listening

6 Would you like to keep in touch with your school friends after you leave school? Discuss in pairs. Think of three reasons why this might be a good idea.

7 🔊 PC1–3.1 Listen to Eve describing how she met her old school friend and complete the sentences. Use 1–3 words in each gap.

Meeting an old school friend

- Eve and Maya met at a café in ¹*the town centre* .
- Eve felt ² _____ when she saw Maya because she looked different. Her clothes were made from ³ _____ .
- When Maya left the school, Eve felt ⁴ _____ about it.
- They talked about the present. Eve's university course includes a project on ⁵ _____ .
- Maya organises events for an ⁶ _____ .

Reading

8 🔊 PC1–3.2 Read the blog post on the right. For each gap (1–5), choose the correct sentence (a–g). There are two extra sentences. Listen and check.

a I'm talking about individual love and attention.
b It's hard to tell young people to switch their screens off.
c This takes time away from family, school work and other important things.
d When teenagers get together, they sometimes make bad choices.
e Maybe it's natural to choose another teenager like themselves instead of a famous singer or sportsperson.
f It helps them find what they're interested in.
g I can see how much it's helped her.

9 In pairs, discuss the questions.
1 What YouTube channels do you follow? What kind of channels would you like to follow?
2 Do you think it's helpful to follow advice from teenage YouTubers? Why?/Why not?
3 Would you like to have your own YouTube channel? Why?/Why not?

Teenage YouTubers: a good thing?

My friend and I both have teenage children and we recently had a serious talk about teenage YouTube channels. She was worried about how much time her son spends watching videos on them. It isn't just gaming channels. He also looks at other topics – anything from fashion to the environment.

I think my friend is worrying a bit too much. It's really good for teenagers to have a lot of things to choose from. ¹_____ It's healthy that they're curious and feel secure enough to see what's out there.

I can give my own daughter as an example. She follows a teenage YouTuber's channel about achieving goals, being positive and making the most of things. ²_____ OK, so maybe I'm a bit upset she didn't get this good advice from me! But it doesn't matter where it came from. The important thing is it worked.

We have to accept that teenagers often look to role models as examples. ³_____ They're about the same age as the person they're following. They probably have some of the same goals and challenges.

I told my friend something important and I would like all parents to remember it. There's one thing you can give your child that a YouTuber never can. ⁴_____ It's what I always remember to do.

One final thought: I'm more concerned about the teenagers that make the videos than the ones that watch them. It takes hours and hours to get ideas, make videos and upload them. ⁵_____ And then there's reading all the comments (and some of them are not very kind). If my daughter asks about having her own YouTube channel, I'll ask her to think very carefully.

Writing

10 You have a friend in Canada who is interested in nature and helping the environment. He has emailed you asking if you are interested in those things too. Reply to your friend's email. Include this information.
- where and when you went
- what environmental topics you are interested in
- the worst environmental problem in your area
- what you would like to do to help
- the name of a beautiful natural place in your country you've visited

Work hard, dream big!

4

VOCABULARY	GRAMMAR
Jobs	Work	Working conditions	Job training	Success at work	Talking about the future	Future Continuous

Pros

1 **Working flexibly.** You can take time off whenever you need to take care of personal stuff, see friends and take the dog for a walk!
2 **Being more productive.** Fewer meetings and workplace chats mean it's easier to concentrate, so you can be more efficient.
3 **Saving money.** You don't need to pay for train tickets or buy lunch in cafés or restaurants.

Cons

1 **Working more.** No separation between work and home means you may end up doing overtime and working too much.
2 **Feeling bored.** You can feel lonely and fed up, and miss the company of your colleagues.
3 **Being less productive.** It's easy to put off work by doing housework or making lunch, so you may work less and fall behind.

WORKING FROM HOME
The pros and cons

4.1 Vocabulary

Work and jobs

1 What do you think are the advantages and disadvantages of working from home?

2 Read the text above. Does it mention any of your ideas from Exercise 1?

3 🔊 4.1 Study Vocabulary box A. Which of the jobs do you think you can do easily from home?

VOCABULARY A — Jobs

accountant blogger cleaner electrician engineer
influencer interpreter librarian mechanic
plumber psychologist translator

Compound nouns

app developer computer programmer fashion designer
film director flight attendant freelance journalist
lab assistant music critic personal trainer
shop assistant travel agent

4 **I KNOW!** In pairs, add more jobs to Vocabulary box A. Say which are easy to do from home.

5 In pairs, take it in turns to describe a job from Vocabulary box A for your partner to guess.
I help people understand each other when they don't speak the same language.

6 Read the emails. What work is Jenny doing now? What's her new job?

✉️

Hey, Sandra,

Did you hear about Jenny? She quit her job as a lab assistant. She didn't feel part of the team in that company and she had no chance of getting a promotion there. For now, she's doing some voluntary work as a shop assistant in a charity shop, but she's applied for lots of jobs and sent off over twenty CVs. She has two interviews tomorrow: one for a job as a translator and the other as an app developer. I hope she gets one of them.

Cheers,
Mark

✉️

Sandra,

Good news! Jenny got the job in the translation agency! She's going to the office tomorrow to sign the contract and to meet her new colleagues. She isn't going to earn a high salary, but she can work from home and she's just happy she's not unemployed anymore.

See you soon,
Mark

Unit 4   50

7 🔊 4.2 **WORD FRIENDS** Find these phrases in the emails in Exercise 6 and write the missing words. Listen and check.

<u>apply</u> for a job
2 be/_____ part of a team
3 _____ unemployed
4 _____ voluntary work
5 _____ a salary/wage
6 _____ a promotion
7 get fired
8 give up/_____ a job
9 _____ an interview
10 _____ your colleagues
11 _____/write a CV
12 _____ a contract

8 Complete the questions with the correct form of verbs from Exercise 7. Then, in pairs, discuss the questions.

1 Do you think you need to mention your hobbies when you <u>write</u> your CV?
2 How do you think most people feel when they _____ an interview? Why?
3 Do you like to _____ part of a team or do you prefer to work alone? Why?
4 Have you ever _____ any voluntary work? Would you like to? If so, what kind?
5 Can you think of some reasons why people _____ fired from their job?
6 Do you think it's more important to _____ a good salary or to have a job you enjoy?
7 How do you think most people feel when they _____ unemployed? Why?
8 Can you think of some reasons why people might _____ up their job and start looking for a new one?

9 Read the advert for the job Jenny got. What do you think attracted her to the job?

Chelsea Communicators

Would you like to be a member of staff in London's best translation and interpreting company? We offer well-paid jobs with permanent contracts, flexible working hours, regular pay rises and five weeks paid holidays a year. If you're ambitious, a hard worker and don't mind doing some overtime, visit our website and send us your CV.

10 🔊 4.3 Study Vocabulary box B. Check you understand the words.

VOCABULARY B — **Working conditions**

do/work overtime   flexible working hours   hourly rate
member of staff   paid holiday   pay rise
temporary/permanent contract   well-paid/badly-paid

11 Choose the correct option.

✉️

Hi Ellie,

I've got a new job working full-time for a translation agency! I'm the newest member of ¹*staff / work*. It's a(n) ²*overtime / temporary* contract for now – just six months, but I'm really happy here. We have flexible ³*permanent / working* hours, so I can work from home three days a week. When we have a big job on, we have to do some ⁴*overtime / rate*, but I don't mind. Firstly, because the hourly ⁵*rate / rise* is higher when you work extra hours and secondly, because I love the work. Translating is fun. It's not ⁶*badly-paid / well-paid* either. The money's a lot better than it was in my old job. And my boss says I'll get a ⁷*pay / voluntary* rise soon. There are quite generous paid ⁸*holidays / wages* too.

So let's start planning our trip in August!

Love,
Jenny

12 Which of the things below do you think are the most important things in a job? Discuss in pairs.

chances of promotion   flexible working hours
friendly boss/colleagues   generous holidays
high salary   interesting work
possibility to work from home

VIDEO ▶ **WIDER WORLD**

13 ▶ 15 Watch five people talking about the jobs below. Which jobs do they think should be better-paid?

bin collector   office worker   soldier
street sweeper

14 Which jobs would you like/not like to do? Which jobs should be better paid? Why? Discuss in pairs.

I wouldn't like to be a mechanic. I hate cars.
I think all jobs should be well-paid.

4.2 Grammar
Talking about the future

1 What are the advantages and disadvantages of an open-air cinema? Do you think it would be fun to work in one?

2 🔊 4.4 Read the email. What is Paolo's plan for the summer?

✉

Hi, Matt!

What are you going to do in the summer? I'm going to Italy. My uncle is starting a new business this summer. It's an open-air cinema and I'm going to work there (I'll send you a photo of the cinema later). My uncle lives next to the sea and I'm not going to work in the morning, so I'll be able to go swimming every day before lunch. I'll probably spend my mornings on the beach with my cousins and then I'll work with my uncle in the evenings. It's going to be great.

My flight leaves the day after we finish school and I fly back to the UK on 30 August, so you'll have to come and visit me before then. I'm going to miss hanging out with my friends, but I'm sure I won't miss the British weather!

Bye for now,
Paolo

---

3 Study the Grammar box. Find more examples of the future forms in the email.

> **GRAMMAR** — Talking about the future
>
> **will**
> I'll send you a photo. (spontaneous decision)
> I won't miss the British weather. (prediction)
>
> **be going to**
> I'm going to work there. (plan)
> It's going to be great. (prediction based on facts)
>
> **Present Continuous**
> My uncle is starting a new business this summer. (arrangement)
>
> **Present Simple**
> My flight leaves the day after we finish school. (schedule)
>
> Look at the future forms of *can* and *must*.
> I can go swimming. → I'll be able to go swimming.
> You must come and visit me. → You'll have to come and visit me.
>
> GRAMMAR TIME > PAGE 129

4 Complete the second sentence so that it means the same as the first one. Use no more than three words.
1 They've arranged to visit their friend at the weekend.
They *are visiting* their friend at the weekend.
2 They're expecting to be well-paid.
They think _____ well-paid.
3 The boat is scheduled to leave at 4 p.m.
The boat _____ at 4 p.m.
4 I'm planning to quit my job.
I _____ quit my job.

5 🔊 4.5 Choose the correct option. Listen and check.
Scott: Are you OK? You look worried!
Fran: I am! My interview at the bakery ¹*will be / is* in half an hour!
Scott: Are you looking for a job?
Fran: Yes. I ²*'m going / 'll go* on holiday next month; it's all booked. My flight ³*leaves / will leave* on the first, so I need to earn some money!
Scott: Oh, right. Where ⁴*do you go / are you going*?
Fran: Ireland. My aunt has invited us, so we ⁵*'re staying / 'll stay* at her house in Dublin.
Scott: Cool. ⁶*Will you be able to / Are you able to* travel around Ireland a bit?
Fran: Definitely. Cork, Galway, Donegal …

YOUR WORLD

6 In pairs, take it in turns to ask and answer questions about your partner's plans for this evening/next weekend/the summer holidays.

Unit 4 | 52 | I can use different tenses to talk about future events.

4.3 Reading and Vocabulary
Virtual reality training

1 Look at the title of the article. What are the advantages of virtual reality training? Read the introduction to the article and check.

2 🔊 4.6 Read the article and answer the questions.

Fearne
1. What kind of surgeon does Fearne want to be?
2. Who gave her help during a virtual operation?
3. Which type of training gives better results?

Sean
1. According to Sean, what improves trainees' results?
2. What has he been learning to avoid recently?
3. What will the VR training allow him to do?

Dylan
1. What job does Dylan want to do in the future?
2. Where is he doing the VR training?
3. What advantage of VR training does he mention?

3 🔊 4.7 Study the highlighted job training phrases in the article. Complete the text with the correct form of the verbs. Listen and check.

I'm ¹*doing* a training course in Travel and Tourism at college. It's a great course. They ² _____ virtual training to ³ _____ students practical experience. I ⁴ _____ part in a VR workshop for the first time yesterday. It was great to ⁵ _____ an opportunity to use my skills in different situations. During the workshop, we ⁶ _____ feedback from the teacher. It's just what I need because I'm ⁷ _____ to be a specialist in hotel management, and with VR I can ⁸ _____ relevant work experience without leaving the college.

YOUR WORLD

4 In pairs, discuss the questions.
1. Would you like to do a VR training course? Why?/Why not?
2. What jobs do you think you will be able to train for with VR in the future?

Training for work with virtual reality

Today more and more people are improving their professional skills thanks to virtual reality (VR). The companies that provide virtual training say it's faster, safer and cheaper than traditional training. It gives trainees practical experience. They can work in teams or independently. And they can learn without worrying about making expensive mistakes. We spoke to three virtual reality trainees.

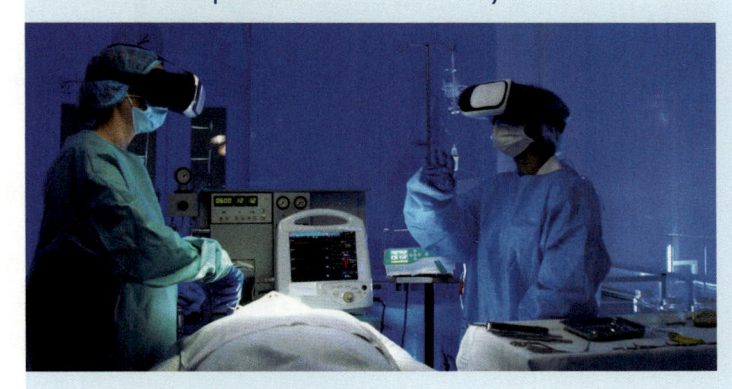

A Fearne, 25, trainee surgeon
'Virtual reality is a valuable tool for the medical profession. I'm a qualified doctor, but I'm training to be a specialist in sporting injuries. Yesterday I took part in a training workshop. I operated on a knee without using a real body. It felt just like the real thing. While we were working on our virtual patients, we were getting feedback from the professor. On the screen, you can see what you've done, what to do next and how well you're doing. It seems that VR training produces better surgeons. In one study, VR trainees' scores were 230 percent higher than those of traditionally trained students.'

B Sean, 20, construction worker
'Virtual training's a great way to gain work experience. It's like playing video games, which is cool because I think you learn better when you're enjoying yourself. It's so real. You totally feel as if you're six floors up on a building site. This week we've been learning how to avoid dangerous situations like falling off a high building. That's really important because there are a lot of workplace accidents in the construction industry. I've done a few training courses, but this is the best I've ever done. I'm sure this qualification will help me get a good job.'

C Dylan, 21, computer programmer
'My job's OK. I recently got a promotion. But it's not what I want to do. I want to be a pilot. The problem is flying lessons are expensive. So, when I heard there was a vacancy on a VR training course for pilots at my local college, I applied and I was lucky enough to be accepted. I'm so happy to have got an opportunity to fly. It's not exactly like the real thing, but it's pretty good. And, of course, it's totally safe. The other day I crashed when I was landing at the airport, and nobody got hurt.'

I can understand an article about virtual reality.

4.4 Grammar
Future Continuous

1 Look at the picture in the blog post. Which jobs do you think robots will take over in the next few years?

I think we'll have robot cleaners in a few years' time.

TERRY'S BLOG

In ten years' time

I recently saw a documentary about the future. It predicted that in ten years' time robots and computers will be doing almost all of today's jobs. That got me thinking about my life. So here are a few of my predictions.

- This time next year I'll be speaking with a Scottish accent. (I'm going to study in Edinburgh, the Scottish capital!)
- In five years' time I'll be celebrating the end of my university studies.
- In ten years I'll be earning a fortune. I'll be working as an app developer.
- I won't be living in Bedford. I'll be living somewhere exciting like London or Paris.
- I won't be doing any housework. My personal robot will be doing it all for me.

What about you? What will you be doing in five years? Where will you be living? Will you be working in ten years' time or will you be watching robots do your job? Send in your comments now!

2 🔊 4.8 Read the blog post and mark the sentences T (true) or F (false).
1. ☐ Terry's living in Scotland now.
2. ☐ He's got big plans.
3. ☐ He's worried he'll be unemployed because of robots.

3 Study the Grammar box. Find more examples of the Future Continuous in the blog post.

GRAMMAR Future Continuous

I'**ll be speaking** with a Scottish accent.
I **won't be living** in Bedford.
What **will** you **be doing**?
Will you **be working**? Yes, I **will**./No, I **won't**.

Time expressions
this time next month/year, this/next weekend/week, in five years/in five years' time, at 9 p.m. tonight, in the future

GRAMMAR TIME > PAGE 129

4 🔊 4.9 Complete the dialogue with the Future Continuous form of the verbs in brackets. Listen and check.

Terry: I'll be in France next week.
Sally: What ¹*will you be doing* (you/do) in France?
Terry: I ² _____ (work).
Deepak: Where ³ _____ (you/work)?
Terry: In a hotel at a ski resort. This time next week I ⁴ _____ (ski) down a mountain!
Deepak: You won't have time to ski. You ⁵ _____ (work) all the time.
Terry: No, I won't. Just wait and see. In a few years I ⁶ _____ (ski) in the Olympics!

5 Make questions in the Future Continuous. Then, in pairs, ask and answer the questions.

1. what subjects / you / study / next year / ?
   What subjects will you be studying next year?
2. you / work / abroad / in the future / ?
3. you / do / work experience / next summer / ?
4. your friends / go / to university / after school / ?
5. you / celebrate / your birthday / soon / ?
6. you / meet / your friends / tomorrow / ?

VIDEO WIDER WORLD

6 ▶ 16 Watch six people talking about the future. What will they be doing at the times below?

| 11 p.m. tonight | in five years | next summer |
| this weekend | | |

7 In pairs, say what you will be doing at the times in Exercise 6.

In five years I'll be living and working in …

Unit 4 54 I can use the Future Continuous to talk about actions in progress in the future.

4.5 Listening and Vocabulary
Success at work

1 Have you ever won a prize? What was it? What was it for?

2 🔊 4.10 Study the Vocabulary box. Then match the words with the definitions below.

> **VOCABULARY** ▸ **Success at work**
>
> award   candidate   career   diploma   employer   speech

1 a prize that you get for doing something well: *award*
2 a job that you have trained for and have done for a long time: _____
3 a formal talk to a group of people: _____
4 a document that shows you have completed a course: _____
5 someone who wants to be chosen for a job or a prize: _____
6 a person or company that pays you to work: _____

3 Cover Exercise 2. In pairs, describe a word from the Vocabulary box for your partner to guess.
A: It's something you win when you do something well.
B: An award?

4 🔊 4.11 Listen to the first part of a recording. Answer the questions.
1 What type of event is taking place?
2 What's going to happen later in the evening?

5 Look at the photos of Claire and Stuart. What do you think their jobs are?

6 🔊 4.12 Listen to the second part of the recording and check your ideas.

7 🔊 4.12 Listen again and choose the correct answer.
1 When she was on TV, Claire appeared
   a embarrassed.   b calm.   c nervous.
2 Claire got her diploma when she was
   a sixteen.   b seventeen.   c eighteen.
3 Where was Stuart when he designed his app?
   a at home   b at a friend's
   c in the mountains
4 Stuart's dad
   a owns a sports shop.
   b works in a sports shop.
   c has a job in a bank.
5 What does Claire consider her mum to be?
   a an employee   b a colleague
   c a friend
6 How long will Stuart be working with a famous app developer in New York?
   a a week   b a month   c a weekend

8 In pairs, compare and contrast Claire and Stuart's stories.
Stuart is only fifteen and he's an app developer. Claire is older and she's a personal trainer.

> **YOUR WORLD**
>
> 9 In pairs, think of a simple idea for a new business. Explain your idea to the class. Use these questions to help you.
>   1 What is the business?
>   2 Why is the business a good idea?
>   3 How many people are in the business?
>   4 What's the future for your business?

I can understand a conversation about success at work.

4.6 Speaking
Warnings, recommendations and prohibition

VIDEO ▶ BEA'S NEWS BULLETIN

Bea has a work experience job at a radio station. The boss, Jo, is showing her around.

Jo: You'll be sitting here. This is your computer. Watch out: it crashes a lot, so remember to back up your files regularly. Oh, sorry. Yes? OK, bye. Bea, we've got a problem. Our newsreader's going to be late. She won't be able to read the next news bulletin. It's in half an hour. I know it's your first day with us, but can you do it?

Bea: Er … I suppose so.

Later …

Jo: Now pay attention. This is important. See that green light? After a few minutes it'll turn red. If you're not careful, you'll miss it, so make sure you keep an eye on it.

Bea: And then what do I do?

Jo: Read the news. You mustn't speak too fast. Be sure to speak clearly. And whatever you do, don't shout. Just speak normally. OK? Good luck!

Bea: This is the news. The town council has …

Later …

Bea: Oh, I'm really sorry about the bottle! I suppose I'm not allowed to come again.

Jo: Of course you are. You did a great job and we can try it again tomorrow. Just watch out for your bottle!

SOUNDS GOOD! Keep an eye on it. • Good luck! • You did a great job.

1 Look at the photo. Where is Bea? What is she doing?

2 ▶ 17 ◀)) 4.13 Watch or listen. What does Jo ask Bea to do? Why?

3 Study the Speaking box. Find examples of the phrases in the dialogue.

SPEAKING | Warnings, recommendations and prohibition

Warning
Pay attention!   Mind your head!
Look out!   Watch out!   Be careful (you don't …).
If you're not careful, you'll …

Recommending
Remember to …   Don't forget to …
Make sure (you) …   Be sure to/not to …

Prohibiting
Whatever you do, don't …
You can't/mustn't …   You're not allowed to …

---

4 How well does Bea do on the first day of her work experience at the radio station?

SET FOR LIFE

5 What do you think are the three greatest benefits of work experience for young people? Use these ideas to help you.
- You find out what it's like to work with other people.
- It can help you when you apply to go to university.
- It helps you identify what you like and what you're good at.

6 ◀)) 4.14 Complete the instructions with one word in each gap. Use the Speaking box to help you. Listen and check.
1 *Remember* to wash your hands. Make _____ your knives are sharp. And _____ careful you don't burn yourself. It's hot.
2 Watch _____ ! That camera is worth a fortune! Now pay _____ . You're not _____ to speak while we're filming.

7 What kind of work experience is taking place in each situation in Exercise 6?

YOUR WORLD

8 In pairs, write a dialogue for one of the work experience jobs in Exercise 6. Use the Speaking box to help you.

I can give warnings, make recommendations and express prohibition.

4.7 Writing
A job application letter

1 Do you think summer jobs are a good idea? Why?/Why not?

2 Go to page 136 and read the job ads. Then read Rohan's application letter. Which job is he applying for? Do you think he is a good candidate? Why?/Why not?

Dear Sir/Madam,

① I am writing in response to your advertisement. I am interested in applying for the job of summer receptionist at the Arts Centre. I am currently in my final year at high school, and I will be studying Art at college from September. Therefore, I am very keen to gain work experience.

② Regarding the post of receptionist, I have some experience in dealing with customers at a local shop, where I worked on Saturday mornings. In addition, I think I would be suitable for the position because I am a good speaker and very sociable. I am a frequent visitor to the Arts Centre, and I am working on a school project about your recent Kandinsky exhibition. I will be able to work at weekends this summer.

③ Thank you for taking the time to read my application. I hope you will consider me for the post. I am available for an interview at any time.

④ I look forward to hearing from you.

Yours faithfully,
Rohan Patel

---

3 Study the Writing box. Find similar phrases in Rohan's letter.

WRITING   A job application letter

Reason for writing
1 I am writing to apply for the position of …
   I would love to gain experience in this sector.

Describe your experience and personal qualities
2 I am currently studying Science at school.
   I have worked in a library.
   I have a working knowledge of these applications: …
   I am a very good team player.

Thank the reader
3 Thank you in advance for considering my application.

End your letter
4 Please feel free to contact me if you need any further information.
   Yours sincerely,

---

4 Study the Language box. Find formal equivalents of the informal phrases below in Rohan's letter.

LANGUAGE   Formal style

Use formal language to start and finish.
Dear Sir/Madam, → *Yours faithfully,*
Dear Mrs Collins, → *Yours sincerely,*

Use formal phrases.
Regarding the post of …
I look forward to hearing from you.

Don't use contractions.
I am very keen to …

Use formal connectors to explain and add ideas, e.g. *therefore, as well as, in addition.*

1 Hi there, *Dear Sir/Madam,*
2 I have worked with customers
3 See you soon,
4 Interview me now.
5 I hope you answer me.
6 I saw your job ad
7 about the job
8 I really want the job

WRITING TIME

5 Write an application letter for one of the jobs advertised on page 136.

1 Find ideas
Make notes for your letter. Think about:
- your reasons for wanting the job.
- what you are doing now.
- your experience and personal qualities.

2 Plan
Organise your ideas into paragraphs. Use Rohan's letter to help you.

3 Write and share
- Write a draft of your letter. Use the Language box and the Writing box to help you.
- Share your letter with another student for feedback.
- Write the final version of your letter.

4 Check
- Check language: have you used a formal style?
- Check grammar: have you used future tenses correctly?

I can write a job application letter.

Vocabulary Activator

WORDLIST 🔊 4.15

Jobs
accountant (n)
blogger (n)
cleaner (n)
electrician (n)
engineer (n)
influencer (n)
interpreter (n)
librarian (n)
mechanic (n)
plumber (n)
psychologist (n)
translator (n)

Jobs: compound nouns
app developer (n)
computer programmer (n)
fashion designer (n)
film director (n)
flight attendant (n)
freelance journalist (n)
lab assistant (n)
music critic (n)
personal trainer (n)
shop assistant (n)
travel agent (n)

Word friends (work)
apply for a job
be part of a team
be unemployed
do voluntary work
earn a salary
earn a wage
feel part of a team
get a promotion
get fired
give up a job
have an interview
meet your colleagues
quit a job
send off a CV
sign a contract
write a CV

Working conditions
badly-paid (adj)
do overtime
flexible working hours (n)
hourly rate (n)
member of staff (n)
paid holidays (n)
pay rise (n)
permanent contract (n)
temporary contract (n)
well-paid (adj)
work overtime

Job training
do a training course
gain work experience
get an opportunity to
get feedback from
give practical experience
improve professional skills
provide virtual training
take part in a training workshop
train to be a specialist

Success at work
award (n)
candidate (n)
career (n)
diploma (n)
employer (n)
speech (n)

Extra words
agency (n)
application (n)
charity shop (n)
complete a course
concentrate (v)
construction worker (n)
deal with customers
do housework
earn a fortune
efficient (adj)
fall behind (v)
make a career of something
management (n)
newsreader (n)
part-time position
personal qualities (n)
profession (n)
put money into something
qualification (n)
qualified (adj)
receptionist (n)
surgeon (n)
take time off
train for a job
trainee (n)
vacancy (n)
work as a team
work from home
work independently
workplace accident (n)

---

1 Choose the odd one out.
1 mechanic   employer   librarian   plumber
2 contract   CV   diploma   career
3 wage   hourly rate   voluntary work   salary
4 award   candidate   CV   interview

2 The jobs below have got mixed up! Rearrange them.

app agent   computer director   film developer
flight trainer   personal attendant   travel programmer

app developer

3 Use the wordlist to find these things.
1 three phrases for leaving a job *get fired, …*
2 two jobs related to a foreign language
3 three jobs in which people fix things
4 two phrases about the money you get for work

4 Find words in the wordlist to match the definitions.
1 a talk you give to an audience: *speech*
2 a person who has applied for a job: _____
3 without a job: _____
4 working more than your normal work hours: _____
5 information that helps you improve: _____
6 a person who tries to change how you think: _____

5 🔊 4.16 **PRONUNCIATION** Listen to words 1–4. Then write the words below in the correct group according to their stress pattern.

interview   mechanic   professional   unemployed

1 ooO: engineer, _____
2 oOo: accountant, _____
3 Ooo: candidate, _____
4 oOoo: experience, _____

6 🔊 4.17 **PRONUNCIATION** Listen and check. Then listen again and repeat.

Unit 4 58

Revision

Vocabulary

1 Read what each person says and write their job.
1 'The book you're looking for is on the history shelf.' _librarian_
2 'Water is coming out of the shower head because it's broken.' _____
3 'Croatia is beautiful, with lots of accommodation choices.' _____
4 'Please stay in your seats while the "Seatbelt fastened" lights are on.' _____
5 'These numbers show what profits your firm made last year.' _____
6 'Fans won't be disappointed with the new album.' _____

2 Choose the correct option.
1 I've got an *experience / opportunity* to work for a famous magazine.
2 They both *earn / gain* a good salary.
3 I might get a pay *rise / rate* next year.
4 I got a job by sending *up / off* my CV to different companies.
5 When there is a lot of work, you might have to *do / make* overtime.
6 You can improve by taking *place / part* in training.
7 Jo has decided to give *out / up* her job.

3 Complete the text with the words below.

| apply | ~~career~~ | experience | have | send |
| sign | work | write | | |

Let's say your life plan is to have a ¹_career_ designing clothes. So ² _____ for some jobs, but don't be disappointed if you have no success at first. Think about doing voluntary ³ _____ because it looks great on your CV. When you ⁴ _____ your CV, put any practical ⁵ _____ on it, even if it's not about clothes. Then ⁶ _____ it off to different employers. Sooner or later you'll ⁷ _____ an interview and maybe a job offer! But make sure it has everything you want before you ⁸ _____ a contract.

Grammar

4 Complete the sentences with the correct future form of the verbs in brackets. Use *will*, *be going to*, the Present Continuous or the Present Simple.
1 A: Have you got any idea about Greg's future career yet?
  B: I have a feeling it _will be_ (be) in music.
2 A: On no! My pen's stopped working.
  B: It's OK. I _____ (lend) you mine.
3 A: A TV crew has just arrived outside the office.
  B: That's right. They _____ (record) some interviews.
4 A: Do you want to hang out this morning?
  B: Sorry, I _____ (see) the dentist at ten.
5 A: There are too many people on Earth!
  B: Don't worry, we _____ (be able to) live on Mars soon!
6 Our bus _____ (leave) at 2 p.m. tomorrow.
7 Your cat is having trouble climbing down the tree. She _____ (fall)!

5 Complete the sentences with the Future Continuous form of the verbs in brackets.
1 Visit us in July. I _won't be working_ (not work) then.
2 Call me before 8 p.m. tomorrow. After that we _____ (watch) a film.
3 _____ (you/wait) for me at the station?
4 I _____ (not go out) after lunch.
5 This time tomorrow we _____ (fly) to New York.
6 The doctor _____ (not see) patients between 10 and 12 a.m. tomorrow.

Speaking

6 In pairs, follow the instructions.
1 Choose one activity each that you would like to do.
   - explore underground caves
   - cook outside on a fire
   - visit an amusement park
   - attend an open-air music festival
2 Think about how your partner can do his/her activity safely. Think of one warning, one recommendation and one prohibition.
3 Take turns to talk about your plans and reply.
   A: *I'm going to explore underground caves.*
   B: *Nice, but look out for low rocks! If you're not careful, you can hit your head.*

Dictation

7 🔊 4.18 Listen. Then listen again and write down what you hear during each pause.

SET FOR LIFE

A job interview

Have you got a job interview soon?
Listen to my podcast and learn how to make a great first impression.

1 Look at the pictures. In which one is the teenager making a good first impression?

2 Look at the pictures again. Choose the correct option in the advice for making a good first impression.

1 *Wear / Don't wear* smart clothes.

2 *Have / Don't have* messy hair or hair that hides your face.

3 *Smile / Don't smile*.

4 *Look / Don't look* into the interviewer's eyes.

5 *Play / Don't play* nervously with something in your hand.

6 *Sit / Don't sit* with a straight back.

3 🔊 4.19 Listen to the first part of a podcast and check your answers in Exercise 2. Which tips do you think are the most important?

4 🔊 4.19 Match these reasons with the advice in Exercise 2. Then listen again and check.

a [2] The interviewer wants to see you properly.
b [ ] You don't want the interviewer to think that you are hiding something or lying.
c [ ] You want the interviewer to think that you are making an effort.
d [ ] You'll look more confident.
e [ ] The interviewer needs to concentrate on what you are saying.
f [ ] It makes you look friendly.

I can make a good first impression.

5 🔊 **4.20** Listen to the second part of the podcast. Tick (✓) the advice you hear.
1. ☐ Prepare for the interview.
2. ☐ Find out about the business.
3. ☐ List useful experience and interests.
4. ☐ Think about how to answer typical interview questions.
5. ☐ Don't tell the interviewer about your weaknesses.
6. ☐ Don't arrive too early for the interview.
7. ☐ Leave your mobile phone at home.
8. ☐ Show that you're interested in the job.
9. ☐ Show that you already know exactly how to do it.
10. ☐ Show that you are the right kind of person and have the right skills.

6 Choose one of the workplaces below. Then, in pairs, discuss how you might answer the questions in a job interview. Read the Useful phrases to help you.

> café   children's play centre   clothes shop   electronics shop

1. Can you tell me a little about yourself?
2. What are your strengths?
3. What are your weaknesses?
4. Why do you want this job?
5. What have you done in the past that will help you in this job?

7 Which questions did you find the most difficult to answer? Why?

8 Read the Useful tips. Do you think it will be easy to remember all the advice in a job interview? Which things do you think will be hardest for you?

SET FOR LIFE

9 In pairs, role play a job interview. Follow the instructions.

1 Choose one of the workplaces below or use your own idea.

> sports club   animal centre   charity shop
> kids' arts and crafts centre

2 List your strengths, weaknesses, skills and experience.

3 Role play the interview. Use expressions from the Useful phrases box.
- Student A: You are the interviewer. Ask the questions in Exercise 6, in any order. Ask extra questions if you want.
- Student B: You are the person who has applied for the job. Try to answer all the questions and make a good impression.
Then swap roles.

4 Choose one of your interviews and act it out it for the class.

Make a good first impression

USEFUL TIPS

It's important to make a good first impression at a job interview.

Before the interview

- Look smart.
- Prepare answers to typical interview questions.
- Turn off your mobile.
- Arrive on time.

During the interview

- Keep eye contact.
- Smile.
- Explain why you are perfect for the job.
- Show that you are interested in the job.

USEFUL PHRASES

Talking about strengths and weaknesses
I'm really good at …
Unfortunately, I'm not always the most … person, but I'm trying to change that by …ing.

Talking about your experiences
… has given me the chance to improve my … skills.
My time in … (has) taught me …

Showing interest in a job
I'd be excited to work for your company because …
I love the idea of …ing.
It would be great to learn how to …

To the stars and beyond

5

VOCABULARY
Space | Dimensions and distance | Large numbers | Space travel | Space science

GRAMMAR
Zero, First and Second Conditionals | Third Conditional

CITIZEN SCIENCE SPACE PROJECTS

Scientists often need non-scientists to help with projects, especially when they collect lots of data. These are known as 'citizen science' projects, and anybody can get involved. Many projects need volunteers. You can find them on special websites.

TOMATOSPHERE™ PROJECT
A If you are interested in plant experiments, you can help to grow special tomato seeds. These seeds have been into space! Just sign up at Tomatosphere™ to get your own 'space seeds'!

THE GLOBE AT NIGHT PROJECT
B Perhaps you're interested in our use of energy here on Earth. There's a great project called Globe at Night. You need to match the stars you see at night with a picture. This helps to measure light pollution.

THE PLANET HUNTERS PROJECT
C If you're more interested in our galaxy, projects like Planet Hunters involve finding small details in photographs of planets. Humans are sometimes better than computers at understanding this type of data and it's possible to make amazing discoveries.

5.1 Vocabulary

Space

1 Are you interested in space? Have you heard of any new space discoveries or projects recently?

2 What is citizen science? Read the text quickly and find out. Which project sounds most interesting to you?

3 🔊 5.1 Study Vocabulary box A. Which of these things can you see in the photos above?

> **VOCABULARY A** ▶ **Space**
>
> astronaut   astronomer   comet   Earth   galaxy   gravity
> moon   orbit   planet   satellite   solar system
> space station   star   telescope

4 Match words from Vocabulary box A with their definitions.
  1 the force that makes objects fall to the ground: _gravity_
  2 an electronic system in space for communication: _____
  3 a giant space 'snowball' of gas, rock and dust with a long tail: _____
  4 a curved path around a planet, star or moon: _____
  5 the group of planets and stars around our sun: _____
  6 a huge group of many millions of stars and solar systems: _____

Unit 5   62

5 🔊 5.2 **WORD FRIENDS** Complete the sentences with the words below. Listen and check.

> away   length   per   speed   ~~wide~~

1. The smallest satellite is a cube satellite. It is 10 centimetres high/long/*wide*.
2. The height/_____/width of the cube satellite is 10 centimetres.
3. Most satellites are about 36,000 kilometres _____. (= They're 36,000 kilometres from Earth.)
4. Their _____ is 11,000 kilometres/7,000 miles _____/an hour.

6 Complete the sentences with words from Exercise 5.
1. A speed of twenty miles *per* hour is the same as thirty-two kilometres _____ hour.
2. The moon is about 384,000 kilometres _____.
3. The space station's wings are 35 metres long and 12 metres _____.
4. Large satellites can be the height of a school bus: about 2 metres _____.

7 🔊 5.3 Study Vocabulary box B. Listen to the numbers.

VOCABULARY B	Large numbers
100 = a hundred	1,000,000 = a million
1,000 = a thousand	1,000,000,000 = a billion

⚠️ **WATCH OUT!**
How do we say/write numbers?
- We do not use plurals for large numbers.
  4,700 = four **thousand** seven **hundred**
  2,400,000 = two **million** four **hundred thousand**
- In British English, we put *and* between *hundred* and a smaller number that follows.
  1,403 = one thousand four hundred **and** three
- We use a hyphen when we write numbers from 21 to 99.
  twenty-one   ninety-nine
- In writing, we separate billions, thousands and hundreds with a comma.
  3,000   5,000,000
- We can make very big numbers simpler with *point*.
  1,700,000 (one million, seven hundred thousand) = 1.7 million (one point seven million)

8 🔊 5.4 Write the numbers in words. Listen and check.
1. 745 — *seven hundred and forty-five*
2. 9,862 — _____
3. 3,600,000 — _____
4. 5.8 billion — _____
5. 24,222,394 — _____
6. 800,000,000 — _____

9 In pairs, take it in turns to write a number on a piece of paper and show it to your partner. He/She has to read it aloud.

10 🔊 5.5 In pairs, choose the correct option. Listen and check.

SPACE TRIVIA

1. Ancient astronomers believed that the *Moon / Earth* was at the centre of the universe.
2. There are thousands of planets in the universe, but only eight in our *galaxy / solar system*.
3. Two of those eight planets don't have any moons: *Venus / Earth* and Mercury.
4. The Sun is a giant *star / planet*.
5. The Sun is about the same size as one *thousand / million* Earths.
6. The Earth travels around the Sun in a(n) *orbit / height* once every year.
7. The Karman Line marks the end of the Earth's atmosphere and the beginning of space. It's one hundred *thousand / million* metres above the Earth – that's 100 kilometres!
8. Light can travel round the *Earth / solar system* seven times in one second!
9. Mars is millions of kilometres *away / far*, but actually, the distance between Mars and the Earth changes all the time.

YOUR WORLD

11 Make a note of two space facts from this lesson. Make a small change to one fact so it is false. In pairs, take it in turns to share your facts with your partner. He/She guesses which fact is true and which is false.

> A: The Karman Line is one thousand metres above the Earth.
> B: False.

I can talk about space and use large numbers.

5.2 Grammar
Zero, First and Second Conditionals

1 Work in pairs. What skills do you think you need to become an astronaut? Compare your ideas with the class.

2 🔊 5.6 Read the introduction to a podcast and check your ideas from Exercise 1. What other skills and qualifications does the text mention?

TALK TIME with Zac

WOULD YOU BE A GOOD ASTRONAUT?

American Alyssa Carson has always wanted to be an astronaut. If her dreams come true, she'll travel over 200 million kilometres to Mars. But how do you become an astronaut? Would I be a good astronaut if I had the right training? What skills do astronauts need?

Firstly, you have to be good at Science and a lot of other school subjects. For example, you can't become an astronaut unless you speak several languages. Alyssa speaks Spanish, French, Chinese and some Turkish. Also, if you decide to be an astronaut, you'll have to get a certificate in scuba diving and a pilot's licence.

If astronauts pass the tests, they start a special training programme. It takes a long time, but when they complete the training, they are finally able to go to Mars. What would life be like if you were an astronaut on Mars? My friends Jay and Emilia have been finding out more online.

3 🔊 5.7 Listen to the podcast. What interesting facts about life in space does it mention?

4 Study the Grammar box. Find more examples of conditionals in the text. Are they Zero, First or Second Conditionals?

GRAMMAR > Zero, First and Second Conditionals

Zero Conditional: things that are always true
if/when/unless + Present Simple, Present Simple/imperative
When they *complete* the training, they *are* able to go to Mars.

First Conditional: possible situations in the future
if/unless + Present Simple, will + infinitive/imperative
If her dreams *come* true, she'*ll travel* to Mars!

Second Conditional: unlikely or imaginary situations
if/unless + Past Simple, would + infinitive (without *to*)
What *would* life *be* like if you *were* an astronaut?

GRAMMAR TIME > PAGE 130

5 🔊 5.8 Match the sentence halves. Then decide if the sentences are Zero (0), First (1) or Second (2) Conditional sentences. Listen and check.
1 ☐ ☐ If I went to Mars,
2 ☐ ☐ I wouldn't go there
3 ☐ ☐ If astronauts drop something in space,
4 ☐ ☐ I'll grow taller
a it doesn't fall.
b unless I had to.
c if I travel in space!
d I would hate it!

6 Complete the Second Conditional sentences with the correct form of the verbs in brackets.
1 If I _were_ (be) you, I _____ (study) another language.
2 I _____ (not look) at the sun unless I _____ (have) special glasses.
3 What _____ (you/do) if you _____ (win) a trip to space?
4 If I _____ (have) enough time, I _____ (show) you how to use the telescope.
5 She _____ (not go) into space unless somebody _____ (pay) her.

VIDEO — WIDER WORLD

7 ▶ 18 Watch five people talking about space travel. How many would like to go to Mars?

8 Complete the sentences to make them true for you. Then, in pairs, compare your sentences.
1 I wouldn't go to Mars unless …
2 I can become an astronaut if …
3 If my dreams come true, …

I can use the Zero, First and Second Conditionals.

5.3 Reading and Vocabulary
Tourists in space

1 Where is the furthest you've ever travelled? Where else would you like to go?

2 Look at the title of the article and the photo. Where do you think the people are going? Why are there so many windows?

3 🔊 5.9 Read the article quickly. Check your ideas from Exercise 2.

4 Read the article again and choose the correct answer.
  1 What does the article say about people who have been into space?
    a Most were not actually astronauts.
    b Most of them travelled before 1961.
    c There have been fewer than 500 of them.
    d The majority prepared for many years.
  2 Who can become a space tourist?
    a anyone who is famous
    b people who can afford it
    c people who work for certain companies
    d anyone who passes a test
  3 How far above the Earth would a space plane go?
    a 250 kilometres   c 4,000 kilometres
    b 100 kilometres   d 2.5 kilometres
  4 The author believes that
    a all the alternatives to space travel are too expensive.
    b the only way to experience space is to become an astronaut.
    c there are lots of affordable alternatives to enjoy space.
    d alternatives to space travel offer only a virtual reality experience.

5 Look at the highlighted words about space travel in the article. Check you understand them.

6 In pairs, discuss the questions about the article.
  1 What have you learned about space tourism?
  2 How would you summarise the article in one sentence?

7 Write three questions of your own about the article. In pairs, discuss your questions.

YOUR WORLD

8 Which of the space experiences in the article would you most like to try? Why?

Stars in their eyes

Have you ever wondered how many people have been into space? The first person in space was Russian astronaut Yuri Gagarin in 1961. By the end of 2020 a total of 568 people had become space travellers. Most of these were astronauts and they had trained for many years. However, since the beginning of the twenty-first century it has been possible for non-astronauts to travel into space for short flights. The first space tourist was multi-millionaire Dennis Tito. In 2001, at the age of sixty, he paid $20 million to fly to the International Space Station with two astronauts. In 2006 Anousheh Ansari became the first female tourist in space.

Several big companies such as Virgin Galactic and SpaceX have already started test flights. If these are successful, more tourist flights will be possible. There are hundreds of people on the waiting list, including many celebrities. If you want to fly into space with one of these companies, it will cost you a huge amount of money – around $250,000!

The price of the ticket means that space tourism is not possible for most of us. However, if you had the money, what would the experience be like? You wouldn't have to wear a space suit. You would travel in a space plane with large windows so you could see the amazing views. The space plane would travel at a speed of up to 4,000 kilometres an hour! You would fly about 100 kilometres upwards – just past the end of Earth's atmosphere where space begins. At that point you would experience zero gravity for about a minute. Then you'd return to Earth. The whole trip would last for around two and a half hours.

So what can you do if you're interested in space, but can't afford these tourist trips? Luckily, there are lots of great options. You could download an incredible virtual reality app such as *Earthlight Spacewalk*. The app allows you to 'fix' a spaceship like real astronauts do. Alternatively, you can visit a space centre. Many countries have them. There you can experience life as an astronaut without leaving Earth. If you visit these places, you can try a flight simulator or a zero-gravity experience. Or if you're really keen to go to space, you can train as an astronaut, of course!

I can understand an article about space travel.

5.4 Grammar
Third Conditional

1 🔊 5.10 Read the interview quickly. How long did the flight take?

ALL ABOUT SPACE

This week in *Space* magazine, astronomer Guy Greenwood talks about a historic mission to catch a comet.

The Rosetta mission cost 1.7 billion dollars. That's a lot of money! What was your aim?

Our aim was to discover more about comets. The *Rosetta* spacecraft flew 6.4 billion kilometres to comet 67P, which is about four kilometres wide. The flight took ten years!

What would have happened if your calculations had been wrong?

Well, we would have been very disappointed if the mission had failed. If the mission hadn't been successful, we wouldn't have had these incredible close-up photos or this analysis of the comet's surface.

So, tell us more about the lander, the little spacecraft which landed on the comet.

Yes. The lander sent us the first pictures of the icy surface of the comet. If the lander's solar panels had been in sunlight, it would have been OK. But it landed in a large shadow which was quite dark. So it didn't have much power and it went to sleep. Luckily, even though it worked for two hours only, it managed to get enough information.

2 Read the interview again. Answer the questions.
 1 Were the scientists' calculations right?
 2 Was the mission successful?
 3 What was a result of the mission?

3 Study the Grammar box. Find more examples of the Third Conditional in the interview.

> **GRAMMAR** **Third Conditional**
>
> **Unreal situations in the past**
> *if* + Past Perfect, *would* + *have* + past participle
> *If the lander's solar panels **had been** in sunlight, it **would have been** OK.* (They weren't in sunlight.)

GRAMMAR TIME > PAGE 130

4 Match the sentence halves.
 1 ☐ If the lander had had more solar power,
 2 ☐ The Rosetta mission would have been quicker
 3 ☐ If the European Space Agency hadn't spent millions of euros,
 a if the comet had been nearer to Earth during the mission.
 b the scientists would have gathered more data.
 c the Rosetta Mission wouldn't have happened.

5 🔊 5.11 Read the first part of an article. Complete the Third Conditional sentences with the correct form of the verbs in brackets. Listen and check.

MOON LANDINGS FACT OR FICTION?

Some people believe astronauts have never landed on the moon. They believe NASA faked the landing. Here are some of their reasons.

They say that the flag [1] *wouldn't have waved* (not wave) if the astronauts [2] _____ (film) it on the moon because there is no air on the moon. They also think some stars [3] _____ (be) visible if the astronauts [4] _____ (take) the photos on the moon. Another mystery is that although we can see the astronauts' footprints on the surface, we can't see any traces of the landing module. A lot of people think that if the module [5] _____ (land) on the surface of the moon, it [6] _____ (leave) some traces.

6 🔊 5.12 Listen to the second part of the article. What are the arguments against the ideas in the first part? What's your view?

> **VIDEO** ▶ **WIDER WORLD**
>
> **7** ▶ 19 Watch four people talking about past experiences. How do they complete the sentences below? Make notes of some answers.
> 1 If I hadn't met my best friend, …
> 2 If I had/hadn't learned …
>
> **8** Complete the sentences in Exercise 7 to make them true for you. Then, in pairs, discuss your sentences.

Unit 5 | 66 | I can use the Third Conditional to talk about unreal situations in the past.

5.5 Listening and Vocabulary
A record-breaking adventure

1 Would you jump out of a plane or a hot air balloon using a parachute? Why?/Why not?

2 🔊 **5.13** Study the Vocabulary box and check you understand the words.

> **VOCABULARY** — Space science
>
> balloon   capsule   engine   force   helium   oxygen
> parachute   sound barrier

3 Look at the pictures in the infographic. Which words from the Vocabulary box can you see?

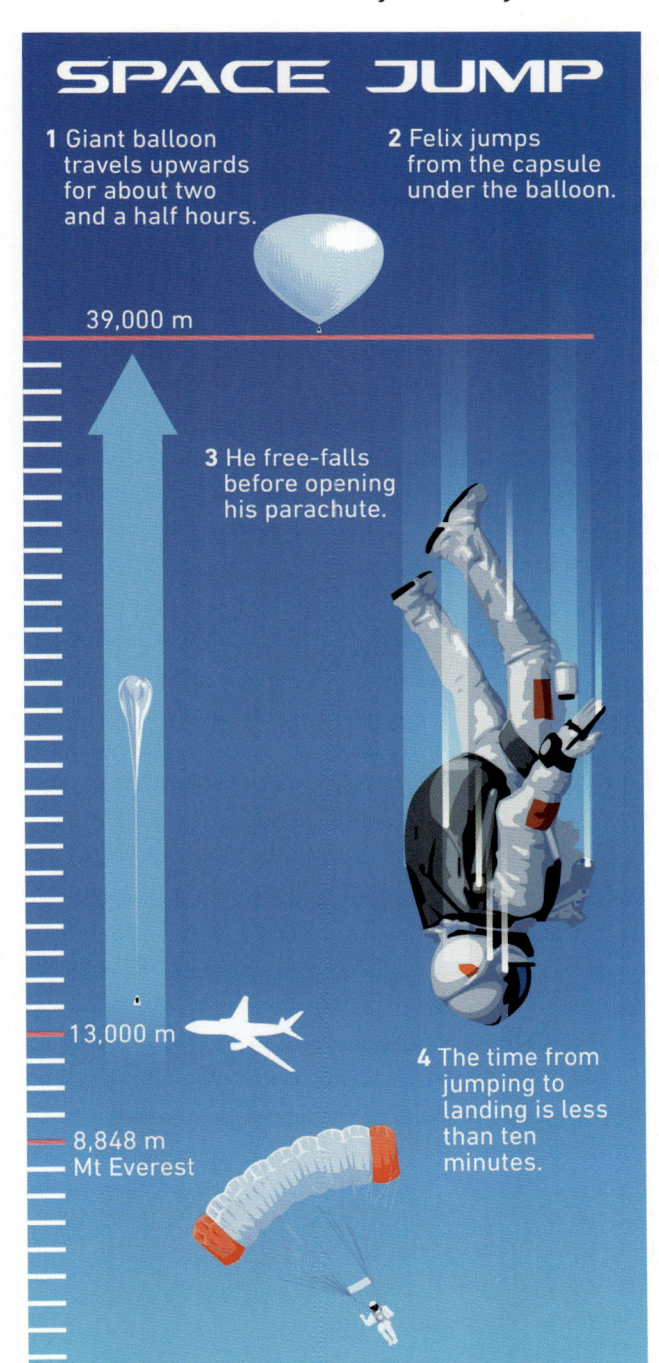

SPACE JUMP

1 Giant balloon travels upwards for about two and a half hours.
2 Felix jumps from the capsule under the balloon.
39,000 m
3 He free-falls before opening his parachute.
13,000 m
4 The time from jumping to landing is less than ten minutes.
8,848 m Mt Everest

4 Choose the correct option.
1 Humans need *oxygen / helium* to breathe.
2 The *Concorde* was a jet plane which broke the *engine / sound* barrier.
3 The *capsule / force* which attracts objects towards the Earth is gravity.
4 *Oxygen / Helium* is a very light gas which is used in balloons.
5 A jet *engine / balloon* is very powerful.
6 If you jump out of a plane, you need a *balloon / parachute*.

5 Read the infographic in Exercise 3. What do you think happened? Why?

6 🔊 **5.14** Listen to the first part of a report about Felix Baumgartner and check your ideas from Exercise 5. Then summarise what happened. Use these prompts to help you.
1 First, Felix put on …
2 Then he got into …
3 The balloon took him …
4 When he reached the right height, …
5 Finally, he opened …

7 🔊 **5.15** Listen to the second part of the report and complete the notes.

Name:	Felix Baumgartner
Date of jump:	14 ¹October 2012
Location:	² _____ , USA
Nationality:	³ _____
Age:	42
Height of jump:	about ⁴ _____ kilometres
Speed:	⁵ _____ kilometres per hour
Time in free fall:	⁶ _____ minutes and _____ seconds
Cost:	⁷ _____ of US dollars

8 What is your opinion of Felix's achievement?

YOUR WORLD

9 In pairs, talk about what you would do and how you would feel if:
1 you had to climb ten metres up a climbing wall to win a big prize.
2 you won a bungee jump as a prize in a school lottery.
3 your friend invited you to fly in a hot air balloon.
   If I had to climb ten metres up a climbing wall, …

I can understand a radio programme about a scientific achievement.

5.6 Speaking
Instructions

VIDEO ▶ I HOPE IT WORKS

Carla: Right, time to test the rover. This is our last chance before the competition!
Bea: Sure. First, I need to check the code.
Carla: Awesome! What do you want me to do?
Bea: Well, we have to set up the obstacle course.
Carla: That seems fun. I'll do that. Where do you want it?
Bea: How about just here?
Carla: OK. No problem.
Bea: Remember: it's important to have a small hill, a stone obstacle and a ramp.
Carla: Right, I hope it works. Now what?
Bea: Next, we have to check if my programming works. I hope I got it right and the rover can go over all the obstacles!
Carla: Let's go for it! The first obstacle: the hill. That seems easy.
Bea: Now going over the stones. I'm worried I haven't programmed enough power to the wheels. Phew! Finally, we need to test it on the ramp.
Carla: It's the toughest one.
Bea: Wow! It looks good.
Carla: Bea, we've got a problem!
Bea: Yeah, I think we need to work on this a bit more.

SOUNDS GOOD! Let's go for it! • It looks good. • Phew!

1 Have you ever entered a competition? What was it for?

2 Look at the photo. What competition have the girls entered?

3 ▶ 20 🔊 5.16 Watch or listen and answer the questions.
   1 What is Bea doing? What is Carla doing?
   2 What goes wrong?

4 How do Bea and Carla divide the tasks between them? Why?

SET FOR LIFE

5 In teamwork, is it better to do a task you can do well? Or should you do new tasks so you can learn something new? Discuss in pairs.

6 Study the Speaking box. Find examples of the phrases in the dialogue.

SPEAKING ▶ Instructions

Giving instructions
First, …   Second, …   After a few minutes, …
After that, …   Then …   Next, …
The last thing you need to do is …   Finally, …
Never/Always check the program.   You/We need to …
I/We have to …   It's important (not) to …
Try (not) to …

Responding to instructions
That seems fun/easy.   Of course.   OK.
Sure.   No worries.   No problem.
What next?   Now what?   Then what do I do?
I hope it works/I get it right.

7 🔊 5.17 Complete the dialogue with words from the Speaking box. Listen and check.

Ben: I want to build one of the robots from this kit.
Ivy: ¹*First*, decide which model you want to build.
Ben: Of course. Then ² _____ ?
Ivy: After ³ _____ , check you have all the pieces.
Ben: OK, I'll check them. That ⁴ _____ easy.
Ivy: Oh, and you ⁵ _____ to put the batteries in.
Ben: No problem. I ⁶ _____ it works!

YOUR WORLD

8 In pairs, take it in turns to choose one of the situations below and tell your partner what to do. Use the dialogue in Exercise 7 to help you.
- how to download an app
- how to enter a competition

Unit 5   I can give and respond to instructions.

5.7 Writing
A for and against essay

1 In pairs, make a list of the advantages and disadvantages of space travel.

2 Read Taylor's essay. Number the sections in the order they appear in the essay.
- a ☐ conclusion
- b ☐ advantages
- c ☐ introduction
- d ☐ disadvantages

3 Study the Writing box. Find similar phrases in Taylor's essay.

> **WRITING** — A for and against essay
>
> **Introduction**
> 1. Nowadays, many/more and more people …
> Many people believe/hoped/have travelled …
> But is … really useful/good/a good thing?
> Is … worth … ?
>
> **Arguments for and against**
> 2. On the one hand, … On the other hand, …
> Firstly, … Secondly, …
> One/Another/The main advantage/disadvantage is (that) …
> One/Another reason for … is …
> Finally, …
>
> **Giving and justifying opinions**
> 3. I believe (that) … In my opinion/view, …
> It seems … For example, … This is because …
>
> **Conclusion**
> 4. To sum up, … In conclusion, …

4 Study the Language box. Find examples of linkers of addition in Taylor's essay.

> **LANGUAGE** — Linkers of addition
>
> We can use linking words and phrases to add more ideas.
> - and/also/as well (as)
> - apart from/besides
> - both … and …
> - in addition/moreover
> - not only … , but also …
> - what is more

5 In pairs, make a list of the advantages and disadvantages in Taylor's essay. Compare them with your ideas in Exercise 1.

Space travel is a good thing. Do you agree?

1 Since the first space flight in 1961 many people have travelled into space, and we have learned a lot from their journeys. However, in my opinion, space travel is not always a good thing.

2 On the one hand, it's true that humans have seen the benefits of space travel. For example, solar panels were first used for satellites, but now they help us to save energy on Earth as well. In addition, space science is one of the main reasons we have developed smaller, more powerful computers. Another advantage of space travel is that we can test new technology, like robots. In future, it might also be useful if we can find another planet to live on.

3 On the other hand, space travel has many disadvantages. It is not only dangerous, but it also creates a lot of air pollution. Moreover, there are thousands of pieces of metal 'space rubbish' from satellites and spaceships. Apart from that, I believe it wastes money that we should spend on things like hospitals and education.

4 To sum up, the arguments against space travel are stronger, in my view. Although it's interesting, it's more important to look after planet Earth.

WRITING TIME

6 Space tourism is a good thing. Do you agree? Write an essay.

1 Find ideas
Make notes for your essay. Think about:
- a short introduction and conclusion.
- your reasons for and against, and your final decision.

2 Plan
Organise your ideas into paragraphs. Use Taylor's essay to help you.

3 Write and share
- Write a draft of your essay. Use the Language box and the Writing box to help you.
- Share your essay with another student for feedback.
- Write the final version of your essay.

4 Check
- Check language: have you used linkers of addition?
- Check grammar: have you used any conditionals?

I can write an essay discussing advantages and disadvantages.

Vocabulary Activator

WORDLIST 🔊 5.18

Space
astronaut (n)
astronomer (n)
comet (n)
Earth (n)
galaxy (n)
gravity (n)
moon (n)
orbit (n)
planet (n)
satellite (n)
solar system (n)
space station (n)
star (n)
telescope (n)

Word friends
(dimensions and distance)
10 km per hour
be 10 cm high/long/wide
be 10 km away/from
height (n)
length (n)
speed (n)
width (n)

Large numbers
100 = hundred (n)
1,000 = thousand (n)
1,000,000 = million (n)
1,000,000,000 = billion (n)

Space travel
flight simulator (n)
space plane (n)
space suit (n)
space tourism (n)
space tourist (n)
space traveller (n)
test flight (n)
zero gravity (n)

Space science
balloon (n)
capsule (n)
engine (n)
force (n)
helium (n)
oxygen (n)
parachute (n)
sound barrier (n)

Extra words
analysis (n)
appear (v)
atmosphere (n)
bright stars (n)
calculation (n)
data (n)
discovery (n)
dust (n)
experiment (n)
float (v)
footprint (n)
free fall (n)
globe (n)
ground (n)
jet plane (n)
land (v)
landing module (n)
manned flight (n)
Mars (n)
Mercury (n)
mission (n)
mystery (n)
on board

orbit (v)
push limits
record breaker (n)
robot (n)
rover (n)
scientific achievement (n)
scientist (n)
signal (n)
skydiver (n)
solar panel (n)
sound wave (n)
space rubbish (n)
space science (n)
spacecraft (n)
spaceship (n)
speed of sound (n)
surface (n)
universe (n)
Venus (n)
visible (adj)

1 Use the wordlist to find these things.
1 three parts of the solar system *moon, …*
2 two jobs
3 two things moving around the Earth
4 two gases

2 Complete the compound nouns with the words below.

> barrier   flight   gravity   simulator   ~~station~~   system

1 space *station*
2 flight _____
3 sound _____
4 zero _____
5 test _____
6 solar _____

3 Choose the odd one out.
1 long   fast   high   wide
2 star   comet   gravity   galaxy
3 comet   engine   planet   moon
4 balloon   force   capsule   plane

4 Write the numbers in the sentences as figures.
1 Comets travel at about three thousand kilometres per hour. *3,000 km*
2 The Earth is about twelve thousand, seven hundred kilometres wide. _____
3 Mars is about three hundred and forty-four million kilometres from Earth. _____
4 The moon is about three hundred and eighty-four thousand metres above the Earth. _____
5 The speed of sound is just over one thousand two hundred kilometres per hour. _____

5 🔊 5.19 **PRONUNCIATION** Listen to the sentences. Are the underlined words stressed?
1 Would you buy a ticket <u>to the</u> moon?
2 If I <u>were an</u> astronaut, I'd miss my friends on Earth.
3 The space travellers would <u>have</u> got lost in space without their star map.
4 Sound travels <u>at</u> three hundred <u>and</u> thirty-three metres <u>per</u> second.
5 What's the width <u>of the</u> Earth?

6 🔊 5.19 **PRONUNCIATION** Listen again and repeat.

Unit 5   70

Revision

Vocabulary

1 Complete the sentences with words formed from the words in brackets.
1. After a successful test *flight* (**FLY**), the rocket took astronauts into space.
2. What's the _____ (**WIDE**) of your door? Will the piano go through it?
3. Every space _____ (**TRAVEL**) needs special training and equipment.
4. What's the _____ (**HIGH**) of the Eiffel Tower?
5. What's the _____ (**LONG**) of this river?
6. Astronauts train with a flight _____ (**SIMULATE**).
7. Space _____ (**TOURIST**) will become cheaper for holidaymakers.

2 Label the photos with the words below.

> capsule   ~~comet~~   parachute   satellite   space plane   telescope

1. *comet*
2. _____
3. _____
4. _____
5. _____
6. _____

Grammar

3 Complete the questions with the correct form of the verbs in brackets. Use the Zero, First or Second Conditional. Then, in pairs, ask and answer the questions.
1. If you could travel in time, when in the past *would you travel* (you/travel) to?
2. If you _____ (have) time, do you ever look at the stars in the night sky?
3. If your friend invited you on a space trip in ten years' time, _____ (you/go)?
4. If you _____ (be) an astronaut, what job would you do on a space station?
5. _____ (you/be) happy if there's a space documentary on TV tonight?

4 Rewrite the sentences using the Third Conditional to make a story. Then write two more Third Conditional sentences to continue the story.
1. We were in an unknown part of space, and we discovered a new planet.
   If we hadn't been in an unknown part of space, we wouldn't have discovered a new planet.
2. We had almost no fuel. But we survived because we landed here.
3. We didn't leave the spaceship that day because we were too tired.
4. The next day we started exploring and we met intelligent life.

5 Choose the correct answer.
1. If you had the read the instructions more carefully, you ___ so many mistakes.
   a wouldn't make   b don't make
   c wouldn't have made
2. If water goes into the air in zero gravity, it ___ round balls.
   a will form   b forms
   c would form
3. Unless you ___ a lot of money, you won't be able to go into space.
   a paid   b 'll pay   c pay
4. We wouldn't have got lost if you ___ used the map app on your phone.
   a had   b would have   c have
5. Nobody can enter this part of the building unless they ___ permission.
   a 'll have   b have   c had
6. If astronauts ___ receive special training, they wouldn't be able to work effectively in space.
   a don't   b didn't
   c wouldn't
7. If you could afford a holiday in space, ___ you go?
   a would   b will   c did

Speaking

6 In pairs, do the speaking task. Student A, go to page 136. Student B, go to page 142. Follow the instructions.

Dictation

7 🔊 5.20 Listen. Then listen again and write down what you hear during each pause.

BBC CULTURE

Pushing the limits

EXPLORATION AND ADVENTURE

Some people are challenging what is possible on Earth and in space. We're going to meet two of them. Tim Peake has been an astronaut on the International Space Station (ISS). His work there didn't stop him doing the sports he loves. Believe it or not, in 2016 he took part in the London Marathon – from space! He did it to raise money for charity. How? Easy: a rope kept him tied to the running machine.

The ISS is a zero-gravity lab where a crew of six people live and work. They travel in the space station, which orbits the Earth every ninety minutes at a speed of 28,800 km per hour. So Tim Peake not only ran the usual 42 km, but also travelled more than 100,000 km during his marathon run!

Peake isn't the only astronaut to explore what is possible when playing their favourite sport. American astronauts often play weightless baseball or basketball and sometimes even golf. Zero gravity makes things slower, but they still work. You can even throw a boomerang and it returns to you in orbit, just like on Earth!

Talking of Earth, some people are finding that there are still many places to explore here too. Ocean depths and hidden unknown places in far mountains and forests still call to people looking for adventure.

For TV adventurer Steve Backshall, that call is stronger than prospects of potential problems and difficulties. His team recently filmed in the tabletop mountains of Venezuela to explore the little-known area at the top. They went down the vertical sides of the mountains on ropes. Floating in mid-air and viewing the world spread out below has curious similarities to the feelings of weightlessness and distance in space. Exploring space or far mountains isn't for everyone, but an attitude of looking for adventure has led to new discoveries and possibilities.

adventure (n) an exciting new experience
crew (n) a group of people working together
surroundings (n) places and things near you
vertical (adj) in a straight line up and down
weightless (adj) having no weight in zero gravity

1 Look at the photos and the title of the article. In pairs, discuss the questions.
  1 Who do you think the people are?
  2 How is a rope helping them?
  3 What do you think these two men have in common?

2 🔊 5.21 Read the article and check your answers to Exercise 1.

3 Read the article again and answer the questions.
  1 Why did Tim Peake run the London Marathon in space?
  2 How many people are in the International Space Station?
  3 What are American astronauts' favourite sports in space?
  4 What is different about doing sport in space instead of on Earth?
  5 What are some of the places on Earth people can still explore?
  6 In what ways can climbing with a rope be similar to being in space?

4 In pairs, discuss the questions.
  1 Which of the sports mentioned in the article would you like to do? Why?
  2 Which wild places on Earth would you like to visit and explore? Why?
  3 Why do you think some people like the idea of exploring new places?

BBC ▶ Exploring the unknown

5 Look at the photo and discuss the questions.
1 Where do you think this place is?
2 Why do you think the mountain in the photo is called a 'tabletop' mountain?
3 How could people visit it?
4 What might there be inside the mountain?

6 ▶ 21 Watch Part 1 of a TV programme about tabletop mountains and check your answers to Exercise 5.

7 ▶ 22 Watch Part 2 of the video and mark the sentences T (true) or F (false).
1 ☐ Steve feels scared when he is abseiling down.
2 ☐ Steve sees the biggest waterfall in the world.
3 ☐ Steve's team need a lot of abseiling stages to get down the mountain.
4 ☐ There aren't many more places left to explore there.

8 ▶ 22 Answer the questions about Part 2 of the video. Watch again and check.
1 How does Steve react when he sees Angel Falls?
2 How high is Angel Falls?
3 Where are Steve and his team when they reach the bottom?
4 What are they planning to do?

9 Which parts of the team adventure would you like to try? Why? Discuss in pairs.

10 **VISIBLE THINKING** It is now possible to reach a new beautiful unexplored area. Discuss how the people below might feel about this.
CONSIDER DIFFERENT VIEWPOINTS
- a person looking for adventure
- close family of the adventurer
- local people living in the area
- a tourist operator in the country

PROJECT TIME

11 In groups of four, create an online advert for a day trip to the tabletop mountains. Follow these steps.

1 In your group, discuss who will find information about the activities in the advert: abseiling, exploring the caves, walking in the jungle and photographing nature. Find answers to these quesitons.
- What do you need to know about the tabletop mountains?
- How do you need to prepare for the activity (e.g. safety training)?
- What equipment and how much time do you need for each activity?
- What can you gain from this experience?

2 Individually, prepare your part of the advert.
- Find answers to your question(s) and write a short text.
- Find photos to illustrate the information.

3 In your group, create your advert. You can use online ad maker.
- Put all the texts and photos together.
- Decide on a layout.
- Think of a title for the advert.
- Check and edit your advert.

4 Share your advert with the class.
- Answer other students' questions.
- Ask questions and comment on the other adverts.

Good health
6

VOCABULARY
Health problems | First aid kit | Word building: health and illness | Health improvement | Extreme sports

GRAMMAR
Reported statements and questions | Reported commands and requests

Today	Tomorrow	Thursday	Friday
7.00 p.m.	7.45 p.m.	**Island Life** 8.00 p.m.	8.30 p.m.

Island Life

Episode 6: *In Sickness and in Health*

Channel 9, Tuesday 23 April, 8.00 p.m.

When you live in a remote island community, what do you do when you fall ill or suffer a serious injury? If the nearest GP* is a long, difficult boat ride away, you can't just visit the doctor's surgery any time you feel ill or need to get a blood test. You need to know how to take care of yourself. You need a basic knowledge of medicine and a first aid kit including more than just a thermometer, a few headache pills, an antiseptic cream for insect bites and an old packet of sticking plasters. In this week's episode of *Island Life*, we find out how the islanders cope when they have a broken bone, a serious infection or a cut that won't stop bleeding. We see how they get to hospital when they need to have an operation or get emergency treatment. And we report on how drones are helping to improve health care on the island.

*GP (General Practitioner) = a doctor that treats people in a particular area

6.1 Vocabulary
Sickness and health

1 How do you feel today? Choose from the phrases below. Share your answer with the class. Then look at the photo in the text. How does the girl feel?
- I've never felt better.
- I can't complain. I feel fine.
- Not bad, I suppose.
- I don't feel very well, to be honest.
- I've got a bit of a cough.
- I feel awful. I think I need to go home.

2 Read the text and answer the questions.
1. What kind of TV programme is *Island Life*?
2. What is this episode about?

3 🔊 6.1 Study Vocabulary box A. Which three health problems do you think are the most serious?

VOCABULARY A	Health problems
asthma broken bone bruise chest/ear/eye infection	
cut fever insect bite migraine rash virus	

Unit 6 74

4 **I KNOW!** In groups, add more words to Vocabulary box A.

5 Check you understand the verbs in bold. Then complete the sentences with health problems from Vocabulary box A.
1 You may **cough** or **sneeze** when you have (a/an) _____ .
2 You may **bleed** when you have (a/an) _____ .
3 You may **faint** when you have (a/an) _____ .

6 🔊 6.2 Study Vocabulary box B. When do you use a first aid kit? Which of the things in the box can you see in the photo below?

VOCABULARY B	First aid kit
antibacterial spray antiseptic cream bandage	
cough medicine painkiller pill	
sticking plaster thermometer	

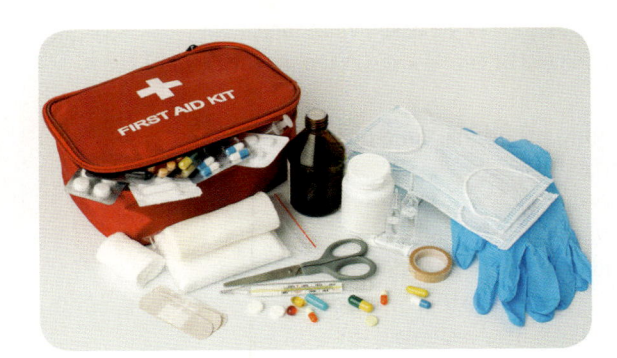

7 🔊 6.3 **WORD FRIENDS** Complete the phrases with the words below. Listen and check.

~~bone~~   ill   injury   operation   test   treatment

Illnesses and accidents
1 break a *bone*
2 fall _____
3 feel dizzy
4 have an accident/a serious _____
5 hurt your arm/back/leg
6 lose your appetite/voice
7 your muscles ache

At the doctor's
8 ask for/make an appointment
9 describe your symptoms
10 get a blood _____
11 get a prescription
12 take your temperature

At the hospital
13 get emergency _____
14 have an _____

8 🔊 6.4 Listen to three extracts from the TV programme in Exercise 1 and answer the questions.
Extract A
1 What are Malcolm's symptoms?
2 What does the doctor think he has?
Extract B
3 What happened to Cameron last week?
4 What happened to Heather last night?
Extract C
5 What happened to Alex last month?
6 What happened after he called for help?

9 In pairs, talk about health problems you have had. How did you feel? What did you do?
I had a broken bone in my foot once. I went to the doctor's and she sent me straight to the hospital.

10 🔊 6.5 Study Vocabulary box C. Check you understand the words.

VOCABULARY C	Word building: health and illness			
Adjectives	blind	deaf	ill	sick
Nouns	blindness	deafness	illness	sickness
Verbs	infect	injure	operate	
Nouns	infection	injury	operation	
Nouns	allergy	depression	pain	
Adjectives	allergic	depressed	painful	

11 🔊 6.6 Complete the text with words from Vocabulary box C. Listen and check.

Did you know?
- Your whole body can feel ¹p*ain* except for the brain. That's why doctors can ²o_____ on somebody's brain while they're awake!
- Some people have an ³a_____ to pets, but cats and dogs can also be ⁴a_____ to people!
- When you cut your finger, put sugar on it. It can stop an ⁵i_____ from developing.
- If you suffer from travel ⁶s_____ when travelling in a car, try sitting in the front.
- Many adolescents suffer from ⁷d_____ – check out our website for tips on how to feel more cheerful and less ⁸d_____ .

VIDEO — **WIDER WORLD**

12 ▶ 23 Watch five people talking about having a cold. What remedies do they recommend?

13 In pairs, say what you think are the best remedies for a cold, an allergy and car sickness.

I can talk about health problems.

6.2 Grammar

Reported statements and questions

1 Have you had an eye test recently? Why is it important to check your eyes regularly?

2 🔊 6.7 Look at the photo and read the text quickly. What problem does George have?

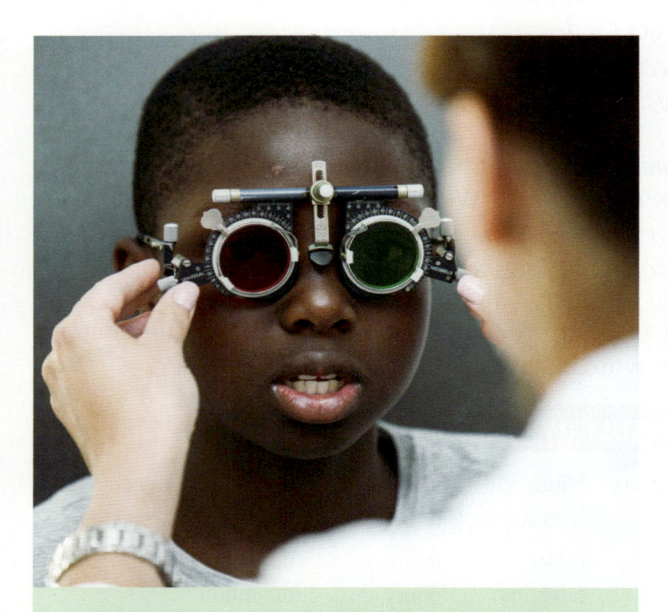

When ten-year-old George said that he was getting headaches at school, his dad made an appointment for an eye test. The optician showed him some coloured images and asked him what numbers he could see, but George found the task difficult. The optician then asked George what his plans were for the future. George replied that he hoped to be a pilot. 'That might be difficult,' explained the doctor, 'because you're colour blind'. She told George that he probably wouldn't be able to fly planes in the future. He was very disappointed.

Later, his mum told him that colour blindness ran in the family and said his grandad had the same problem, but that he had learned to live well with it. She said that he couldn't tell the difference between red and green. George asked whether that was why his grandad didn't drive. 'No,' replied his mum. 'You can drive when you're colour blind. He just didn't like driving!'

3 Study the Grammar box. Find more examples of reported speech in the text.

GRAMMAR — Reported statements and questions

Present Simple → Past Simple
'I have a headache.' → He said (that) he had a headache.

Present Continuous → Past Continuous
'I'm getting better.' → She said (that) she was getting better.

Past Simple → Past Perfect
'I left home at six.' → He said (that) he had left home at six.

will → would
'My mum will do it.' → He said (that) his mum would do it.

can → could
'I can't see anything.' → She said (that) she couldn't see anything.

Questions
'What time is it?' → He asked what time it was.
'Do you know Dr Lee?' → She asked me if/whether I knew Dr Lee.

Changing pronouns, time phrases and place adverbials
now → then   here → there
this month → that month
yesterday → the previous day/the day before
tomorrow → the next/following day
'My dad was here yesterday.' →
He said (that) his dad had been there the day before.

GRAMMAR TIME > PAGE 131

4 Rewrite the sentences in reported speech.
1 'What time does the doctor finish?' I asked.
   I asked what time the doctor finished.
2 'When are they leaving?' Rachel asked.
3 'It hurts,' he told the nurse.
4 'I took the medicine this morning,' she said.
5 'Did Emma see the doctor?' I asked.
6 'Can I make an appointment?' Liam asked.
7 'I'll make an appointment with Dr Fox,' he said.
8 'I'm feeling much better,' Lisa said.

YOUR WORLD

5 In pairs, take it in turns to tell your partner about the last time somebody gave you some important news. What did they say? How did you feel?

My friend told me she was going to live in a different town. I was really sad.

Unit 6 76 I can report what somebody else has said.

6.3 Reading and Vocabulary
Health apps

HEALTHY AND HAPPY?

In a recent report, over sixty percent of young people said that they had used a health-related mobile app. By using these apps, you can take control of your health and fitness. Do you have problems sleeping? Try a sleep app. Do you want to work on your running? Download a training app. There are some fantastic apps out there, but which ones work?

Bella, who is sixteen, sometimes gets bad headaches called migraines. This condition affects around ten percent of young people. Bella uses a migraine app to manage her symptoms. She inputs data about any food she has eaten so she can identify foods that cause a migraine. The app has shown that she needs to avoid certain foods, like some types of nuts and cheese. The app also gives advice on helpful medications and healthy lifestyle. 'Poor sleep or stress can sometimes cause migraines,' says Bella. 'I also use a relaxation app to stay calm when things get stressful. It's a life changer.'

Nathan, aged fifteen, started using a fitness app last year. Nathan wanted to get fitter, but he couldn't afford to go to the gym. 'I started with a walking app. I wanted something simple and fun,' he explains. Nathan's app shows his walking route on a map. It counts his steps and measures his speed and heart rate. However, he thinks the best thing about the app is the music. Studies show that when walkers and runners match their movement to music, their performance improves. Nathan says he feels happier and less tired while he's exercising with music, so he would definitely recommend it.

Luke's family has had a mixed experience with health apps. 'My sister was using an app to check salt and sugar in food, but then she often didn't eat family meals with us. My mum said that we would try a healthy eating app for the whole family. Now we use the app for recipe ideas. My sister and I enjoy cooking them and our meals are healthier and tastier. We all have more energy too!' Luke's sister's story shows that it's important to get advice before choosing an app. Speak to family and friends first. When you find one that's right for you, it can make a big difference.

1 Have you ever used an app for any of the things below? Was it helpful?

> fitness   healthy eating   medical use   sleep

2 Look at the phone screen above. What information does it show?

3 🔊 6.8 Read the article quickly. What type of app does each person talk about? Whose app is on the phone screen above?

4 Read the article again and complete the sentences. Use no more than three words in each sentence.
1. The article states that health-related apps are popular with _____ .
2. Lack of sleep, certain foods or _____ can cause migraines.
3. Nathan didn't have enough money to go _____ .
4. Exercising to music can result in much better _____ .
5. Luke's family are now eating much healthier _____ .
6. It's a good idea to ask other people before you _____ .

5 Look at the highlighted phrases related to health improvement in the article. Check you understand them. Use a dictionary if necessary.

YOUR WORLD

6 In pairs, discuss the questions. Think about the information in the article and your own experience.
1. Which type of health or fitness app would you like to use? Why?
2. What kind of app would you like someone to invent?

I can understand an article about health apps.   77   Unit 6

6.4 Grammar
Reported commands and requests

Sandra's blog – It's a funny old world

'I asked the doctor to help me get fit. She gave me a small bottle of water and told me to take it for a 10 km walk every day.'

Funny health stories

Bad health isn't usually funny, but there are times when stories of injuries or illnesses can make us laugh.

For example, the other day I was at my friend Carol's and we were making lunch. Carol asked me to open a tin of sardines, but while I was doing it, I cut my finger. Carol told me to put it under the tap, but when I saw the blood in the water, I fainted. After a few seconds, I woke up and my finger was still bleeding – a lot! I asked Carol to do something. I was very upset. She told me not to panic and then ran to get her first aid kit. She asked me not to move while she put a sticking plaster on the cut. But after she'd done it, my finger was still bleeding. She'd put the plaster on the wrong finger!

Have you got any funny health stories? Why not share them with us?

Barry321

One time when I was little, I hurt my ankle. It was sore, so I asked my mum to make it better. She asked my sister Jodie to get the first aid kit. Then she told me to sit down so she could put a bandage on it. Just then, the doorbell rang. Mum told us not to do anything and went to the door. Jodie took the bandage and started putting it on me. I asked her to stop, but she told me not to worry. She said she knew what she was doing. When Mum came back, she started laughing. Jodie had put the bandage round both my legs, from my ankles to my knees. I couldn't walk!

1 Look at the cartoon in the blog post. Why is it funny?

2 🔊 **6.9** Read the blog post quickly. What happened to Sandra? What happened to Barry?

3 Study the Grammar box. Find more examples of reported commands and requests in the blog post.

> **GRAMMAR** Reported commands and requests
> **Commands**
> 'Do more exercise.' → She told him to do more exercise.
> 'Don't worry!' → She told me not to worry.
> **Requests**
> 'Can you give me something, please?' → I asked the doctor to give me something.
> 'Please don't shout! → She asked him not to shout.
>
> GRAMMAR TIME > PAGE 131

4 How did Sandra report these sentences in her story in the blog post?
1 Carol said to me, 'Can you open a tin of sardines?'
 Carol asked me to open a tin of sardines.
2 Carol said to me, 'Put it under the tap.'
3 I said to Carol, 'Please do something.'
4 She said to me, 'Don't panic.'
5 She said to me, 'Please don't move.'

5 🔊 **6.10** Report these commands and requests from a conversation between a female doctor and a male patient. Listen and check.
1 'Come in.'
 She told him to come in.
2 'Take a seat.'
3 'Please don't be nervous.'
4 'Relax.'
5 'Can you tell me what the problem is?'
6 'Explain where you were hurt.'
7 'Please show me which part of your body hurts.'

YOUR WORLD

6 In pairs, tell your partner about a time when you hurt yourself or felt unwell. What did people ask you or tell you to do?

Once I fell off my bike and cut my knee. My mum told me to wash it and put a plaster on it and then she asked me to be more careful next time!

Unit 6 · I can report commands and requests.

6.5 Listening and Vocabulary
Extreme sports

1 Which of the sports in photos A–D looks the most exciting?

2 🔊 6.11 Study the Vocabulary box. Which sports can you see in photos A–D?

> **VOCABULARY** Extreme sports
>
> abseiling   BMXing   free running   hang-gliding
> kitesurfing   paddleboarding   parachuting
> sandboarding   whitewater rafting   ziplining

3 Write the words from the Vocabulary box in the correct categories.
1. on land: _abseiling_ , _____ , _____ , _____
2. in the air: _____ , _____ , _____
3. on/in the water: _____ , _____ , _____

4 Complete the sentences with words from the Vocabulary box.
1. I love _BMXing_ , so my parents got me a new bike for my birthday.
2. On our holiday in Tunisia last year, we went _____ in the desert.
3. We're going _____ on the Salmon River – I hope I don't fall in!
4. My dad tried _____ once, but he was too scared to jump out of the plane!
5. We do _____ around our town. It's a mix of athletics and acrobatics.
6. I tried _____ for the first time today. We wore ropes and went down a ten-metre wall.

5 🔊 6.12 Listen to Ed talking about extreme sports. Number the parts of the body in the order you hear them.
a ☐ brain   b ☐ lungs   c ☐ heart   d ☐ muscles

6 🔊 6.12 Listen again and answer the questions.
1. Why does Ed think extreme sports are good?
2. Who does he say should be careful about doing extreme sports?

7 🔊 6.13 Listen to Zara leaving a message. Which sports are they going to do at her party?

8 🔊 6.13 Listen again and complete the notes.

> **Zara's extreme party!**
> - Where: 'The Climbing Wall' opposite ² _____ and next to the leisure centre
> - When: Saturday, ³ _____ a.m.
> - Tell Zara's mum about any ⁴ _____ .
> - Must wear: ⁵ _____ and trousers
> - Phone Katy's mum about lift (mobile no.: ⁶ _____).

VIDEO **WIDER WORLD**

9 ▶ 24 Watch five people talking about sports. Which sports do they mention?

10 In pairs, discuss the questions.
1. Have you ever tried an extreme sport? Which one? How did you feel?
2. If not, would you like to try? Why?/Why not?

I've never tried an extreme sport, but I'd like to try hang-gliding because I think it's the nearest thing to flying.

I can understand a talk about extreme sports.

6.6 Speaking
Asking for and giving advice

VIDEO ▶ **I WISH I COULD HELP!**

Bea: Listen, guys, Carla's got a First Aid test tomorrow. How can we help her to revise for it?
Abe: I know. Let's do it in a practical way, right?
Eren: Yeah, that's a great idea.
Carla: Sorry I'm late.
Eren: No worries. Here, catch the frisbee, Carla!
Bea: No, no! Throw it to me! Oh, my nose! Should I keep my head up?
Carla: No, you'd better sit down, lean forward and breathe through your mouth.
Bea: That's better, thanks. You carry on.
Abe: Good throw, Eren. I've got it.
Eren: Are you all right, Abe? That was a nasty fall.
Abe: My ankle really hurts. What shall I do?
Carla: You need to put your foot up on my bag. And try pressing this cold bottle on your ankle. That should help.
Eren: Agh! What's that? I think a bee stung me on my neck! It really hurts!
Carla: Oh gosh! I wish I could help, but I haven't got a cream with me.
Eren: Carla, I'm fine. We're just helping you to revise First Aid!
Carla: Oh, I see!

SOUNDS GOOD! You carry on. • Are you all right? • Oh gosh!

1 Look at the photo. What do you think is happening?

2 ▶ 25 🔊 6.14 Watch or listen. Are Bea's, Abe's and Eren's injuries real?

3 How do Carla's friends help her revise for a First Aid test?

SET FOR LIFE

4 In pairs, discuss the questions.
 1 Do you remember things better when you revise in creative ways?
 2 Think of a creative way you can revise for your next test or exam.

5 Study the Speaking box. Find examples of the phrases in the dialogue.

SPEAKING Asking for and giving advice

Asking for advice
What do you think I should do?
If you were me, what would you do?
What shall I do?   Should I keep my head up?
Have you got any ideas (what to do)?

Giving advice
If I were you, I'd make a doctor's appointment.
You'd better/It might be a good idea to lean forward.
You should/ought to/need to put your foot up.
Let's rest.
Have you tried/thought about putting some ice on it?
Try pressing your nose.
I'd recommend/advise/suggest taking an aspirin.

Being unable to give advice
I don't know what to advise/suggest/do, I'm afraid.
I wish I could help, but …
I'm afraid I can't really help you.

6 🔊 6.15 Listen to three people describing problems. Respond with your advice in each situation. Use phrases from the Speaking box.

7 🔊 6.16 Listen and compare the speakers' advice with your own.

YOUR WORLD

8 In pairs, choose one of the problems below. Take it in turns to ask for and give advice.

a bad headache   a sore throat   sneezing

Unit 6 80 I can ask for and give advice.

6.7 Writing
A forum post about an experience

Mason Jarvis online
A learning experience: whitewater rafting

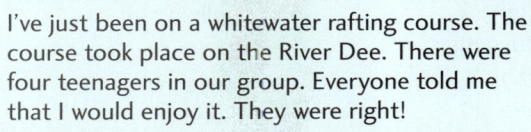

1. I've just been on a whitewater rafting course. The course took place on the River Dee. There were four teenagers in our group. Everyone told me that I would enjoy it. They were right!

2. First of all, our professional trainer, Dave, told us about safety and comfort on the raft. He explained that we had to wear helmets and wetsuits. Dave also reminded us to always wear our lifejackets.

3. After that, we went onto the raft. Our trainer showed us how to paddle and demonstrated how to swim in the river. He also warned us not to panic or jump off the boat. Dave advised us to practise moving the raft slowly. About thirty minutes later, we were ready to go.

4. As we started moving, I felt excited and scared. Soon, we were rafting quickly down the river. It was amazing!

5. I had never been rafting before. It was a fantastic learning experience. If you enjoy having fun outdoors, I encourage you to try it.

1 Have you ever been on a course to learn something new?

2 Read Mason's post. What did he do? What did he learn? Did he enjoy it?

3 Study the Writing box. Find similar sentences in Mason's post.

WRITING — A forum post about an experience

1. **Get your reader's attention and basic details**
   Let me tell you about a rock-climbing course I've just done.
   It was in the Welsh mountains.

2. **Report on the training/event**
   Our trainer explained how to climb safely …
   She advised us to test our equipment …
   Karen told us to be careful …

3. **Describe what happened next**
   After the …, we tried to …
   Soon after, we were ready to start …

4. **Describe what happened in the end**
   Eventually, we arrived at the top of the …
   It was awesome!

5. **Summary recommendation**
   If you really want to try rock climbing, I highly recommend this course.

4 Study the Language box. Find examples of reporting verbs in Mason's post.

LANGUAGE — Reporting verbs

We use reporting verbs to report what someone has said.

advise   ask   encourage   explain   persuade
remind   tell   warn

5 Write five sentences to report what your teachers told you to do last week. Use reporting verbs from the Language box.

Last week our teacher advised us to revise for the end-of-term exam.

WRITING TIME

6 Write a post about a learning experience. Choose one of the ideas below or your own.

after-school club   arts course   language classes

1. **Find ideas**
   Make notes for your post.

2. **Plan**
   Organise your post into paragraphs. Use Mason's post to help you.

3. **Write and share**
   - Write a draft of your post. Use the Language box and the Writing box to help you.
   - Share your post with another student for feedback.
   - Write the final version of your post.

4. **Check**
   - Check language: have you used reporting verbs?
   - Check grammar: have you used reported speech correctly?

I can write a post about a learning experience.

Vocabulary Activator

WORDLIST 🔊 6.17

Health problems
asthma (n)
broken bone (n)
bruise (n)
chest/ear/eye infection (n)
cut (n)
fever (n)
insect bite (n)
migraine (n)
rash (n)
virus (n)

First aid kit
antibacterial spray (n)
antiseptic cream (n)
bandage (n)
cough medicine (n)
painkiller (n)
pill (n)
sticking plaster (n)
thermometer (n)

Word friends
(illnesses and accidents)
break a bone
fall ill
feel dizzy
have a serious injury
have an accident
hurt your arm/back/leg
lose your appetite/voice
your muscles ache
(at the doctor's)
ask for an appointment
describe your symptoms
get a blood test
get a prescription
make an appointment
take your temperature
(at the hospital)
get emergency treatment
have an operation

Word building
(health and illness)
allergic (adj)
allergy (n)
blind (adj)
blindness (n)
deaf (adj)
deafness (n)
depressed (adj)
depression (n)
ill (adj)
illness (n)
infect (v)
infection (n)
injure (v)
injury (n)
operate (v)
operation (n)
pain (n)
painful (adj)
sick (adj)
sickness (n)

Health improvement
avoid certain foods
count your steps
give advice
have more energy
make a big difference
manage your symptoms
measure your heart rate
measure your speed
show a walking route
stay calm
take control of your health and fitness

Extreme sports
abseiling (n)
BMXing (n)
free running (n)
hang-gliding (n)
kitesurfing (n)
paddleboarding (n)
parachuting (n)
sandboarding (n)
whitewater rafting (n)
ziplining (n)

Extra words
ankle (n)
bleed (v)
brain (n)
chemist's (n)
colour blind (adj)
condition (n)
cough (v)
doctor's surgery (n)
emergency services (n)
eye test (n)
faint (v)
fall (n)
health care (n)
lung (n)
nosebleed (n)
sneeze (v)
sore throat (n)
stomach ache (n)
suffer (an injury) (v)
take care of yourself

1 Complete the words in the sentences.
1 My app showed me a long walking r<u>oute</u> yesterday. When I walked it, the app counted 24,152 s_____ . My muscles a_____ today!
2 When my friend had a chest i_____ , she needed c_____ medicine.
3 I h_____ my arm playing basketball. It wasn't a s_____ injury, but it was too p_____ to finish the game.

2 Complete the phrases with the verbs below. Which phrases describe a problem (P) and which are things that can help (H)?

| break   fall   feel   give   have   ~~measure~~   stay   take |

1 [H] <u>measure</u> your heart rate
2 [ ] _____ your temperature
3 [ ] _____ ill
4 [ ] _____ a bone
5 [ ] try to _____ calm
6 [ ] _____ dizzy
7 [ ] _____ a friend advice
8 [ ] _____ an accident

3 Find words in the wordlist to match the definitions.
1 a document from the doctor with medicine and instructions: <u>prescription</u>
2 when a doctor cuts into your body to help you: _____
3 not being able to see: _____
4 you need a kayak and a fast river for this sport: _____
5 a kind of headache; sometimes people feel sick with it too: _____

4 🔊 6.18 **PRONUNCIATION** Sentence stress falls on the important information in a sentence. Read the dialogue and underline the important information that you think is stressed. Listen and check.
A: I have an insect bite on my foot.
B: Are you sure?
A: I think so.
B: Can I take a look?
A: Sure, it's just there.
B: I can see it. I'll put some cream on it.

5 🔊 6.18 **PRONUNCIATION** Listen again and repeat. Then, in pairs, practise the dialogue.

Revision

Vocabulary

1 Choose the correct answer.
1. Sheila isn't feeling well. She has lost her ____ and doesn't want to eat.
   a voice   b bite   c appetite
2. Always remember that regular exercise ____ a big difference to your health.
   a gives   b does   c makes
3. In ____ , the wind pulls you across the water.
   a kitesurfing   b ziplining   c hang-gliding
4. Take this ____ to the chemist's tomorrow morning to get your medicine.
   a receipt   b prescription   c infection
5. My grandma ____ an operation on her eyes.
   a made   b did   c had
6. I have an app which measures the distance of my walking ____ .
   a route   b way   c path
7. People with allergies must ____ some kinds of food and drink.
   a manage   b avoid   c lose
8. When Olivia said she was ____ dizzy, I told her to lie down.
   a having   b making   c feeling
9. In ____ , you go down a rock by sliding down a rope.
   a abseiling   b BMXing   c ziplining
10. This app helps you measure your heart ____ .
    a speed   b rate   c route

2 Complete the dialogue with the words below.

> appointment   bone   injury   kit   painkillers   plasters
> symptoms   thermometer   treatment   ziplining

Parent: How do you take care of students' health in this summer school?
Director: There is a twenty-four-hour first aid officer with a first aid ¹*kit* . He can give a few ² _____ for a headache, use the ³ _____ to take temperatures or use bandages and sticking ⁴ _____ if someone's bleeding.
Parent: But you have some extreme sports here, like ⁵ _____ . What happens with a more serious ⁶ _____ ?
Director: The hospital is a ten-minute drive for emergency ⁷ _____ – for example, if someone breaks a ⁸ _____ . If it's less serious, students describe their ⁹ _____ and we can ask for a quick ¹⁰ _____ with a doctor.

Grammar

3 Choose the correct option.
1. My friend offered me a sandwich, but I told him *I'm not / I wasn't* hungry.
2. I asked a man *where was the post office / where the post office was*.
3. The shop assistant told me she *sold / had sold* her last sun cream.
4. Amy said she *will help / would help* us paint the bedroom, but she isn't here.
5. The teacher asked *had we completed / whether we'd completed* our projects.
6. Bill told me he *is watching / was watching* birds when I met him in the park.
7. Someone was feeling dizzy on the bus, so I said I *know / knew* how to help.

4 Complete the reported commands and requests in the sentences.
1. When I felt dizzy in class the other day, the teacher *told me to lie down* (tell/lie down).
2. Mum _____ (ask/get) her prescription when I was at the shops.
3. When a bee flew near my face, my friend _____ (tell/not move).
4. The doctor _____ (ask/not move) my head when she was examining my ear.
5. When we saw a bear in the forest, our leader _____ (tell/not run).
6. The doctor _____ (ask/describe) my symptoms.

Speaking

5 In pairs, do the speaking task. Student A, go to page 137. Student B, go to page 142. Follow the instructions.

Dictation

6 🔊 6.19 Listen. Then listen again and write down what you hear during each pause.

Unit 6

SET FOR LIFE

Take action!

1 Match the statements with photos A–D.
1. ☐ Getting around should be easier for people who use wheelchairs.
2. ☐ It's terrible that there's so much rubbish in this beautiful place.
3. ☐ It's a shame there isn't anything fun for young people to do in this town.
4. ☐ It's sad that so many older people are lonely.

2 In pairs, discuss the questions.
1. Are there similar problems to the ones in Exercise 1 in your community?
2. What other problems are there?
3. What can young people do to make a difference in their community and help to solve these problems?

3 🔊 6.20 Listen to a radio interview. Which problem is it about? Did the speakers mention any of your ideas from Exercise 2?

4 🔊 6.20 Mark the sentences T (true) or F (false). Then listen again and check.
1. ☐ Ash said that he had started his campaign because of a conversation with his grandmother.
2. ☐ He said that he had talked to different companies in his town about the problem.
3. ☐ He said that one of the main reasons for the problem was that some older people didn't live near their families.
4. ☐ He said that he had organised a petition for better bus transport in his town.
5. ☐ He said that he had raised money to teach old people about social media.
6. ☐ He said that the posters in his school had helped him to get a lot of volunteers.
7. ☐ He said that doctors had given older people leaflets about the club.
8. ☐ He didn't think his campaign made a difference.

I can make a difference.

Make a difference

5 Read what some people have done to make a difference. Complete the sentences with the words below.

> campaign   leaflet   petition   poster   ~~sponsored run~~   volunteers

1. I organised a <u>sponsored run</u>. My friends and I ran 100 kilometres in ten days, and our friends and family paid us. We raised enough money to buy a community piano for the leisure centre.
2. I designed a _____ to advertise a new club for children with disabilities. Then I put it up in lots of places around town.
3. I got together a team of _____ and we picked up a lot of rubbish in the park.
4. I started a social media _____ to persuade people to walk instead of driving cars.
5. I started an online _____ . It asked the council not to close our sports centre, and thousands of people signed it.
6. I made a _____ about safe cycling and gave it to children in my town's primary school.

6 In pairs, discuss how you might help to solve the problems in the other photos on page 84. Use the ideas in Exercise 5 and the Useful phrases to help you.

7 Read the Useful tips. In pairs, discuss the questions.
1. Which of the suggestions in the tips do you think are the easiest to organise?
2. Which might make the biggest difference?
3. Are there any other tips that you'd like to add?

SET FOR LIFE

8 In small groups, plan how to make a difference in your community. Follow the instructions.

1 Choose one of the problems in Exercise 1.

2 Discuss what you can do to make a difference and list at least three ideas. Use expressions from the Useful phrases box.

3 Prepare a presentation to tell the class about your plans. Include:
- the reason(s) you have chosen this problem.
- the actions you are going to take.
- the results you hope to achieve.

4 Give your presentation to the class.

USEFUL TIPS

To make a difference in your community, choose a problem, find out more about it and take action.

- Find some volunteers to help.
- Tell people about the problem through posters, leaflets or social media.
- Raise money through a cake sale, a sponsored sports event or a quiz night.
- Start an online petition.
- Write to politicians, businesspeople or newspapers.

USEFUL PHRASES

Suggesting
I think we should start a …
It might be a good idea to write …
Let's get together a team of volunteers to …
Maybe we could ask … (not) to …

Responding to other people's suggestions
Great idea.
Yes, that could work.
That's a nice idea, but I'm not sure it will work because …

Talking about your plan
We're going to …
We hope to raise enough money to …
We want to persuade people to …

Progress Check Units 1–6

Vocabulary and Grammar

1 Choose the correct answer.
1 If your boss asks you to ____ overtime at work, ask for more money!
   a make   b do   c earn
2 If I ____ the opportunity, I would certainly learn more about first aid.
   a have   b 'd had   c had
3 Objects fall towards the Earth because of the ____ of gravity.
   a energy   b size   c height
4 I voted ____ him in the last election.
   a on   b for   c to
5 Put some antibacterial ____ on that cut.
   a plaster   b pill   c spray
6 Let's eat a quick lunch at the museum. We need to ____ the most of our time there.
   a make   b take   c get
7 At her job interview, they asked Sandra whether ____ done voluntary work.
   a had she   b she had   c did she

2 Complete the text with one word in each gap.

I ^{1}*ve* always been interested in fashion design. I had applied ^{2}_____ a lot of jobs, but I had never been successful. But last week a big company asked me ^{3}_____ I could come in for an interview. The interview went well – they offered me the job and I've already ^{4}_____ the contract! This time ^{5}_____ year I'll be designing my own clothes! But I need more training, so in the first month I'm going to take part ^{6}_____ a series of workshops. It's a good thing I kept ^{7}_____ trying. If I'd given up, I wouldn't ^{8}_____ had this opportunity.

3 Complete the sentences with words formed from the words in brackets.
1 Derek was pleased to start a new job. He had been *unemployed* (EMPLOY) for months.
2 I hurt myself when I fell from the tree, but I didn't have any _____ (BREAK) bones.
3 We need an _____ (ELECTRICITY) because our kitchen lights don't work.
4 My brother is very _____ (COMPETITION). He takes winning too seriously!
5 Don't worry, the treatment for your knee isn't _____ (PAIN).
6 We need to protect the giant panda because it is an _____ (DANGER) animal.
7 If you speak another language really well, you can be a _____ (TRANSLATE).

Speaking

4 Complete the dialogue with the words below.

| need   next   seems   ~~should~~   so   that's |
| were   would |

A: I'm going to help in a city library one day next week. It's part of learning about different jobs at school.
B: That's great! But it might be a good idea to prepare first.
A: Really? What do you think I ^{1}*should* do?
B: First, find out something about the work. ^{2}_____, think about what you would like to learn. Write some questions.
A: That ^{3}_____ easy.
B: I guess ^{4}_____. Do you ^{5}_____ a hand?
A: That ^{6}_____ be great, thanks!
B: If I ^{7}_____ you, I'd ask how they choose new books.
A: I think ^{8}_____ a good idea.

5 In pairs, help each other prepare for a day of practical work experience. Follow these steps.
1 Student A, choose a job that you would like to get work experience in. Tell Student B.
   I'm going to be a librarian for a day next week!
2 Student B, suggest ideas about how Student A can prepare for their work experience.
   It might be a good idea to …/You should …
3 Student A, respond to Student B's suggestions.
   I think that's a good idea./What next?
4 Change roles.

Listening

6 🔊 PC1–6.1 Listen to a museum guide and complete the text. Use 1–3 words in each gap.

SPACE MUSEUM TOUR

The first room in the space museum tour is ^{1}*the planet room*. In this first room, visitors can see our ^{2}_____ on the wall facing them.
In the second room, visitors can learn about astronauts. Astronauts do the work of ^{3}_____ outside the space station. Visitors can also try a computer app. It shows how astronauts can ^{4}_____ to get help for health problems.
In the third room, you can do an experiment with helium gas. It's light, so it makes a balloon ^{5}_____.
In the large room, visitors learn that there are ^{6}_____ million stars in our galaxy.

Reading

7 🔊 **PC1–6.2** Read the blog post and choose the correct answer.

1 Why did the head teacher want parents to come to the school early?
   a She wanted to ask the parents some questions.
   b She wanted to learn about the parents' jobs.
   c She wanted the parents to share their job experiences with students.
   d She wanted the parents to make some decisions about their children's future.

2 What did Genna's friends think about a librarian's job?
   a They all thought it was boring.
   b They didn't think it was a useful job anymore.
   c It made some of them consider doing the job in the future.
   d They realised it includes visiting members of the library.

3 What did Genna's best friend learn about the work of an app designer?
   a It was exactly how she imagined it.
   b It didn't seem so attractive after she had talked to them.
   c The most important thing in the job is imagination.
   d It's not important to work as part of a team.

4 What did Genna think about the lab assistant?
   a She wasn't very focused.
   b She was unfriendly.
   c She seemed to apologise about her job.
   d She was encouraging.

5 What is the best way to sum up the last paragraph?
   a It shows how important it is to see the practical side of a job.
   b It explains how the lab assistant created a new kind of medicine.
   c It describes all the ways computers help a lab assistant's work.
   d It shows that first impressions about a job are always right.

GENNA'S BLOG
Career Day

At our last parents' evening, the head teacher thought it would be a good idea for parents to come in a couple of hours earlier. The idea was for the students to meet parents with different jobs, learn about them and maybe ask some questions. If the students found out about jobs from people who did them, it would help them make their own decisions in the future.

My mum didn't want to do it at first. She's a librarian and she thought that nobody would come and talk to her because they would think it was a boring job. She decided to come in the end, and many of my friends talked to her. Later they told me it made them think about how useful her work was. She advises all members of the community who visit the library. Some of my friends have started thinking about becoming librarians now!

My best friend really likes computers and spent time talking to an app designer – she'd like to design apps herself. But she was surprised by how much more there is to the job than just being creative. The designer has to work as part of a team. He gets feedback from colleagues at each stage in the project and has to change things. Sometimes he has to start all over again. My friend has started thinking about other jobs now!

I talked to a lab assistant. When she was describing her work, it was difficult for me to concentrate and she could see that. So she started talking about other things instead: her sons, food, TV and stuff. She smiled and said she could see I wasn't very interested in her job. I felt a bit bad and said I was sorry. So she asked me to come to her work and find out more about it. 'Give it a chance!' she said.

So, a few days later, I did. She showed me one way her research team use computers to develop medicine. It was hard to follow what she was saying. But then she asked me to sit in front of the computer and try making my own medicine! To me, it made a big difference when I had a go myself. Maybe I would like to do that as a job one day. But if she hadn't introduced me to it, I never would have thought about it.

Writing

8 Write a for and against essay on this question: is it a good idea to do voluntary work? Include this information.
- an introduction saying why voluntary work is important, and a few examples of voluntary work
- some advantages of doing voluntary work
- some disadvantages
- a summary of your opinion, saying how you might decide to do voluntary work

Beyond words 7

VOCABULARY
Effective communication and body language | Word building: communication | The media | Advertising

GRAMMAR
The passive: Present Simple, Past Simple, Present Perfect, modal verbs | The passive with *will*

How to be a good communicator

We all prefer talking to people who are interested in what we say. Follow these tips to learn how to listen actively and communicate well.

- Stand up straight or sit forward to show you're paying attention.
- Make eye contact, but don't look someone in the eye all the time. That can make people uncomfortable.
- Ask questions and use phrases like 'I see', 'I know' and 'that's right' to show you're following the conversation.
- If the topic of conversation doesn't interest you, don't shrug your shoulders. Try changing the topic politely.
- Listen, even when someone's views are different from yours.
- Use your hands to help you describe or explain things. But don't point your finger – it's rude.
- Nod your head to show you understand or agree. But if you disagree, try not to shake your head too much and never raise your voice.
- Don't fold your arms in front of you. It might suggest you don't have an open mind.
- And finally, smile. People like a happy face!

7.1 Vocabulary

Communication and body language

1 Are you a good communicator? What can you do to communicate better?

2 Read the text. Does it mention any of your ideas from Exercise 1?

3 🔊 7.1 **WORD FRIENDS** Check you understand the phrases. Find twelve of them in the text.

fold your arms
follow a conversation
have an open mind
look someone in the eye
make eye contact
nod/shake your head
pay attention
point your finger
raise an eyebrow
raise/lower your voice
shrug your shoulders
stand up straight

Unit 7

4 Complete the sentences with phrases from Exercise 3. Do you agree with the sentences? Why?/Why not?
1 You can't really understand someone if you don't *pay attention* to what they say.
2 If you want people to trust you, keep your head up and _____ them _____.
3 When you're angry with someone, don't _____ your _____ at them; keep your hands down. And try not to shout or _____.
4 If someone asks you what you want to do and you don't really mind, don't _____ your _____. It suggests you don't care.
5 You can _____ one _____ to show you're a little surprised; if you raise two, it shows you're shocked.
6 It's better to _____ an _____ than to be closed to new ideas.

5 Choose the correct option. Then, in pairs, discuss the questions.
1 Do you usually *raise / stand up* straight?
2 Are you good at *having / making* eye contact with other people? Is it easy to talk to people who don't *look / point* you in the eye?
3 Are there any situations where it is necessary to *raise / shake* your voice?
4 Is it always rude to *point / shrug* your shoulders? Do you ever do it?
5 How do you feel when someone *nods / points* their finger at you during an argument? Does it bother you?
6 How do you show you disagree with someone? Do you *fold / shake* your head? Do you *fold / shake* your arms in front of you?
7 Can you *follow / pay* a conversation at the same time as checking your phone?
8 Is it possible to *have / make* an open mind about everything?

6 🔊 7.2 Study the Vocabulary box. Write the nouns formed from the verbs. Use a dictionary if necessary. Listen and check.

VOCABULARY	Word building: communication
Verb	**Noun**
communicate	*communication*
define	_____
describe	_____
discuss	_____
explain	_____
express	_____
inform	_____
pronounce	_____
suggest	_____

7 Complete the sentences with the correct form of words from the Vocabulary box.
1 My new dictionary app gives me a d*efinition* of any word I don't know.
2 It took me a long time to remember the correct p_____ of 'Edinburgh'.
3 I went to bed late because my parents wanted to d_____ my future plans.
4 Anna tried to e_____ to Matt why she was late, but he didn't listen.
5 After lots of s_____ from everyone, we decided to stay in and watch a film.
6 I was able to give the police a good d_____ of the thief.

8 🔊 7.3 Complete the blog post with the correct form of words from the Vocabulary box. Listen and check.

FACE TIME OR SCREEN TIME?

We watched a documentary in class yesterday about non-verbal ¹c*ommunication*. There was a lot of interesting ²i_____ about body language. An expert from Canada ³d_____ the meaning of different movements. Her ⁴e_____ was clear and entertaining. She had a great accent. I loved the way she ⁵p_____ some words, and she used some Canadian ⁶e_____ that I'd never heard before. Afterwards, we had a lively ⁷d_____ on how we prefer to ⁸c_____ with friends. I ⁹s_____ that it's easier to ¹⁰e_____ your feelings when you're physically with other people rather than talking to them on a screen.

VIDEO — **WIDER WORLD**

9 ▶ 26 Watch seven people taking about communication. When do the speakers find communicating difficult?

10 In pairs, discuss in which situations you find communicating difficult. Use the ideas below to help you.

> face-to-face   in a foreign language
> in a video conference   on the phone
> with large groups of people   with strangers

Talking on the phone is hard because you can't use body language.

I can talk about effective communication and body language.

7.2 Grammar
The passive

1 Have you ever been in an escape room? What happens there? Is an escape room a good place to improve your communication skills? Why?/Why not?

2 🔊 **7.4** Read the introduction to a podcast and answer the questions.
1. When did the Beat It escape room open?
2. How many players can play *CommunicOut*?
3. What's the key to winning the game?
4. How long do you have to finish the game?

TALK TIME with Mel and Zac

ESCAPE ROOMS

Have you ever been to an escape room? I've just been to one called Beat It. It opened a year ago and since then, thousands of customers have been challenged by their fantastic games. Their newest game is called *CommunicOut*. It's designed for groups of 2–6 and it must be finished within one hour. The game was specially created by experts to improve communication skills. Role plays are used, so each player can experience various roles and situations. Before you start, you are told to listen carefully and to observe everything. Everyone in the group should be heard because the game can't be won unless you work as a team. Listen to today's podcast as I tell Mel how I got on.

3 Study the Grammar box. Find more examples of the passive in the text.

GRAMMAR — The passive

Present Simple
The game **is designed** for groups of 2–6.
Prizes **are given out** to the winners at the end.

Past Simple
The game **was created** by experts.
We **were invited** to an escape room recently.

Present Perfect
This new room **has** already **been visited** by hundreds of players.
Thousands of customers **have been challenged** by their games.

Modal verbs
The game **must be finished** in one hour.
It **can't be won** without teamwork.
Everyone **should be heard**.

GRAMMAR TIME ▶ PAGE 132

4 Write the past participle form of the verbs below.

> ~~be~~ do find gave hear keep know lose make say see show speak take teach tell win write

be – been

5 🔊 **7.5** Complete the second sentence using the passive. Listen and check.
1. Zac joins me.
   I *'m joined* by Zac.
2. Bad weather delayed my train.
   My train _____ by bad weather.
3. They give out some instructions.
   Some instructions _____ .
4. You must complete the game in an hour.
   The game _____ in an hour.
5. You can't do it if you don't share ideas.
   It _____ if you don't share ideas.
6. Someone invited you to an escape room.
   You _____ to an escape room.
7. My cousin Mike took me there.
   I _____ my cousin Mike.
8. Nobody has ever invited me to do something like that.
   I _____ to do something like that.
9. We raised our voices once or twice.
   Our voices _____ once or twice.

YOUR WORLD

6 Complete the sentences so they are true for you. Then, in pairs, compare your sentences.
1. In my family, birthdays are usually celebrated in …
2. The best game I've ever played was given to me by …
3. I've never been invited to …
4. Something that can't be done without teamwork is …

Unit 7 — I can use verbs in the passive.

7.3 Reading and Vocabulary
April Fool's jokes

APRIL FOOL'S DAY IN THE MEDIA

Newspapers are usually reliable sources of news. So are radio stations and TV channels. ¹___ In Spain it's on 28 December. But in most of the world, including the UK, it's on 1 April and it's known as April Fool's Day.

One of the earliest April Fool's Day reports on British television was shown on the BBC in 1957. ²___ The reporter on location explained they were picking spaghetti from the trees before putting it in the sun to dry. Many viewers believed the story and sent letters asking where spaghetti trees could be bought.

In 1971, on French radio, it was revealed that drivers would have to begin driving on the left. The reason given? To help British tourists.

On 1 April 1976, on BBC Radio 2, the famous astronomer Patrick Moore reported that the position of two planets was going to reduce the effect of gravity. ³___ Moore invited his listeners to jump in the air at precisely 9.47 a.m. to experience a floating feeling like astronauts. Many did.

More recently, in 2008, the BBC reported on flying penguins in Antarctica. The birds were filmed apparently preparing for their long flight to the Amazon.

Many April Fool's jokes have been printed in the press. In 1931 a Berlin journalist wrote an article with a photo of a bus that was four floors high. ⁴___ And one year, on 28 December, a local newspaper in the Spanish city of Granada talked about free helicopter rides from the city centre to the Sierra Nevada ski resort. Hundreds of excited skiers turned up with their skis.

Should the media play jokes like these on their audiences? They're funny, but some people think it's not right for news organisations to tell lies and make fun of people. Some of the skiers in Granada, for example, were angry that they'd wasted their time and been made to look silly.

Finally, there's one more problem with April Fool's Day. ⁵___ For example, in 1946 many people in Hawaii and Alaska ignored warnings about a tsunami because it was 1 April. 165 people were killed.

1 Have you ever heard any strange or funny stories reported in the media? What were they?

2 Read the article quickly. Answer the questions.
  1 Which story do you find the funniest?
  2 Which is the hardest to believe?

3 🔊 7.6 Read the article again. For each gap (1–5), choose the correct sentence (a–h). There are three extra sentences. Listen and check.
  a At first, it didn't seem such a strange story.
  b It showed farm workers in a field in Switzerland.
  c It wasn't explained how it passed under bridges.
  d People might believe a serious story is just a joke.
  e As a result, people would feel lighter for a few seconds.
  f Most people just laugh when they hear stories like that.
  g But it's not a good idea to believe everything you see or hear.
  h However, there is one day every year when false stories are reported.

4 In pairs, ask and answer about the media in your country. Use the highlighted media words in the article.
What's your favourite TV channel?

5 🔊 7.7 Listen to a girl talking about her brother's April Fool's Day tricks. What four tricks does she describe?

6 Which of the tricks in Exercise 5 do you think is the funniest? Why? Discuss in pairs.

YOUR WORLD

7 In pairs, discuss the questions.
  1 Is it all right to have April Fool's jokes in the media? Why?/Why not?
  2 Have you ever played an April Fool's trick on someone? What was it?
  3 Has anyone ever played an April Fool's trick on you? What was it?

I can understand an article about April Fool's jokes in the media.

7.4 Grammar

The passive with *will*

1 Does your school offer sign language classes? If not, do you think it would be a good idea to add them? Why?/Why not?

2 🔊 7.8 Read the leaflet. Who can take the sign language course? What level is it? Where and when will it take place?

MEADOWBANK High School

LEARN SIGN LANGUAGE

We are pleased to report that from September to December free sign language classes will be offered to parents, teachers and students at Meadowbank High. The classes will be aimed at beginners. The course, which will be taught by a professional teacher, will be held in room 1H on Mondays at 4.30 p.m. All materials will be provided. You won't be expected to do homework, but there will be online exercises on the school website for further practice. If numbers are not high enough, the classes won't be continued in January.

3 Study the Grammar box. Find more examples of the passive with *will* in the leaflet.

> **GRAMMAR** — The passive with *will*
>
> The classes **will be aimed** at beginners.
> You **won't be expected** to do homework.
> **Will** we **be given** homework?

GRAMMAR TIME > PAGE 132

> ⚠️ **WATCH OUT!**
> Sometimes you can form two passive sentences from one active sentence.
> **Active:** The school **will offer** free classes to parents.
> **Passive:** Free classes **will be offered** to parents.
> Parents **will be offered** free classes.

4 Complete the sentences with *will* and the passive form of the verbs in brackets.
1 The course <u>will be offered</u> (offer) for free.
2 The alphabet _____ (write) on the board.
3 Dictionaries _____ (not need).
4 Some mistakes _____ (make).
5 _____ (a video/show)?
6 The classes _____ (not film).

5 Rewrite each of these sentences in two different ways in the passive.
1 We will give the students handouts.
   The students will be given handouts.
   Handouts will be given to the students.
2 We will send more information to you by email.
3 We won't give the students exams.
4 Will they provide us with tea and biscuits?

6 🔊 7.9 Read the text. Complete the sentences below using the passive with *will*. Listen and check.

> We believe that large companies will use Mandarin Chinese more often in the future. So from next week teachers from Beijing will teach Mandarin at our school. They will give great importance to pronunciation and speaking in the classes. They won't test students, but they will organise a weekly quiz. At the end of the course they will prepare a Chinese meal to celebrate.

1 Mandarin Chinese <u>will be used by large companies</u> more often in the future.
2 So from next week Mandarin _____ .
3 Pronunciation and speaking _____ .
4 The students _____ , but a weekly quiz _____ .
5 At the end of the course a Chinese meal _____ .

YOUR WORLD

7 Make questions using the passive with *will*. Then, in pairs, ask and answer the questions.
1 when / your next school trip / organise / ?
2 do you think / we / give / any homework / today / ?
3 sign language / teach / in your school / one day / ?
4 do you think / a big party / organise / for the end of the term / ?

A: *When will your next school trip be organised?*
B: *I hope it'll be organised soon, but I don't know.*

I can use the future form of the passive.

7.5 Listening and Vocabulary
Advertising

1 What type of advertising do you most often see or hear?

2 🔊 **7.10** Study the Vocabulary box. Which things from the box can you see in the photo above?

> **VOCABULARY** Advertising
>
> billboard   brand   commercial   leaflet   logo   poster
> slogan   target audience

3 Complete the sentences with the correct form of words from the Vocabulary box.
1. There's a huge *billboard* near the stadium. It's advertising an energy drink.
2. The _____ for this sports company is 'Everyone's a winner'.
3. The _____ for that clothing company is a green crocodile.
4. A man is handing out _____ for the music festival next weekend.
5. There are too many _____ on TV. It's annoying when you're watching a film.
6. The _____ for this advert is children, so it's shown after school.
7. I have a big _____ of Rafael Nadal advertising that product on my wall.
8. I always buy the same _____ of shampoo.

4 🔊 **7.11** Listen to five extracts from TV commercials. Match the extracts (1–5) with the products (a–h). There are three extra products.
- a ☐ chocolate
- b ☐ trainers
- c ☐ perfume
- d ☐ toothpaste
- e ☐ washing-up liquid
- f ☐ nail varnish
- g ☐ a hamburger
- h ☐ a mountain bike

5 🔊 **7.11** Listen again. Which commercial would be the most successful? Why? Discuss in pairs.

6 🔊 **7.12** Listen to four short dialogues. Choose the correct answer.
1. You will hear a girl telling her mother about a pair of jeans she wants to buy. What does she say about them?
   - a She had a pair like that when she was younger.
   - b She likes the TV commercial for them.
   - c They have a logo with a silver star on it.
2. You will hear two friends talking about a restaurant. What does the girl like about it?
   - a You can drink as much as you like for free.
   - b There's a good choice of salads.
   - c The pizzas are the best she's ever had.
3. You will hear two friends talking about a poster for a music festival. Where do they think is the best place to put it up?
   - a in a supermarket
   - b in a music shop
   - c at the school
4. You will hear a boy talking to his father. Why can't his father take him to football training?
   - a He's working that day.
   - b He has to take the boy's sister to swimming lessons.
   - c He won't be able to use the car at that time.

VIDEO **WIDER WORLD**

7 ▶ **27** Watch seven people talking about their favourite TV commercials. Match the adjectives below that they use to describe them with four of the products (1–5).

> brilliant   complex   cool   emotional   fantastic
> funny   hilarious   interesting   nice   smart   weird

1. John Lewis department store: _____
2. Dairy Milk chocolate: _____
3. *Chanel* perfume: _____
4. a car: _____
5. Cadbury chocolate: _____

8 In pairs, tell each other about your favourite TV commercial. Describe it and say why you like it. Use the adjectives in Exercise 7.

I can understand short TV commercials.

7.6 Speaking
Clarifying and rephrasing

VIDEO ▶ **WHAT DO YOU MEAN?**

Eren: Thanks for helping me practise my speech.
Carla: No problem. Go on then!
Eren: Some people think there's a …
Carla: Great, but how about slowing it down a bit?
Eren: OK. Some people think …
Bea: Nice, but it would be better if you didn't just read your speech.
Eren: Are you suggesting I have to learn it?
Carla: Yes.
Bea: Yes.
Eren: Like this? Some people think there's a secret formula to …
Carla: That's much better, but who are you looking at?
Eren: What do you mean? I'm not looking at anyone.
Bea: Exactly. What we're saying is don't look down. That's to say, look at the audience, not at the floor!
Eren: OK. Some people think there's a … .
Carla: Fantastic!
Bea: But … maybe take your hands out of your pockets.
Carla: Yes. And use some body language.
Eren: OK, I get it!

The next day …

Eren: … and that's the secret to a memorable speech. Thank you very much.

SOUNDS GOOD! Go on then! • OK, I get it!

1 ▶ 28 🔊 7.13 Watch or listen and answer the questions.
1. How well did Eren do when he was practising?
2. How did he do when he finally gave the speech?
3. What advice do Eren's friends give him?

SET FOR LIFE

2 In groups, discuss the best advice to help someone speak in public. Use these ideas to help you.
- Don't repeat yourself too often.
- Practise with friends.
- Take deep breaths and try to relax.
- Be positive – tell yourself that you can do this.

3 Study the Speaking box. Find examples of the phrases in the dialogue.

SPEAKING Clarifying and rephrasing

Asking for clarification
(What) do/did you mean … ?   Like this?
Are you saying/suggesting … ?
When you say/said … , (what) do/did you mean … ?

Giving clarification
Sorry, I meant to say …   What I meant was …
What I am/was saying/trying to say is/was …
When I said … , I meant …
No, I don't/didn't mean …
That's not what I mean/meant.

Rephrasing
In other words, …   That's to say …
Let me put it another way.

4 🔊 7.14 Complete the dialogue with words from the Speaking box. Listen and check.
A: ¹*Are you saying* my speech was boring?
B: No, sorry, I ²_____ it was boring.
A: Well, what ³_____ , then?
B: What I was ⁴_____ is it was too long.
A: In ⁵_____ , you thought it was boring!

5 🔊 7.15 Study the Language box. Then listen and write down the correct question tag for each statement.

LANGUAGE Question tags

We use question tags to check if something is true or when we expect someone to agree with us.
Positive statements have negative tags.
That was good, **wasn't it**?
Negative statements have positive tags.
You haven't got a sore back, **have you**?

6 🔊 7.16 Listen and check.

Unit 7 | 94 | I can ask for and give clarification and rephrase what I say.

7.7 Writing
A review

1. Which of these language learning aids do you consider most effective or enjoyable?

   > books/films in original language   coursebooks
   > dictionaries   flashcards   phone apps   websites

2. Read Jamie's review. What is he reviewing and what does he think of it?

3. Order the information as it appears in the review.
   a ☐ Jamie gives his overall opinion and recommendation.
   b ☐ Jamie says what he is reviewing and why he chose to review it.
   c ☐ Jamie describes the advantages and disadvantages of the product.

4. Study the Writing box. Find similar phrases in Jamie's review.

   WRITING — A review

   1 What you are reviewing and why
   I've often been asked about …
   … is one of the most popular … , but is it as fantastic as they say?

   2 Advantages and disadvantages
   I particularly (dis)like …
   Unfortunately, …
   It looks attractive/confusing.
   3 There's a wide variety of …
   It's easy to use.
   There are one or two disappointing things.

   4 Personal opinion and recommendation
   All in all, I think …
   I would/wouldn't recommend it.
   It's probably (not) the best …
   This is (one of) the best … I've ever …

5. Study the Language box. Find examples of prepositional phrases in Jamie's review.

   LANGUAGE — Prepositional phrases

   at all/first/last/least/once/the moment/times
   by accident/chance/hand/mistake/the time
   in a hurry/addition to/danger/the end/time/trouble
   on average/foot/purpose/sale/time

6. Write six sentences using prepositional phrases from the Language box. Then, in pairs, compare your sentences.

JAMIE'S REVIEW SITE

Is Wordfit the right app for you?
★★★★☆

1. So many language learning apps have been created that at times it's hard to know which to choose. Wordfit is one of the most popular apps, but is it as fantastic as they say?

2. I like the design. It looks really attractive and is easy to use. There's a wide variety of fun activities like quizzes and games. I particularly like the fact that it lets you chat with other language learners. It's a brilliant idea.

3. However, there are one or two disappointing things. Some listening practice is provided, but not enough. Also, unfortunately, I couldn't hear it very well. At first, I thought I'd put the volume too low by mistake. But the problem was the sound quality. It's very poor. I think it was recorded in a hurry. Finally, if you're looking for pronunciation practice, you're in trouble because there is none.

4. All in all, I think Wordfit is pretty good. At least it's not boring. I would definitely recommend it. However, if you need to practise listening and pronunciation, it's probably not the best app for you.

WRITING TIME

7. Write a review of an app, coursebook, website or language course that you have used to study a language.

   1 Find ideas
   Make notes for your review. Think about:
   • the way you studied the language and what it was like.
   • its advantages and disadvantages.
   • your personal opinion and whether you would recommend it.

   2 Plan
   Organise your review into paragraphs. Use Jamie's review to help you.

   3 Write and share
   • Write a draft of your review. Use the Language box and the Writing box to help you.
   • Share your review with another student for feedback.
   • Write the final version of your review.

   4 Check
   • Check language: have you included prepositional phrases?
   • Check grammar: have you used the passive correctly?

I can write a review and offer opinions and points of view.

Vocabulary Activator

WORDLIST 🔊 7.17

Word friends
(effective communication and body language)
fold your arms
follow a conversation
have an open mind
look someone in the eye
lower your voice
make eye contact
nod your head
pay attention
point your finger
raise an eyebrow
raise your voice
shake your head
shrug your shoulders
stand up straight

Word building
(communication)
communicate (v)
communication (n)
define (v)
definition (n)
describe (v)
description (n)
discuss (v)
discussion (n)
explain (v)
explanation (n)
express (v)
expression (n)
inform (v)
information (n)
pronounce (v)
pronunciation (n)
suggest (v)
suggestion (n)

The media
audience (n)
journalist (n)
listener (n)
on location
print (v)
radio station (n)
reliable source
report (v)
reporter (n)
the press (n)
TV channel (n)
viewer (n)

Advertising
billboard (n)
brand (n)
commercial (n)
leaflet (n)
logo (n)
poster (n)
slogan (n)
target audience (n)

Extra words
accent (n)
advert (n)
April Fool's joke (n)
argument (n)
change the topic
chat (v)
communication skills (n)
complex (adj)
design (n)
emotional (adj)
graphics (n)
hilarious (adj)
humour (n)
ignore (v)
instruction (n)

left-handed (adj)
loudly (adv)
meaning (n)
news organisation (n)
observe (v)
play a trick
podcast (n)
politely (adv)
reason (n)
record (v)
role play (v)
rude (adj)
share ideas
shocked (adj)
shout (v)
sign language (n)
sit forward
sound quality (n)
speak clearly
speech (n)
tell a joke
tell lies
trust (v)
volume (n)
warning (n)
write an article

1 What body language could you use when you say these things? Use phrases from the wordlist.
1 'Look at that over there!' *point your finger*
2 'I don't know.' _____
3 'Yes, I agree.' _____
4 'I'm surprised.' _____
5 'No, I disagree.' _____
6 'Are you listening to me?' _____

2 Use the wordlist to find these things.
1 three actions where your arms need to move
   fold your arms, …
2 two jobs
3 two things you often see on advertising posters
4 two phrases with *eye*

3 Choose the odd one out.
1 explain   discuss   print   suggest
2 audience   poster   listener   viewer
3 follow a conversation   fold your arms
   have an open mind   pay attention
4 leaflet   brand   attention   billboard

4 Find words in the wordlist to match the definitions.
1 You see it on walls. It tries to sell you things. It's a big poster. *billboard*
2 It's two words. The press gets its information from here because they can trust it. _____
3 It's a small piece of paper with one or two pages. It advertises something. _____
4 You do this with words when you try to say them clearly. _____
5 A kind of product made by a particular company with a particular name. _____

5 🔊 7.18 **PRONUNCIATION** Listen and underline the sound the words below all have in common.

communication   expression   shrug   special

6 🔊 7.19 **PRONUNCIATION** The most common way of spelling the /ʃ/ sound is *sh*, but we also sometimes spell it *ci*, *si* or *ti*. Find examples of each spelling of /ʃ/ in the wordlist and write them in the correct group. Listen and check.
1 Words with *sh*: *shrug, …*
2 Words with *ci*: *special, …*
3 Words with *si*: *expression, …*
4 Words with *ti*: *communication, …*

Unit 7   96

Revision

Vocabulary

1 Complete the sentences with words for parts of the body.
1. When you shrug your _shoulders_, it can mean you don't care.
2. I didn't eat the last piece of cake. Don't point your _____ at me!
3. Could you look someone in the _____ and tell them a lie?
4. When dad said he was a good singer, it raised a few _____ .
5. I know you can't talk now, but just nod your _____ for 'yes'.
6. When you're giving a presentation, try to make _____ contact with the audience.

2 Complete the sentences with words formed from the words in brackets.
1. Lee's brother is a news _reporter_ (REPORT).
2. Jo made an interesting _____ (SUGGEST).
3. Do you know how to _____ (PRONUNCIATION) this word?
4. We had a very interesting _____ (DISCUSS) about advertising today.
5. Could you _____ (LOW) your voice, please?
6. No one understood his _____ (EXPLAIN).

3 Choose the correct option to complete the comments by people who work in media.

> The programmes on our TV ¹*audience / channel* must be good because there are so many others. They're all competing for ²*viewers / listeners*. It's hard, but it feels great when it works well.

> I like going on ³*travel / location* to different places. Talking to people directly always gives me more reliable ⁴*sources / headlines* for all my stories. Being ⁵*a journalist / an interpreter* is an interesting job.

> I create ⁶*logos / descriptions*. They go on everything – from giant ⁷*commercials / billboards* to paper ⁸*leaflets / expressions* in your mailbox. I need the ⁹*target / brand* audience to remember them. I write ¹⁰*expressions / slogans* too. People hear them on TV or on a radio ¹¹*station / source*.

Grammar

4 Make passive sentences. What product do they describe? Go to page 137 and check your answer.
1. it / discover / farmers / in Africa
   It was discovered by farmers in Africa.
2. it / drink / since the fifteenth century
3. it / drink / millions of people these days
4. milk and sugar / can / add / to it
5. it / serve / chilled or hot

5 Write four sentences like the ones in Exercise 4 about a product/object. In pairs, share your sentences with your partner. Can he/she guess the product/object?

6 Complete the dialogue with the correct passive form of the verbs in brackets.

Teacher: Our lessons ¹*will be moved* (move) to a new classroom tomorrow.
Student: What about our books?
Teacher: They ²_____ (should/take) too. New computer equipment ³_____ (must/install).
Student: Can we see the equipment?
Teacher: It ⁴_____ (not deliver) yet, but I ⁵_____ (inform) by the company that it ⁶_____ (deliver) tomorrow.
Student: When ⁷_____ (the work/finish) so we can come back?

Speaking

7 In pairs, follow the instructions.
1. Choose one of these topics to tell your partner about.
   - your hobby (how you started, why you like it, how you do it)
   - food you like (how you discovered it, when you eat it, how you prepare it)
   - a pet you like (why you like it, what it needs, what it's like)
2. Start speaking. Use phrases to help your partner understand (e.g. *What I meant was … , In other words … , Let me put it another way.*).
3. Ask for clarification when your partner is speaking (e.g. *What do/did you mean?, Are you saying … ?*).

Dictation

8 7.20 Listen. Then listen again and write down what you hear during each pause.

Unit 7

BBC CULTURE
How languages evolve

English never stops changing

All languages are in flux. In other words, they are constantly changing. This is especially true of English, which is a real global language. There are now three times more non-native speakers of English than natives. About one billion people speak it as a foreign language, while only 360 million speak it as a mother tongue. So why is English changing and is this a good thing?

One reason is globalisation. Today business meetings can be held with people from all over the world – for example, Brazil, Nigeria and Japan. Nearly always, the only common language spoken will be English. This has led to the creation of a new language variety called International English. It's a kind of English which speakers from all countries can use to talk to each other.

English plays a different role in different countries. In Singapore, Hong Kong and the Philippines, English is spoken as a second language. In the Philippines, Tagalog (the country's main language) and English merge to create a variety called Taglish. But some local languages don't merge with official languages in this way, and they are in danger because fewer people speak them.

The use of slang also changes a language. For example, colloquial terms such as *innit?* (*isn't it?*) and *like* are used so much in contemporary English that they are now a kind of punctuation. But if people use these terms to communicate, maybe they should count as real words.

The fact is that a language evolves because new words are constantly being added to it. Nouns such as *emoticon*, *spam* or *blog* and verbs like *google*, *photoshop* or *skype* have all been introduced into the English language thanks to digital technology, and they will be with us for a long time. There is much discussion about whether these words should be in the dictionary or not – and some new words never make it into dictionaries. But at the same time, some words and languages that have been with us for a long time are disappearing.

---

contemporary (adj) belonging to the present time
merge (v) join to become one
mother tongue (n) the language you learn and speak as a child
punctuation (n) signs that organise text

---

1 **VISIBLE THINKING** In pairs, follow these steps.
CONNECT
1 Look at the photo. What language(s) could the people be speaking?
EXTEND
2 Does your language have different varieties or dialects?
3 Do you use any English words in your language? If so, which ones?
CHALLENGE
4 Why do you think so many people speak English? How do you feel about this?

2 🔊 7.21 Read the article and answer the questions.
1 Why is English considered to be a global language?
2 How many people speak English as a second language?
3 What is International English?
4 Why are some local languages in danger?
5 How does slang change a language?
6 Why are words like *emoticon*, *spam* or *blog* now part of the English language?

3 In pairs, discuss the questions.
1 Do you think your language is changing as much as English? If so, how?
2 Should we try to control what new words are introduced to our language?
3 What could be done to help languages with fewer speakers?

BBC ▶ Keeping languages alive

4 Look at the photos from a TV programme about languages and discuss the questions.
1. What countries could the photos be from?
2. What languages do you think are spoken there?
3. Are any small regional languages spoken in your country? If so, what are they?
4. Do you think it is important to keep them alive? Why?/Why not?

5 ▶ 29 Watch the TV programme and answer the questions.
1. What languages are spoken in Ireland?
2. How many local languages are spoken in Kenya?
3. What is English used for in our global world?
4. Why is it important to keep local languages alive?

6 ▶ 29 Choose the correct option. Then watch the video again and check.
1. There are *hundreds / thousands* of different languages in the world today.
2. English is spoken by *millions / billions* of people.
3. English is studied as a second language by 1.5 *million / billion* learners.
4. *80,000 / 8,000* people speak Irish.
5. The Irish language has *fewer / more* words than English.
6. 35,000 children in Ireland go to *English / Irish* primary schools.
7. The Turkana people use *two / three* different languages.
8. In their own community, *English / Turkana* is their first choice.

PROJECT TIME

7 In groups of four, create a digital presentation about an endangered language. Follow these steps.

1 In your group, choose an endangered language. Decide who will find information about these things.
- the origins and a short history of the language
- where and how the language is used now, and a few example words
- how the number of speakers has changed and future hopes
- the influences of English or other languages on this language

2 Individually, prepare your part of the presentation.
- Find the information and photos for the slideshow.
- Write a short text for each slide and add photos.

3 In your group, create your presentation. You can use presentation software.
- Put the slides together and think of a title for the presentation.
- Check and edit your presentation.
- Practise giving your presentation as a group.

4 Share your presentation with the class.
- Answer other students' questions.
- Ask questions and comment on the other presentations.

Experience art

8

VOCABULARY
Visual arts | Describing art |
Literature and books |
Painting | Journalism

GRAMMAR
Modal verbs for ability |
Modal verbs for obligation and
prohibition

I love the arts!

I'm Holly. I love all creative arts, from design and sculpture to literature. In this blog, I share my latest art discoveries.

AN ART EXPERIENCE

Last week I was excited to go to an exhibition of Van Gogh's paintings. He was influenced by the French Impressionists. I expected to see lots of portraits and landscapes in a gallery, so I was surprised to see an art installation instead. The paintings had become a light show. There was music and sound effects too. As we moved around, it was like walking through Van Gogh's work. It was a really memorable experience!

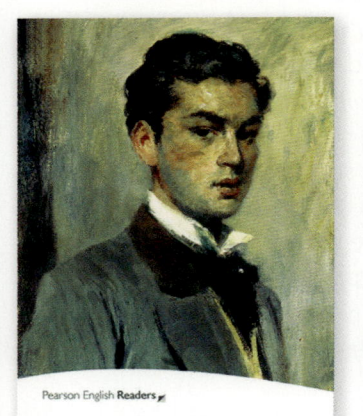

THE STORY OF AN UNUSUAL PICTURE

I'm just reading *The Picture of Dorian Gray*, which I chose because of the classic art style painting on the cover. At first, I thought the book was a biography, but actually, it's fiction. An artist paints a fantastic picture of Dorian, the main character, when he is young and good-looking. As time passes, Dorian remains young, but his portrait changes and becomes old. I don't know how it ends yet, but it's quite a scary story.

8.1 Vocabulary

Art and literature

1 Read the blog post. Would you like to see the exhibition or read the book? Why?/Why not?

2 🔊 8.1 Study Vocabulary box A. Find words from the box in the blog post.

VOCABULARY A — **Visual arts**

Styles of painting
abstract art   classic art   impressionist art
modern art   pop art

Art forms
architecture   art installation   design
film-making   photography   sculpture

---

3 🔊 8.2 Complete the sentences with words from Vocabulary box A. Listen and check.
1 <u>Sculpture</u> is the art of creating objects out of stone, wood, metal, clay, etc.
2 _____ is the art of producing pictures using a camera.
3 _____ is a style of painting that uses objects from ordinary life. It was very popular in the 1960s.
4 _____ is a style of painting that uses mainly shapes and lines and does not show people or things in a realistic way.
5 _____ is the art of designing buildings.
6 An _____ is a piece of art that is made using light, sound, etc. as well as objects.

4 🔊 8.3 **WORD FRIENDS** Study the phrases and check you understand them. Use a dictionary if necessary.

<mark>create an impressive/a memorable/a powerful work of art
choose/use bright/clear colours
design a colourful/an unusual building
have a mysterious/unique/warm atmosphere
paint a landscape/portrait/scene
perform a dance/piece of music
publish a book/a newspaper/poems
visit an art exhibition</mark>

5 Choose the correct option.

Comments

Jacob_M
I think your blog's great, Holly. Did you know the famous architect Gaudi ¹*designed / published* the colourful sculptures in Park Guell in Barcelona, Spain? It's a huge place, so it's actually like an art installation. Gaudi ²*performed / used* bright colours and interesting shapes for his works of art. This place ³*chooses / has* a unique atmosphere because it's very different from anywhere else. The first time I came here, I decided to study architecture!

However, my favourite sculptures are in Trafalgar Square in London. I was very small the first time I saw the four huge lions in the square. I remember seeing these strong black shapes – I wanted to climb up and hug them! The artist who ⁴*created / visited* these impressive works of art was a painter called Edwin Landseer. He usually ⁵*performed / painted* portraits of animals, but his sculptures of lions are famous now and thousands of tourists take photographs next to them. Keep up the good work!

6 🔊 8.4 Study Vocabulary box B. Check you understand the words.

VOCABULARY B | **Literature and books**

author autobiography biography chapter character
cover fiction non-fiction novel novelist plot
short story title

7 🔊 8.5 Choose the correct option. Listen and check. Then, in pairs, say if the sentences are true for you.

1 If a *novel / character* is boring, I stop reading it.
2 I often read a couple of *chapters / plots* of a book at bedtime.
3 Interesting *novelists / characters* are more important than a good plot.
4 I prefer reading *fiction / non-fiction* such as science books.
5 I often choose a book because I like the *biography / cover*.
6 *Short stories / Authors* are more fun to read than non-fiction.

8 🔊 8.6 Complete the book reviews with the correct form of words from Vocabulary box B. Listen and check.

Books by young writers

A Christine Mari Inzer published her first non-fiction book when she was fifteen. *Diary of a Tokyo Teen* is an ¹<u>autobiography</u>. It tells the true story of a year she spent in Tokyo. As well as being the ² _____ of the book, Christine is a skilled artist, so she drew some impressive pictures of her life in a foreign country. Her art appears on the ³ _____ of her book too.

B Christopher Paolini was fifteen when he started writing fiction about dragons. The ⁴ _____ of his first book was *Eragon*. Eragon, the main ⁵ _____ , is a boy who goes on an adventure with a dragon. Christopher obviously enjoyed writing: *Eragon* has fifty-nine ⁶ _____ and is the first novel in a series of five. Christopher is now a well-known novelist.

VIDEO | **WIDER WORLD**

9 ▶ 30 Watch seven people talking about famous artists. How many musicians, sculptors or writers do they mention?

10 In pairs, take it in turns to talk about a famous novelist or artist you really like. Explain why you like him/her.
I like Picasso because he uses bright colours.

I can talk about works of art and books.

8.2 Grammar
Modal verbs for ability

1 Do you like reading comics or graphic novels? Why?/Why not?

2 🔊 8.7 Read the blog post quickly. Why does the writer think graphic novels are a good idea?

3 Study the Grammar box. Find more examples of modal verbs for ability in the blog post.

> **GRAMMAR** — Modal verbs for ability
>
> **Present**
> She *can*/*can't* paint.
> They*'re able to*/*aren't able to* read quickly.
>
> **Past**
> I *could*/*couldn't* follow the plot.
> Jack *was*/*wasn't able to* go to the library.
> He *managed*/*didn't manage to* read the book in a day.
>
> **Future**
> I*'ll be*/*won't be able to* finish this today.
>
> **Questions**
> *Can*/*Could* he paint?   No, he *can't*/*couldn't*.
> *Is*/*Was* she *able to* read quickly?   Yes, she *is*/*was*.
> *Will* you *be able to* read more books?   No, I *won't*.
> *Did* he *manage to* finish the book?   Yes, he *did*.
>
> **Use**
> We use *could* to describe general ability in the past.
> We use *managed to* to describe specific achievements in the past.
>
> GRAMMAR TIME > PAGE 133

4 🔊 8.8 Complete the dialogues with the correct form of *can*, *could*, *be able to* or *manage to*. Listen and check.

Mum: What's the matter, love?
Oscar: I ¹*couldn't* sleep last night and now I ² _____ concentrate.
Mum: Why don't you read before you go to sleep? A good book ³ _____ help you to relax.

The next day …

Oscar: Hi, Mum. I ⁴ _____ get a great book from the library.
Mum: Oh, that's good. Tonight you'll ⁵ _____ read it in bed and you'll soon fall asleep.
Oscar: It's a horror story!
Mum: That's no good, Oscar! You ⁶ _____ sleep after that!

BOOKS COME ALIVE!

I have always loved comics. I started collecting superhero comics like *Spiderman* when I was about ten. I loved manga comics and tried to copy the drawings, but I couldn't do them very well. When I started to read novels, I couldn't always follow the story and missed the pictures. Then I discovered graphic novels. They're great if you aren't able to read very quickly and the pictures keep you interested. We've just started reading Shakespeare's play *Hamlet* at school. At first, I couldn't follow the plot. Now my dad has managed to find a graphic novel of it in the library, so I'll be able to understand the story and the characters. This doesn't mean I won't be able to read longer novels in the future. It just means that I'll be able to enjoy types of books that I wouldn't normally read.

5 Complete the questions with the correct form of the verbs in brackets. Then write answers that are true for you.
1 *Did you manage to* (you/manage to) fall asleep quickly last night?
2 _____ (you/can) swim when you were four years old?
3 _____ (your best friend/can) dance?
4 _____ (you/be able to) do homework and listen to music at the same time?
5 _____ (you/be able to) finish this exercise before the end of the lesson?

YOUR WORLD

6 Write four questions with *manage* or *can*/*could*/*be able to*. Then, in pairs, ask and answer your questions. Use the ideas below or your own.

> draw manga cartoons   paint a portrait
> read books in English   remember a poem
> take great photos   write scary stories

A: Could you read books in English when you were ten?
B: No, I couldn't.

8.3 Reading and Vocabulary

A young artist

Express yourself!

As a kid, Tyler Gordon used to love watching his mom paint. One day when he was ten, he asked her if he could do a painting. The only spare paint was black, but she gave him that and a canvas. She left the room for twenty minutes and when she returned, she couldn't believe her eyes. Although he'd never done a portrait before, Tyler had produced an amazing image of the principal at his school.

Tyler was born deaf, but after an operation he could hear in one ear. Like many young kids, Tyler loved sports. However, he was still deaf in one ear and had a speech problem, so he wasn't able to communicate well with his teammates. For this reason, Tyler was told he couldn't play on his youth football team. Although he was disappointed, Tyler managed to find a positive solution: he became a cheerleader and won many prizes!

Tyler's love of sports led him to create powerful portraits of sports stars. When he was twelve, Tyler painted a portrait of basketball player Kevin Durant and he shared it on social media. Durant saw the picture and decided to meet Tyler and buy the painting! Of course, this appeared in the news and soon pop stars like Jennifer Lopez and Janet Jackson were asking for portraits. He has also painted US president Joe Biden and vice president Kamala Harris.

Tyler doesn't normally paint landscapes. He enjoys creating large pictures, but they aren't usually colourful. His typical style uses strong, simple lines and blocks of colour. He works really fast. A painting can be finished in half an hour, but he's not afraid to start again if something goes wrong. Tyler also creates self-portraits, often when he's had a difficult day at school. He's experienced some bullying because of his speech problem, so painting is a great way to express his emotions.

Tyler enjoys sharing his art on social media and he often posts videos to teach people how to paint. He also does paintings in front of a live audience. If you are ever in San José, California, make sure you visit the local art gallery, where you can see Tyler's work on display.

1 Do you enjoy visiting art exhibitions? Why?/ Why not?

2 🔊 8.9 Read the article. What two types of pictures does Tyler paint?

3 Read the article again and answer the questions.
1. Who was in Tyler's first painting?
2. What health problem did Tyler have as a baby?
3. At what age did Tyler first paint a famous basketball player?
4. Where did other celebrities see Tyler's work?
5. What size artwork does Tyler like to paint?
6. What does Tyler do after a bad day at school?
7. How does Tyler share his art?

4 In pairs, look at the highlighted words and phrases related to painting in the article. Check you understand them.

5 Complete the questions with four of the highlighted words/phrases in the article. Then, in pairs, ask and answer the questions.
1. How old was Tyler when his mum gave him a _____ ?
2. Where is the _____ with a display of Tyler's work?
3. Why do you think Tyler paints _____ after a bad day?
4. What kind of lines and colours are Tyler's typical _____ ?

YOUR WORLD

6 In pairs, discuss the questions. Then share your ideas with the class.
1. If you were an artist, what type of painting would you do? Why?
2. Who or what would you paint?

I can understand an article about an artist.

8.4 Grammar
Modal verbs for obligation and prohibition

Poet's corner
BY SAFIYE – RAP ARTIST AND POET

Since I started doing poetry presentations last year, people have been asking me the same questions, so I wanted to share my answers here.

How do I write poems?
If you want to write poems, you must read poems. Also, you mustn't try to please other people. You have to do this for yourself. And don't worry, poems don't have to rhyme and they don't have to be long. In fact, it's a good idea to start with a short poem. When you're writing poems, just say what you feel.

How do I do poetry presentations?
Of course, you don't have to read your poems to other people, but performing to an audience is a nice way of sharing your work and getting feedback. I was nervous before my first reading, so I had to practise for hours in front of the mirror! Think about the message you want to give. Then, when you have an audience, you're allowed to use notes, so you don't have to memorise every word! If you decide to share poems in future, you'll have to be ready for criticism. It's the best way to improve your poems.

1 Do you write poems? Could you read them aloud in public? Why?/Why not?

2 🔊 8.10 Read the blog post. What's Safiye's advice on how to write good poems?

3 Study the Grammar box. Find more examples of modal verbs for obligation and prohibition in the blog post.

GRAMMAR | **Modal verbs for obligation and prohibition**

Obligation
You *must*/*have to* read.
They *had to* read.
I *will have to* read.
Do/*Did*/*Will* you *have to* read?
Yes, I *do*/*did*/*will*.

Lack of obligation
You *don't have to* come.
She *didn't have to* come.
He *won't have to* come.

Prohibition
You *can't* go.
You *mustn't*/*aren't allowed to* go.
I *wasn't allowed to* go.
He *won't be allowed to* go.
Are/*Were* you *allowed to* stay late?
Will you *be allowed to* stay late?

Must and *mustn't* don't have past or future forms. We use *had to* or *will have to* instead. In question forms, we usually use *have to*.

---

4 Write questions about the blog post. Then answer them.
1. poets / have to / please other people / ?
   Do poets have to please other people?
   No, they don't.
2. poems / have to / rhyme / ?
3. why / Safiye / have to / practise / in front of the mirror / ?
4. poets / be allowed to / use / notes in a presentation / ?
5. poets / have to / learn / to accept criticism / ?

5 Complete the second sentence so that it means the same as the first one. Use the correct form of the verbs in brackets.
1. The audience weren't allowed to talk. (have to)
   The audience *had to be* quiet.
2. It was necessary to use a microphone. (have to)
   The speakers _____ a microphone.
3. You mustn't write in your book. (allowed)
   You _____ in your book.
4. You have to learn all your lines. (must)
   You _____ all your lines.
5. It will be necessary to remember the words. (have to)
   You _____ the words.

6 **YOUR WORLD** Think of a time when you gave or watched a performance. In pairs, take it in turns to tell your partner about the experience. Use *had to* and *was*/*were allowed to*.

I was a dancer in the school show. We had to practise every day and we weren't allowed to change the dance moves in any way.

GRAMMAR TIME > PAGE 133

I can talk about obligation and prohibition in the past, present and future.

8.5 Listening and Vocabulary
A day as a newspaper journalist

1 Who in your family listens to or reads the news?

2 🔊 8.11 Study the Vocabulary box and complete it with the headings below. Listen and check. Can you add more words?

> In the news   People   Types of publishing

VOCABULARY — Journalism

_____
newspaper   magazine   news app
online news site

_____
advert   celebrity gossip   headline
local/national news   weather forecast

_____
designer   editor   paparazzi

3 Complete the sentences with words from the Vocabulary box.
   1 My sister works as an _editor_ in a fashion magazine.
   2 My dad doesn't buy newspapers. He has a _____ on his phone.
   3 This magazine is all about _____ – things like famous people's clothes, holidays and lifestyle.
   4 The _____ says it will rain tomorrow.
   5 The _____'s job is to make the magazine look good.

4 In pairs, discuss the questions. Then share your answers with the class.
   1 What do paparazzi do?
   2 What's the difference between a reporter and an editor?
   3 Why is a good headline important?

5 Look at the photos below. Guess what newspaper stories they might go with.

6 🔊 8.12 Listen to Freddie talking to Ava about his experience. Check your ideas from Exercise 5.

7 🔊 8.12 Listen again and choose the correct answer.
   1 Freddie won second prize in
      a a photography competition.
      b a cinema competition.
      c a story competition.
   2 The first-prize winner was
      a late.   b unwell.   c friendly.
   3 In the office, Freddie
      a met some journalists.
      b watched TV programmes.
      c wrote a long story.
   4 What was Freddie's headline about?
      a a new brand of crisps
      b menus at local cafés
      c bad habits of birds
   5 Why was the footballer disappointed?
      a There were too many paparazzi there.
      b No photographers turned up.
      c Nobody took his photograph.
   6 The owner of the pony
      a wanted it to be in the paper.
      b made a lot of noise in reception.
      c was looking for his pony.

8 In pairs, tell each other what you remember about Freddie's day at the newspaper office.
First, he met …

YOUR WORLD

9 Can you think of a funny or interesting story that has been in the news recently? Explain it in a few sentences.
I heard about a clever cat on the local radio news. It …

I can understand a conversation about the press.

8.6 Speaking
Comparing ideas and expressing opinions

VIDEO ▶ THIS ONE IS THE BEST!

Abe: All of your pictures look great, Carla. Here! You've got even more.

Carla: Oh no, not those ones. They are not finished yet. OK, I think this one's the best – it looks brighter than the others. I'll get this one framed.

A few days later …

Carla: OK, time to unwrap the package. Oh no, it's not the one I chose! How did this happen? This one's really awful!

Abe: But this drawing's amazing! If you ask me, it's really original.

Carla: Are you kidding me? Look, it's not finished, these colours are too dark and the background's too plain. This is a total disaster!

Abe: I could be wrong, but it looks more interesting than the other one. Anyway, it's too late now.

Later …

Man: … and the winner in the category of Best Portrait is … Carla Silva. Congratulations!

Carla: What? I can't believe it!

Abe: I told you it was brilliant! It's totally different from the others.

SOUNDS GOOD! Are you kidding me? • This is a total disaster!

1 Which of your artworks are/were you proudest of? Discuss in pairs.

2 ▶ 31 🔊 8.13 Watch or listen. What are Carla and Abe doing? What goes wrong?

3 How is Abe trying to help Carla to confront a difficult situation?

SET FOR LIFE

4 In pairs, discuss the questions.
1. What can you do to control your negative feelings when something bad or unexpected happens?
2. How can you help a friend who is experiencing a difficult situation?

5 Study the Speaking box. Find more examples of the phrases in the dialogue.

SPEAKING — Comparing ideas and expressing opinions

Comparing ideas
On the one hand, … but on the other hand, …
(Personally,) I think … is better/more interesting than …
… is the best idea because …
It's exactly/almost the same as …
… is totally different from …

Expressing opinions
In my opinion, … is brilliant/amazing/awful.
As I see it, …   I think you're right.
As far as I can see, …   As far as I'm concerned, …
It seems to me that …   If you ask me, …
I'm not sure …   I could be wrong, but …

6 🔊 8.14 Listen to two short dialogues. What do the people decide to do in each one?

7 🔊 8.14 Listen again. Which phrases from the Speaking box do the speakers use?

VIDEO ▶ WIDER WORLD

8 ▶ 32 Watch a man talking about his favourite songs. How many songs and versions does he mention?

9 In pairs, take it in turns to give your opinion about:
- your favourite song or film.
- the best book or poem you've ever read.

Unit 8 106 I can compare ideas and express opinions.

8.7 Writing
A comparison

1 Read the comparison. According to the writer, how are the paintings similar and different?

A comparison of two paintings by Claude Monet

1. At the beginning of the twentieth century Monet created a series of paintings of the Houses of Parliament in London. Although all the paintings show the same view, Monet managed to make each painting different. I will compare the paintings *Sunset* and *Fog*.

2. Both paintings are oil paintings and are painted in the impressionist style. The first painting, *Sunset*, is far more colourful than the second painting, *Fog*. In it, you can see gold, yellow and red colours, which represent the sunset. You can also see the reflection of this light on the waves of the river.

3. The second painting, *Fog*, on the other hand, has got darker grey and blue colours, and a pale orange sun in the sky. It is not as bright as the first painting and the Houses of Parliament are less clear. Despite being a less colourful picture, I think the fog is beautifully painted in it.

4. I love both paintings, but on balance, I prefer *Sunset* because it has much more energy and colour compared to *Fog*.

2 Study the Writing box. Find similar phrases in the comparison.

> **WRITING**   A comparison
>
> **Introduction with background information**
> 1. I am going to compare … with …
> The song was first recorded by …
>
> **Making comparisons**
> 2. The first photo is not as colourful as the second.
> The film is as good as the book.
> 3. This landscape is much/far more interesting than …
> This work is less famous than …
> This is by far the best work by …
> Of the two, the second is less attractive.
>
> **Conclusion and personal comment**
> 4. My personal favourite is … because …
> I prefer the original recording of the song because …

3 Study the Language box. Find examples of linkers of contrast in the comparison.

> **LANGUAGE**   Linkers of contrast
>
> We use *despite* and *in spite of* with a noun or *-ing*.
> **In spite of** the rain, we went to the beach.
> We use *although* and *even though* with a clause.
> **Even though** he had a cold, he went to the beach.

4 Choose the correct option.
1. *Although / Despite* it is an old painting, it looks very modern.
2. *In spite of / Even though* all the details, I find this image relaxing.
3. *Although / Despite* being one of his early works, it is brilliant.
4. *Despite / Even though* this is a great film, I prefer the book.

WRITING TIME

5 Write a comparison of two works of art (e.g. paintings, songs, photos, books).

1. **Find ideas**
   Make notes for your comparison. Think about:
   - information for your introduction.
   - a description of the two works of art, including similarities and differences.
   - your conclusion about which you prefer and why.

2. **Plan**
   Organise your ideas into paragraphs. Use the comparison in Exercise 1 to help you.

3. **Write and share**
   - Write a draft of your comparison. Use the Language box and the Writing box to help you.
   - Share your comparison with another student for feedback.
   - Write the final version of your comparison.

4. **Check**
   - Check language: have you used linkers of contrast?
   - Check grammar: have you used modal verbs for ability correctly?

I can write a comparison of two works of art.

Vocabulary Activator

WORDLIST 🔊 8.15

Visual arts
abstract art (n)
architecture (n)
art installation (n)
classic art (n)
design (n)
film-making (n)
impressionist art (n)
modern art (n)
photography (n)
pop art (n)
sculpture (n)

Word friends
(describing art)
choose bright/clear colours
create an impressive/
  a memorable/a powerful
  work of art
design a colourful/
  an unusual building
have a mysterious/unique/
  warm atmosphere
paint a landscape/portrait/
  scene

perform a dance/piece of
  music
publish a book/
  a newspaper/poems
use bright/clear colours
visit an art exhibition

Literature and books
author (n)
autobiography (n)
biography (n)
chapter (n)
character (n)
cover (n)
fiction (n)
non-fiction (n)
novel (n)
novelist (n)
plot (n)
short story (n)
title (n)

Painting
art gallery (n)
block of colour (n)

canvas (n)
image (n)
on display
self-portrait (n)
simple line (n)
typical style (n)
work (n)

Journalism
advert (n)
celebrity gossip (n)
designer (n)
editor (n)
headline (n)
journalist (n)
local news (n)
magazine (n)
national news (n)
news app (n)
newspaper (n)
online news site (n)
paparazzi (n)
reporter (n)
weather forecast (n)

Extra words
comic (n)
craft (n)
criticism (n)
do an interview with
express emotions
graphic novel (n)
impressionism (n)
inspiration (n)
light show (n)
microphone (n)
oil painting (n)
piece of art (n)
poet (n)
process (v)
rap artist (n)
read aloud
represent (v)
rhyme (v)
shape (n)
skilled (adj)
sound effects (n)
true story (n)
visual information (n)

1 Answer the questions with words from the wordlist. Then write two more questions. In pairs, take it in turns to ask your partner your questions.
  1 What uses text and images to make you want to buy something? *advert*
  2 What is a room or building with paintings?
  3 What is the part of a book you see before you open it?
  4 Who writes a book?
  5 When someone writes a book about their life, what is this book called?
  6 When someone paints themselves, what kind of painting is it?
  7 When someone paints a painting showing natural scenery, what kind of painting is it?

2 Complete the questions with words from the wordlist. Then, in pairs, ask and answer the questions.
  1 Do you like visiting art e*xhibitions*?
  2 What kind of fiction do you prefer to read: a n_____ or a s_____ s_____?
  3 Which actor plays your favourite film c_____?
  4 How often do you read or listen to the weather f_____?
  5 Would you like to pose for a p_____?
  6 Do you prefer to read national n_____ or c_____ gossip?

3 Complete the news headlines with words from the wordlist.

Police arrest ¹p*aparazzi* for taking private photos of pop star

YOUNG FICTION AUTHOR WINS PRIZE FOR FIRST ²N_____

POPULAR NEW SCHOOL SUBJECT: ³FILM-M_____!

Expensive painting missing from ⁴a_____ gallery

LOCAL ARTIST MAKES ⁵N_____ NEWS WITH LIFE-SIZE ⁶S_____ OF FOOTBALLER

4 🔊 8.16 **PRONUNCIATION** Listen and repeat.

1 Oooo	2 oOoo	3 ooOo
criticism	unusual	exhibition

5 🔊 8.17 **PRONUNCIATION** Write the words below in the correct column in Exercise 4 according to the stress pattern. Listen and check.

architecture   celebrity   installation   memorable
mysterious   paparazzi   photography

Unit 8

Revision

Vocabulary

1 Choose the correct option.
1. The artist has *chosen / created* bright colours for this painting.
2. We have just published a *canvas / book* about classic art.
3. My friend enjoys *typical / impressionist* art.
4. I love reading celebrity *gossip / fiction* and learning about stars' lives.
5. Has the *journalist / author* of this novel written any other books?
6. I like to listen to *national / classic* news.
7. The class has to perform a *dance / display*.
8. This artist painted *installations / landscapes* on paper.

2 Complete the course descriptions with the words below. Then, in pairs, take it in turns to tell your partner which course you would be interested in and why.

> architecture   character   design   editor   image
> magazine   news   novelist   photography   plot
> ~~reporter~~   sculpture

Journalism
A ¹*reporter* writes the stories and the ² _____ checks them and usually makes some changes before they are published on ³ _____ sites. This course teaches you both jobs.

Fiction
A good story needs a ⁴ _____ that keeps the reader interested. You'll learn to write one, and also create a ⁵ _____ exactly like a real person. You could be a famous ⁶ _____ one day!

⁷ _____
Forget paparazzi! In this course, you'll learn to provide a memorable ⁸ _____ for a quality ⁹ _____ article.

¹⁰ _____
You'll ¹¹ _____ useful and unusual buildings.

¹² _____
Learn how to create models of people, animals or objects in 3D.

Grammar

3 Choose the correct option.
1. Last year my three-year-old sister *can't / couldn't* climb the stairs on her own, but now she can.
2. We *don't have to / mustn't* take lunch with us because there will be a café.
3. The sandwich was so big that I didn't *able / manage* to eat it all.
4. Before cars, people *must / had to* walk everywhere.
5. Joan *can't / isn't able* use the stairs. Can you call the lift?

4 Complete the questions with the correct form of the verbs in brackets. Then, in pairs, ask and answer the questions.
1. *Did you manage* (you/manage) to do all your homework yesterday?
2. What tasks _____ (you/have to) help with at home?
3. How long _____ (you/be allowed) to play games on your computer?
4. _____ (your family/have to) prepare their own food on your last holiday?
5. _____ (you/be able to) run a business one day?

5 Complete the second sentence with the word in bold so that it means the same as the first one.
1. We mustn't go in until they call us. **HAVE**
   We *have to* wait outside until they call us.
2. Could you ride a bike when you were five? **ABLE**
   _____ ride a bike when you were five?
3. The homework was too hard for me to understand. **MANAGE**
   I _____ understand the homework.
4. Will it be OK to take photos in the gallery? **ALLOWED**
   Will _____ take photos in the gallery?
5. We'll need a larger flat next year. **HAVE**
   Next year we _____ move to a larger flat.

Speaking

6 In pairs, do the speaking task. Go to page 137 and follow the instructions.

Dictation

7 🔊 8.18 Listen. Then listen again and write down what you hear during each pause.

SET FOR LIFE

Good thinking!

A On days when people buy a lot of ice cream, they are more likely to get sunburnt.
Conclusion: I'm never going to eat ice cream again. It causes sunburn!

B Fires with a lot of firefighters at them do more damage than fires with only a few firefighters.
Conclusion: The firefighters make the damage worse!

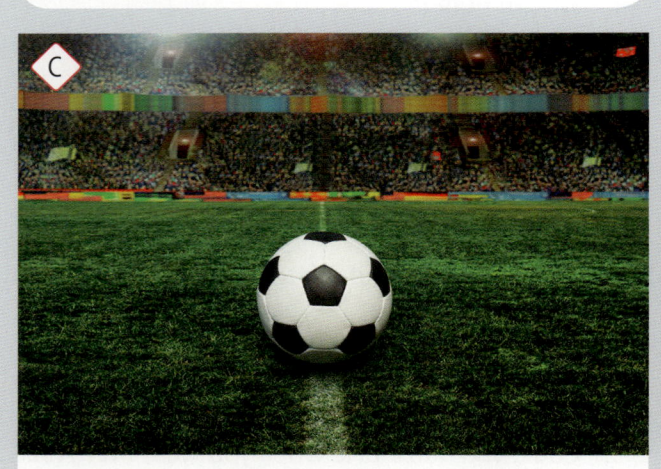

C In the 2018 football World Cup only countries with six or seven letters in their name got into the quarter-finals.
Conclusion: Countries needed the right number of letters in their names to do well in that competition.

D Physical inactivity causes serious health problems such as heart disease.
Conclusion: If I want a long, healthy life, I need to be more physically active.

1 Read sentences A–E. Then complete descriptions 1–4 with letters B–E.
A I woke up late this morning.
B I missed my bus to school.
C My friend Leah woke up late this morning.
D I couldn't turn on my bedroom light this morning.
E My alarm didn't work this morning.
1 ____ is a cause of A.
2 ____ is an effect of A.
3 ____ is probably a coincidence. It isn't a cause or an effect of A.
4 ____ and E are both effects of something else – a problem with the electricity.

2 In pairs, talk about photos A–D. Do you agree with the conclusions? Why?/Why not? Use the words *cause*, *effect*, *coincidence* and *something else* in your discussion.

3 🔊 8.19 Listen to a conversation. Match the conclusions in photos A–D with these sentences.
1 ☐ The cause and effect are the wrong way round.
2 ☐ There's no cause or effect. It's a coincidence.
3 ☐ That's correct.
4 ☐ Both things occur at the same time because they are both caused by something else.

Think critically

4 🔊 **8.20** In pairs, read the fact and discuss the questions. Then listen and compare the speakers' ideas with your own.

> On days when people wear bright colours, they feel happier.

1 Is this a coincidence?
2 Are brightly coloured clothes a cause of happiness?
3 Are brightly coloured clothes an effect of happiness?
4 What else might explain this fact?

5 In pairs, read and discuss the facts below. Use the words *cause*, *effect*, *coincidence* and *another explanation* in your discussion. The words under each fact might help you with ideas.

1 Sportspeople who wear their 'lucky socks' are more likely to win a match or competition.

> comfortable   confident   performance

2 People who learn musical instruments get better exam results at school than people who don't learn musical instruments.

> changes in the brain   money for private lessons   personality

3 People with pet dogs live longer.

> city/countryside   exercise   lonely

Some sports shoes improve people's performance. Maybe socks can do this too, so the socks are the cause of winning.

6 Read the Useful tips. In pairs, discuss the questions.
1 Have you ever believed something that you read online, but later found out wasn't accurate?
2 Can you think of any news stories about the causes of something? Do you think the stories were accurate? Why?/Why not?

SET FOR LIFE

7 In small groups, give a presentation. Follow the instructions.

1 Choose a fact from Exercise 5.

2 Discuss possible ways to explain it and write down at least three ideas. Use expressions from the Useful phrases box.

3 Prepare a presentation to explain your ideas to the class. Make sure you explain your thinking clearly.

4 Give your presentation to the class.

USEFUL TIPS

When you read information online, remember that it may not be accurate. If you read that one thing causes another, ask yourself these questions.

- Is it just a coincidence?
- Is the cause-and-effect relationship the right way round?
- Are both facts an effect of something else?
- Is there enough evidence to support the facts?

USEFUL PHRASES

Speculating
It may/might/could be …
It can't be …
There's another possibility.
Maybe both things are caused by …

Responding to suggestions
Good thinking!
Maybe!

111 Units 7–8

Party time!

9

VOCABULARY
Celebrations | Special occasions | Types of celebrations | Phrases to express *likes* | Sense verbs

GRAMMAR
Defining and non-defining clauses | Direct and indirect questions

HAPPY NEW YEAR!

New Year is a special occasion around the world, but it isn't just about parades and firework displays. There are many other customs to bring good luck in the new year.

- The tradition in Denmark on New Year's Eve is for friends to break plates in front of your home. The more broken plates you get, the luckier you'll be in the year ahead!
- Brazilians have a fun New Year's Eve festival. People dressed in white and holding flowers walk into the sea and jump over seven waves.
- In Spain everyone starts the new year by speaking with their mouth full! As the clock strikes midnight, you have to eat twelve grapes – one for each month.
- Don't be scared if you see bears in Romania on 31 December. People dress up in bear costumes to be protected from bad things.
- In Japan the new year begins with a very loud ceremony. They ring bells 108 times. Ding-dong!

9.1 Vocabulary

Celebrations

1 How do you celebrate New Year's Eve in your country? What traditions are there?

2 Look at the photos and read the article. Which traditions do you find the most interesting? Why?

3 🔊 9.1 Study Vocabulary box A. Find the words in the article. How do you say them in your language?

VOCABULARY A Celebrations

ceremony   costume   custom   festival
firework display   parade   special occasion   tradition

Unit 9

4 🔊 **9.2** Read the text and choose the correct option. Listen and check.

New Year is a special ¹*display / occasion* in China too. On New Year's Eve people get together with their families. They prepare a special meal, throw parties, let children stay up late, count down to midnight and enjoy firework ²*ceremonies / displays*. Some people take part in religious ³*ceremonies / costumes*. But how is Chinese New Year different?

Firstly, the date. The Chinese calendar is different, so New Year's Day can be from 21 January to 20 February, depending on the year.

Secondly, the ⁴*customs / fireworks*. Many families follow the ⁵*parade / tradition* of cleaning their house to remove bad luck. Some repaint their houses red. They also hand out money in red envelopes, put up red decorations and the traditional ⁶*costume / custom* is a red dress. The colour red is said to bring good luck. It comes from a legend about the Nian, a monster that used to eat people. A man scared it away with red paper and fireworks.

Finally, in some communities, the ⁷*festival / tradition* can last for fifteen days. On the final day people light candles and walk in a(n) ⁸*occasion / parade* with animal-shaped lamps. Red, of course.

5 🔊 **9.3** **WORD FRIENDS** Study the phrases and check you understand them. How many can you find in the text in Exercise 4?

bring good/bad luck
celebrate a birthday
follow the tradition of
get together with (friends/family)
light/blow out candles
light fireworks
organise/throw a (surprise) party
put up decorations
prepare a meal
stay up late
turn eighteen/a year older
wrap/unwrap presents

6 Complete the quiz with verbs from Exercise 5.

HAPPY BIRTHDAY!

It's normal on your birthday for your family or friends to ¹*throw* a party, ² _____ your favourite meal and sing *Happy Birthday* before you ³ _____ the candles on your cake. But there are some other, unusual birthday traditions around the world. Can you tell which of these are true?

1 In Vietnam you don't ⁴ _____ your birthday on the day you were born. You ⁵ _____ a year older on 'Tet' (New Year's Day) no matter when you were born.
2 In Brazil, on a child's birthday, the parents often ⁶ _____ brightly coloured paper flowers as decorations.
3 Many Jamaicans ⁷ _____ the tradition of 'flouring', or covering the birthday boy or girl in flour.
4 In parts of Canada they rub your nose with butter on your birthday to ⁸ _____ good luck.
5 In Japan and Korea they often ⁹ _____ birthday presents in cloth instead of paper. It's more ecological.
6 In Spain if you ¹⁰ _____ with friends on your birthday, you have to pay for the drinks.

7 🔊 **9.4** Which of the traditions in the quiz in Exercise 6 are true and which are false? Discuss in pairs. Listen and check.

8 🔊 **9.5** Study Vocabulary box B. In pairs, say what you like and dislike about these kinds of celebrations.
I think the carnival is great because I love dancing.

VOCABULARY B — Types of celebration

carnival   fancy-dress party   family get-together
formal dinner   school prom   street party   surprise party
wedding reception

VIDEO ▶   **WIDER WORLD**

9 ▶ **33** Watch four people talking about celebrations. What celebrations do they enjoy and why?

10 In pairs, talk about recent celebrations you enjoyed. Say why.
I had a great time on New Year's Eve. I stayed up really late and …

I can talk about celebrations and special occasions.

9.2 Grammar

Defining and non-defining relative clauses

1 🔊 **9.6** Read the introduction to a podcast and answer the questions.
1. When and where do people celebrate Polar Bear Plunge Day?
2. Would you ever jump into freezing cold water? Why?/Why not? Do you know anyone who has done that? Why did they do it?

TALK TIME with Mel and Zac

SPECIAL FESTIVAL DAYS

Tonight is New Year's Eve, <u>which is always a lot of fun</u>. But there are other special festivals that are not as well-known and there are some people <u>whose idea of fun is a bit unusual</u>. For example, the people <u>who enjoy Polar Bear Plunge Day</u>. This takes place every year on 1 January in countries where it's very cold, like Canada. In Vancouver, <u>where this event started in 1920</u>, about 10,000 people jump into the freezing cold Pacific Ocean. Brrr! On today's podcast, I'm joined by Zac, who has been finding out about some special festivals.

2 Study the Grammar box. Then look at the underlined relative clauses in the text in Exercise 1. Are they defining or non-defining?

GRAMMAR — Defining and non-defining relative clauses

Defining relative clauses explain which person, thing or place we are talking about. The sentence makes no sense without them.
There are some special festivals that/which are not as well-known.
This takes place in countries where it's very cold.

Non-defining relative clauses give extra information about the person, thing or place we are talking about. The sentence makes sense without them.
I'm joined by Zac, who has been finding out about some special festivals.
Mel, whose podcast is quite popular, has a lovely voice.

GRAMMAR TIME > PAGE 134

WATCH OUT!
*The festival **that/which** takes place in Canada is Polar Bear Plunge Day.* (defining relative clause)
*Polar Bear Plunge Day, **which** takes place in Canada, is a lot of fun.* (non-defining relative clause)

3 🔊 **9.7** Complete the sentences with *who*, *which*, *that*, *whose* or *where*. Listen and check.
1. [D] I'm the kind of guy *who/that* prefers lying on a warm beach.
2. [ ] This is Zac, _____ favourite hobby is lying down.
3. [ ] Lots of people enjoy the Festival of Sleep Day, _____ is on 3 January.
4. [ ] The idea is to help people _____ stay up partying too long.
5. [ ] I know a few people _____ would like to celebrate that day.
6. [ ] This is the day _____ gives you the chance to be a pirate.
7. [ ] Do you know anyone _____ idea of fun is to talk like a pirate?
8. [ ] My friend Miguel, _____ lives in Costa Rica, is crazy about pirates.
9. [ ] Is that the place _____ they filmed *Pirates of the Caribbean*?
10. [ ] It was filmed in Pinewood Studios, _____ a lot of British films are made.

4 Mark the relative clauses in Exercise 3 D (defining) or ND (non-defining).

5 In pairs, say which of the special festivals in the podcast you would like to take part in and why.

6 YOUR WORLD Invent a special day to celebrate. Decide when it will take place and what you should/shouldn't do. Then, in pairs, take turns to tell your partner about your day. Use relative clauses.

10/10 Day, which is on 10 October, is a day for being excellent. Anything that you do on that day, you should do as well as you can, e.g. try to get ten out of ten if you do a test.

Unit 9 | 114 | I can be specific about people, things and places.

9.3 Reading and Vocabulary
Turning eighteen

1 🔊 9.8 Read the texts. Which idea would you choose for your birthday celebration? Why?

Ideas for celebrating turning eighteen

A Junction 2
Boston Manor Park is the venue for the Junction 2 music festival, which takes place from midday to 10 p.m. on 4–5 June. Many of the biggest names in house and techno are taking part this year. You must be eighteen or over to attend. Tickets cost £49.50 for Friday 4 June and £65.45 for Saturday 5 June.

B eZeeZee Zorbing
Do you fancy climbing inside a large transparent plastic ball and racing a friend down a hill at fifty kilometres per hour? If so, you should try zorbing at eZeeZee in the New Forest. It's an experience you'll never forget and it's totally safe. Price: £55 for two people. Special weekend offer: £43.

C Warwick Castle
Travel back in time at this impressive medieval castle. A 3D activity trail, scary games to learn about the past, fantastic shows with wild birds, actors and live concerts. It's a magical experience. A one-day ticket costs £22 (£17 if you book ahead). Or you can stay overnight and make a weekend of it.

D Tapas'n'Tacos
Located on the South Bank near the Tate Modern art gallery, Tapas'n'Tacos is London's coolest new restaurant. If you're fond of Spanish and Mexican food and keen on dancing, this is the place to go. There's live music every evening from 8 p.m. and at lunchtime on weekends. Prices are reasonable and there's a twenty percent discount this month. Open every day, from midday to midnight.

2 🔊 9.9 These people are about to turn eighteen. Match them with the most suitable ideas from the texts in Exercise 1 (A–D).

Andy ☐
I'm into art, music and outdoor activities. I want to celebrate my birthday this weekend with my friends. I've got some money, so I can afford to pay for something exciting. There's a music festival I'd love to go to, but my friends aren't old enough. We all love extreme sports.

Emily ☐
I have a passion for music and dancing. I'd like to go out for my birthday on Saturday with a few close friends. There's a family get-together planned for the evening, so it will have to be during the day. We'd like to get a good meal in a nice place, but nowhere too expensive.

Robin ☐
I'm a big fan of extreme sports. I'm also crazy about music and dancing. Unfortunately, I broke my arm last week, so I can't do anything too physical. My birthday's next week and I'd like to do something with my family. Recently, I've really got into English history and fantasy novels.

3 Find six phrases in the texts that mean *like*. Then, in pairs, use them to talk about things you like.

VIDEO ▶ WIDER WORLD

4 ▶ 34 Watch eight people talking about the last attraction they visited. Match the speakers with the attractions and say what they thought of them.
Speakers: Charlie, Carol, Martina and Alberto, Myriam, Monica, Marne, Rudy
Attractions: a church in Notting Hill, a hotel on Phuket Island, a town called Chefchaouen in Morocco, Edinburgh Castle, the London Dungeons, the London Eye, Victor Hugo's house on Guernsey

5 In pairs, talk about attractions, activities and events that you have enjoyed. Use the phrases in Exercise 3 to say why you enjoyed them.
I recently went to a water park. It was great because I'm really into swimming.

I can understand an article about celebrating a birthday.

9.4 Grammar

Direct and indirect questions

1 Describe the photo. Have you ever been to a festival? What was it like?

2 🔊 9.10 Read the messages and answer the questions.
1. Where are Sophie and Meryl going?
2. Why are they going there?
3. What does Sophie want to do during her holiday?

Hi Sophie,

I'm really looking forward to the trip to New Orleans. I've got a few questions, though. I know our flight's on 24 Feb, but can you remind me which terminal we're leaving from? Have you any idea if there's a pool in the hotel? And I'd like to know how long the flight will be. I'm scared of flying. 😨

Oh, and by the way, 'Mardi Gras': do you know what it means? I've just found out.

Love,

Meryl

Hi Meryl,

We're leaving from Terminal 2. I didn't know you were scared of flying. I wonder why you kept it a secret. But don't worry, it's a short flight: just over two hours. 😊 The hotel has an outdoor pool, so bring your swimming costume. By the way, do you mind if I film you during the trip? It's for my YouTube channel.

See you soon,

Sophie

PS I do know what 'Mardi Gras' means. It's French for 'Fat Tuesday'.

---

3 Study the Grammar box. What is the word order in indirect questions? When do we use *if*?

GRAMMAR — Direct and indirect questions

	Direct	Indirect
Wh- questions	Which terminal are we leaving from?	Can/Could you remind me which terminal we're leaving from?
	How long will the flight be?	I'd like to know how long the flight will be.
Wh- questions with do/does/did	What does it mean?	Do you know what it means?
	Why did you keep it a secret?	I wonder why you kept it a secret.
Yes/No questions	Is there a pool in the hotel?	Have you any idea if there is a pool in the hotel?
	Can I film you?	Do you mind if I film you?

GRAMMAR TIME > PAGE 134

4 🔊 9.11 Rewrite the direct questions as indirect questions. Use the words in brackets. Listen and check.
1. What's your name? (could)
   Could you tell me what your name is?
2. Would you two like to hang out with us? (wondering)
3. Where is our hotel? (idea)
4. What street is it in? (remember)
5. Did you have a good time? (like)
6. When does Mardi Gras start next year? (know)
7. Can I take a photo of you? (mind)

YOUR WORLD

5 In pairs, ask and answer indirect questions. Use these ideas or your own.
- how long / film / last?
- how much / cinema ticket / cost?
- rain / tomorrow?
- use / your phone?
- what / do / weekend?
- when / holidays / begin?
- where / you / born?

Do you know what 'bonjour' means?

Unit 9 — I can ask questions politely.

9.5 Listening and Vocabulary

Do you enjoy firework displays?

1 Do you enjoy firework displays? Why?/Why not?

2 🔊 9.12 Listen to the beginning of a radio interview. What is it going to be about? Who is the guest on the programme?

3 🔊 9.13 Listen to the rest of the interview and choose the correct answer.
1. According to the presenter, China
   a. has the most firework displays in the world.
   b. makes the most fireworks in the world.
   c. makes the largest fireworks in the world.
2. According to Professor Cook, the first fireworks came from
   a. China.   b. India.   c. Syria.
3. When fireworks were made by putting powder inside bamboo, they were
   a. hotter.   b. brighter.   c. louder.
4. Assistants at firework displays in England wore hats of leaves because
   a. it made people laugh.
   b. it protected their heads.
   c. it was an English tradition.
5. Italians changed fireworks by
   a. making them colourful.
   b. making them bigger.
   c. making displays safer.
6. The first firework display in the United States was in
   a. 1608.   b. 1776.   c. 1777.

4 🔊 9.14 Study the Vocabulary box. Do you know any other adjectives that are used with the verbs?

> **VOCABULARY** — Sense verbs
>
> feel terrified   look incredible   smell terrible   sound noisy   taste delicious

5 🔊 9.15 Complete the text with the correct form of the phrases in the Vocabulary box. Listen and check.

> Early fireworks [1]_smelled terrible_, like rotten eggs, but they were quiet. They didn't [2]_____ like modern fireworks. Despite that, people often [3]_____ when they saw them. Today we make fireworks with different colours. People love to take photos of them because they [4]_____.
> On American Independence Day people celebrate with fireworks, barbecues and hot dogs that [5]_____.

6 Use the adjectives below to write sentences with the verbs in the Vocabulary box. Then, in pairs, compare your sentences.

> awful   bitter   bright   clear   disgusting   loud
> mild   peaceful   quiet   rough   scared   smooth
> soft   solid   strange   strong   sweet   weak

When my father sings, it sounds awful.

YOUR WORLD

7 Think of the last time you saw a firework display. In pairs, take it in turns to describe the event.

I can understand a radio interview about fireworks.

9.6 Speaking
Being polite

VIDEO ▶ SORRY TO BOTHER YOU

Carla: Excuse me, do you mind if I sit here?
Ellie: Of course not. Go ahead.
Carla: Thanks … Sorry, could you pass me the sugar, please?
Ellie: Yes, of course. Here you are.
Carla: Thanks very much.
Ellie: It's quite all right.

Ellie is on the phone.

Ellie: Hi! Yeah, it's been a great tour so far. Do you know how many people are coming to the show tonight? Great. Bye.

Carla is texting Bea.

Bea, you'll never guess who's in the café with me! Jane McLane, the singer!

Carla: Sorry to bother you, but are there any tickets left for the show tonight? Are they very expensive?
Ellie: Of course. And they're free!
Carla: Really? Free tickets for your concert! I can't believe my luck!
Ellie: My concert?
Carla: Aren't you Jane McLane?
Ellie: No! People often say I look like her, but I'm not a singer. I work for an animal charity. We're giving a talk here tonight. Do you fancy coming? And I wonder if you could hand out these leaflets?
Carla: Er, sure …
Ellie: That's really kind of you. Thanks.

SOUNDS GOOD!
- Go ahead.
- You'll never guess … !
- Do you fancy coming?

1 ▶ 35 🔊 9.16 Look at the photo. Where is Carla? Do you think she knows the woman? Watch or listen and check.

2 What polite expressions does Carla use in the dialogue?

SET FOR LIFE

3 Which of the expressions below would you use a) when having breakfast at home and b) during a formal dinner? What other expressions might you use in these situations?

Excuse me.   Hey!   I wonder if you could …
Pleased to meet you.   What's up?

4 Study the Speaking box. Find examples of the phrases in the dialogue.

SPEAKING ▶ Being polite

Attracting attention
Excuse me, …   Sorry (to bother you), …

Making and responding to polite requests
A: I was wondering if …   Do you mind if I … ?
B: No, go ahead./Sorry, but …
A: Would you mind passing the … ?
B: Of course not.
A: Could you pass me the … , please?
B: Yes, of course. Here you are.
A: Do you happen to know if … ?
B: I'm sorry, I don't know.
A: I wonder if you could do something for me.
B: Sure./Sorry, I can't.

Giving and responding to thanks
A: That's really kind of you.   B: It's quite all right.
A: I really appreciate it.   B: It's no problem.
A: Thanks (so/very much).   B: You're welcome.

5 Complete the sentences with one word in each gap.
a ☐ Do you *happen* to know where I should get off for Elm Street?
b ☐ _____ me. Sorry to _____ you. I was _____ if I could ask you a question.
c ☐ I'm _____ , I don't know. I'm not from here.
d ☐ It's no _____ . Thanks anyway.
e ☐ Yes, of _____ . Go _____ .

6 🔊 9.17 Order sentences a–e in Exercise 5 to make a dialogue. Listen and check. Then, in pairs, practise the dialogue.

7 In pairs, go to page 137 and follow the instructions.

YOUR WORLD

Unit 9 · 118 · I can use polite phrases in conversation.

9.7 Writing
An informal invitation

1 Which of the information below would you give a friend coming to your house for the first time for a party? What other information might you include?

> advice on what to bring   directions to your house
> information about animals in your home
> what you plan to do   when it's planned to start/finish
> who will be there

2 Read David's email. Why is his family having a party?

3 Study the Writing box. Complete gaps 1–5 with phrases from David's email.

> **WRITING** An informal invitation
>
> **Starting your email**
> How are things?
> How are your summer holidays going?
> 1 _____
>
> **Offering an invitation**
> Would you like to come … ?
> Do you want to meet up … ?
> 2 _____
>
> **Explaining your plans**
> I'd like to show/take you …
> I hope we can …
> 3 _____
>
> **Before you finish**
> I hope you can come.
> I'm really looking forward to seeing you (again).
> 4 _____
>
> **Ending your email**
> Hope to see you soon.
> 5 _____

4 Study the Language box and match the phrases below with the underlined phrases in David's email.

> can come   see what something is like
> spend time with   start   wear formal clothes
> would find useful

> **LANGUAGE** Informal writing
>
> In informal writing, your language can be chatty. You can:
> - ask questions.
> - use exclamation marks and emojis (but not too many!).
> - use contractions.
> - use informal language (e.g. *What have you been up to? Do you fancy … ? By the way, …*).

Hi Mark,

How are your summer holidays going? What have you been up to?

My brother Gavin, who has been living in the USA, is coming back home next Saturday (19 August). We're throwing him a surprise party at our house to welcome him home. 😊 It should <u>kick off</u> at about 8 p.m. Do you fancy coming? Mum and Dad said you could stay with us for the weekend if you like.

On the Sunday after the party, we're planning to <u>check out</u> the Atlantis Water Park, which everyone says is an amazing place! So, if you come, you could <u>do with</u> some swimming trunks. We could <u>hang out with</u> my cousins. Remember them? They'll be at the party too.

By the way, you don't need to <u>dress up</u> for the party – you can wear whatever you want. I really hope you <u>can make it</u>. Let me know as soon as you can!

Speak soon,
David

WRITING TIME

5 Write an email inviting a friend to a celebration.

1 Find ideas
Make notes for your email. Think about:
- what kind of celebration you're planning.
- where and when it's taking place.
- some details that might persuade your friend to attend.

2 Plan
Organise your email into paragraphs. Use David's email to help you.

3 Write and share
- Write a draft of your email. Use the Language box and the Writing box to help you.
- Share your email with another student for feedback.
- Write the final version of your email.

4 Check
- Check language: have you used informal language?
- Check grammar: have you used relative clauses correctly?

I can write an email inviting a friend to a celebration.

Vocabulary Activator

WORDLIST 🔊 9.18

Celebrations
ceremony (n)
costume (n)
custom (n)
festival (n)
firework display (n)
parade (n)
special occasion (n)
tradition (n)

Word friends
(special occasions)
blow out candles
bring bad luck
bring good luck
celebrate a birthday
follow the tradition of
get together with
light candles
light fireworks
organise a party

prepare a meal
put up decorations
stay up late
throw a party
turn a year older
turn eighteen
unwrap presents
wrap presents

Types of celebrations
carnival (n)
family get-together (n)
fancy-dress party (n)
formal dinner (n)
school prom (n)
street party (n)
surprise party (n)
wedding reception (n)

Phrases to express likes
be a big fan of
be crazy about

be fond of
be into/get into
be keen on
have a passion for

Sense verbs
feel terrified
look incredible
smell terrible
sound noisy
taste delicious

Extra words
attend (v)
attraction (n)
barbecue (n)
brightly coloured (adj)
calendar (n)
close friend (n)
count down to (v)
dress up (v)
entertain (v)

event (n)
hang out (v)
Independence Day (n)
live concert/music (n)
masquerade ball
meet up (v)
midnight (n)
New Year's Eve (n)
outdoor activity (n)
party (v)
powder (n)
ring a bell
rotten (n)
rub (v)
show (n)
stay overnight
take part
take place
Thanksgiving (n)
traditional (adj)

1 Complete the questions with the correct form of words from the wordlist. Then, in pairs, ask and answer the questions.

1. How are you going to celebrate your birthday when you t_____ eighteen?
2. What birthday c_____ and traditions does your family f_____ ?
3. Do you enjoy having candles on your birthday cake so you can b_____ them out?
4. Would you like someone to throw you a s_____ party?
5. Do you like to help put up d_____ ?
6. What kinds of party food t_____ the most delicious to you?
7. What do you enjoy doing when you g_____ t_____ with friends?
8. Do you like fireworks or are you secretly t_____ of them?

2 Choose the odd one out.

1 fireworks	customs	candles	decorations
2 surprise party	school prom	display	wedding reception
3 mask	costume	fancy-dress	present
4 sound	wrap	smell	look
5 fond	keen	crazy	noisy

3 These phrases about special occasions have got mixed up! Rearrange them.

> blow out a party   follow eighteen   put up a tradition
> stay up decorations   throw presents   turn candles
> wrap late

blow out candles

4 🔊 9.19 **PRONUNCIATION** Listen to the chant and underline the two most stressed syllables in each line.

> I'm fond of festivals
> And I'm keen on customs.
> I'm into fireworks
> And I'm crazy about parties!

5 **PRONUNCIATION** In pairs, practise saying the chant in Exercise 4 in a rhythmic way. Stress the correct syllables. Then change some of the words in the chant to make it true for you.

Revision

Vocabulary

1 Choose the correct answer.
1. I think there's a party going on upstairs. It sounds ___.
   a noisy   b noisily   c noise
2. My sister is really ___ Harry Potter. She has read all the books.
   a for   b about   c into
3. Some people say that the number thirteen ___ bad luck.
   a brings   b prepares   c gets
4. Jim doesn't like going to bed early. He prefers to ___ up late.
   a put   b stay   c turn
5. My mum has always ___ a passion for rare garden plants.
   a followed   b lived   c had
6. I can't wait to ___ my birthday presents!
   a unwrap   b unpack   c undo

2 Write the correct word for each definition.
1. a kind of celebration where people play music and dance in the streets: c*arnival*
2. an end-of-year school party for high school students: school p_____
3. a set of clothes worn by an actor: c_____
4. a party people have after a wedding: r_____
5. something you do to candles on your birthday: b_____ out
6. part of a celebration where people walk together along the street: p_____
7. a kind of party where people have to wear unusual clothes: f_____-d_____ party

Grammar

3 Complete the text with *who*, *which*, *that*, *whose* or *where*.

Every year people from Gloucester in England enjoy the Hill Cheese Rolling Festival, ¹*which* is a kind of race. On a hill near Gloucester, ²_____ the festival happens, people meet at the top. Then they roll a wheel of cheese, ³_____ weighs about three kilos, down the hill. Everybody runs after it and the person ⁴_____ crosses the finish line first wins. The winner, ⁵_____ prize is the cheese, can feel happy that they are encouraging a tradition ⁶_____ has been around a long time.

4 Complete the indirect questions about the Hill Cheese Rolling Festival. Use the verbs in brackets.
1. Where's the cheese festival? (remind)
   Could *you remind me* where the cheese festival is?
2. What kind of cheese do they use? (know)
   I'd _____ what kind of cheese they use.
3. Is it dangerous? (tell)
   Could _____ dangerous?
4. When is the festival? (remind)
   Can _____ the festival is?
5. Can I attend the festival? (possible)
   I wonder _____ for me to attend the festival.
6. Can I take photos there? (mind)
   Do people _____ take photos there?

Speaking

5 A new college has invited young people to an informal open day with food and music, to meet new students. Work in pairs. You don't know each other, but are sitting together at a table. Student A, go to page 137. Student B, go to page 142. Take turns to start the conversation.

Dictation

6 🔊 9.20 Listen. Then listen again and write down what you hear during each pause.

Unit 9

BBC CULTURE
Festivals for Generation Z

The UK's biggest gaming festival

When you think of festivals, do you think street parades, traditional events and colourful costumes? Well, think again. Nowadays it's fashionable to stay indoors with your screens. Why? It's to celebrate video gaming, which is one of the most popular hobbies around. There are lots of big gaming festivals in the world and the UK is one of the main centres because most gamers communicate in English.

Insomnia is the biggest gaming festival in the UK. It is held every year near Birmingham and attracts thousands of young people. It's an amazing get-together, where you can meet the world's most renowned players. Some of these celebrities are only eleven or twelve years old! There are tournaments of popular games, such as *Mortal Kombat*. *Minecraft* is also everywhere, which shows that it is a real cultural phenomenon.

Although the festival happens inside and everyone is glued to screens, these events have a lot in common with traditional festivals. There are many fans who form long queues to watch celebrity gamers on big stages. There are incredible light displays and giant screens everywhere. At first sight, it looks more like a rock concert!

We interviewed two teenagers at the Insomnia Festival in Coventry to see what they thought.

Stuart
'I love it here, but I would rather play video games at home. I'm into more traditional parties where people enjoy themselves together. Here everybody is watching the screen with their headphones on. They're isolated from each other. It would be better to watch it online than go to the event itself.'

Marcela
'This is the best party I've ever been to! I've travelled across the world to be here. There's a real sense of community. I've met a lot of people who I only knew from the internet. We share our love for video games and discuss how best to play them. It's great for my English because that's what everyone speaks online and here too!'

---

be glued to (phr) give something your full attention
indoors (adv) inside a building
isolated (adj) without much contact with other people
phenomenon (n) something that happens in society, culture, nature, etc.
renowned (adj) famous
tournament (n) a series of contests to win first prize

1 Look at the photo and the title of the article. In pairs, discuss the questions.
   1 What kind of event is it?
   2 Would you like to go to an event like this? Why?/Why not?

2 🔊 9.21 Read the article and mark the sentences T (true) or F (false).
   1 ☐ The article says that playing computer games at home is trendy.
   2 ☐ Gaming events are popular in the UK because English is the common language of gamers.
   3 ☐ Some of the famous gamers are children.
   4 ☐ Video game events are similar to traditional events.
   5 ☐ Fans watch celebrity gamers on screen.

3 Decide if each statement shows Stuart's (S) or Marcela's (M) opinion about Insomnia. Read their comments again and check.
   1 ☐ It's a good place to talk to other gamers.
   2 ☐ Parties without screens and headphones are better.
   3 ☐ It's a good opportunity to share game strategy.
   4 ☐ I prefer watching gaming events online.
   5 ☐ It's an opportunity to practise my English.

4 In pairs, discuss the questions.
   1 Which statements from Exercise 3 do you agree with? Why?
   2 Are events like Insomnia popular where you live?

Two different festivals

5 VISIBLE THINKING In pairs, follow these steps.
   SEE
   1 Describe the actions of someone doing one of the activities in the photos to your partner. Be as accurate as you can.
   THINK
   2 Which activity looks more fun/challenging? Why?
   WONDER
   3 What else would you like to know about the activities in the photos?

6 ▶ 36 Watch Part 1 of the video and complete the sentences.
   1 Most of the people at the Insomnia Festival are there to _____ computer games.
   2 One of the teens interviewed thinks that gaming is a legitimate _____.
   3 Last year the global audience was more than _____.
   4 The reporter concludes that gaming is evolving and _____ all the time.

7 ▶ 37 Watch Part 2 of the video and mark the sentences T (true) or F (false). Correct the false sentences.
   1 ☐ BMXing and parkour are part of the Festival of Neighbourhood.
   2 ☐ Stick says that graffiti dates back to very ancient times.
   3 ☐ We see the dance troop Zoo Nation performing outdoors.
   4 ☐ The Festival of Neighbourhood celebrates both music and sport.

PROJECT TIME

8 In groups of four, create a digital leaflet for a festival of street art. Follow these steps.

1 In your group, discuss how your leaflet could attract people to the festival. Then decide who will prepare information about four activites during the festival. The activities might include parkour, street dancing, street painting, BMX biking or your own ideas. Find answers to these questions.
   • When and where will each activity take place?
   • What skills and techniques will the performers present?
   • What are the attractions prepared for the participants?

2 Individually, prepare your part of the leaflet.
   • Find the information and photos for your part of the leaflet.
   • Write a short text about your activity and add photos.

3 In your group, prepare your leaflet. You can use a leaflet maker app.
   • Put all the texts and photos together.
   • Think of a catchy title for your leaflet.
   • Decide on a layout.
   • Check and edit your leaflet.

4 Share your leaflet with the class.
   • Answer other students' questions.
   • Ask questions and comment on the other leaflets.

Progress Check Units 1–9

Vocabulary and Grammar

1 Choose the correct answer.
1 My dad, ____ hobby is writing fiction, has won a prize in a short story competition!
   a whose   b which   c that
2 I didn't want other people to hear what I was saying, so I ____ my voice.
   a raised   b lowered   c reduced
3 Of course they lost the game. They played ____ !
   a terrified   b terrible   c terribly
4 Do you know how long ____ ?
   a will my appointment last
   b will last my appointment
   c my appointment will last
5 Paintings of classic art will be ____ display at the gallery until the end of July.
   a on   b in   c at
6 Let's ____ a surprise party for Jeremy!
   a bring   b put   c throw
7 Our local news stories will ____ after these headlines.
   a show   b shown   c be shown
8 I ____ manage to finish my essay last night.
   a couldn't   b didn't   c wasn't

2 Complete the second sentence with the word in bold so that it means the same as the first one. Use no more than five words.
1 Someone has put up the decorations. **HAVE**
   The decorations *have been put* up.
2 'Do you like rap music?' I asked John. **INTO**
   I asked John _____ rap music.
3 They don't make us play competitive sports at our school. **HAVE**
   We _____ competitive sports at our school.
4 Companies can't leave leaflets in our building. **ALLOWED**
   Companies _____ leave leaflets in our building.
5 We went to bed late last night. **STAYED**
   We _____ late last night.
6 It's a good idea to eat salad with your lunch. **SHOULD**
   Salad _____ with your lunch.

3 Complete the text with one word in each gap.

When all my family ¹*get* together, we take a family photo. Our neighbour, ²_____ is a wedding photographer, takes it. He tells us what to do: smile, stand ³_____ straighter, etc. It's a great photo when we ⁴_____ to get it right. I'm very keen ⁵_____ our family photo tradition. I know that we'll be ⁶_____ to look at the photos in the future and remember good times. But my sister doesn't like it when her photo ⁷_____ taken. I'm surprised because she always ⁸_____ incredible in them. I hope we'll have a photo next month because I'm ⁹_____ eighteen!

Speaking

4 Choose the correct option.
A: Can I help you?
B: That ¹would / can be great, thanks. I was ²asking / wondering what book to buy for my mum's birthday.
A: In my ³idea / opinion, this detective story is good. Do you ⁴happen / mean to know if she likes crime?
B: I'm not ⁵know / sure. She likes fiction, but she's more ⁶keen / interested in art.
A: Oh great! This is the best biography of Vincent Van Gogh, as far as I'm ⁷appreciated / concerned.
B: Sorry, what I ⁸meant / tried was she would like a novel about art.
A: I understand. I don't know what to ⁹suggest / help, I'm afraid.
B: It's no ¹⁰worries / problem. Thank you for your help ¹¹anyway / welcome.

5 In pairs, plan an end-of-year party for your class. Follow these steps.
1 Add more ideas to each group.
   • a gift for your teacher: flowers, …
   • a picture on the card for your teacher: a class photo, …
   • music for the party: disco, …
   • party food: pizza, …
2 Compare the ideas in step 1. Give your opinion and make a decision for each item.
   A: *In my opinion, disco is better because …*
   B: *I think so too.*
3 Decide who will organise what.
   A: *I can organise the food.*
   B: *Thanks, I appreciate it.*

Listening

6 'Life drawing' means looking at real people and drawing them. What do you think might be difficult about it? Discuss in pairs.

7 🔊 PC1–9.1 Listen to an interview with an artist and choose the correct answer.
1. When Hannah describes life drawing, we learn
   a that she needs an art room.
   b that she can do it anywhere where there are people.
   c that festivals are the best places to do it.
2. Why did Hannah decide to draw the man on the train?
   a She was bored.
   b He didn't know she drew him.
   c Her mum asked her to do it.
3. What is true about the pictures Hannah gave to advertisers?
   a The people in her life had liked them.
   b They told her what kind of people they needed on them.
   c They were later shown in an art gallery.
4. What is true about how Hannah draws?
   a We can only see people in her pictures.
   b She only uses ideas from photographs when they show the right moment.
   c It is important how she feels about what she's drawing.
5. The people Hannah draws don't cause problems because
   a she always sends them a copy of the drawing later.
   b they often don't realise what's happening.
   c she only draws them when they're asleep.

Reading

8 🔊 PC1–9.2 Read the article. Complete the gaps with sentences a–g. There are two extra sentences. Listen and check.
   a The people were already getting ready.
   b There were flowers everywhere to show that.
   c There are parades through their streets.
   d People need to show their love and they need to laugh.
   e People celebrate in their houses too.
   f That's why not everyone is into celebrating special occasions.
   g It isn't just about flowers – spring and summer is when our fruit and vegetables grow.

DON'T FORGET MAY DAY!

We all know and enjoy the biggest events of the year, like New Year, for example. People always remember April Fool's Day and Valentine's Day. The reason is that these days are connected to the strongest things we like to feel. ^{1}____ So they are still as popular as ever. But I want to give some examples of less well-known holidays and explain why it's important to celebrate those too.

Some people disagree because they say we already have enough celebrations. Organising festivals and celebrations is an expensive business. Decorations and costumes need to be bought, and people have to take time off work. ^{2}____ They prefer to stay at home, ignore tradition and not take part in the dancing and fun. But maybe they should try it!

That's what I did recently at a May Day celebration in Oxford, and I came away with a much more positive opinion. May Day celebrates the power of the sun to make things grow. ^{3}____ The May Queen even wore some in her hair. The May Queen, dressed up in white, walked at the head of the parade. People were dancing and folk music was playing.

Another old traditional festival is St George's Day, which, in England, is connected to the story of how Saint George killed a terrible dragon. Since then, England has had wars and other problems – more real than dragons! St George's Day gives the nation hope in difficult times, and many towns and villages still celebrate it. ^{4}____ Some people look forward to the atmosphere and the costumes. Unfortunately, many others don't even know the date: 23 April.

May Day, St George's Day and other less well-known celebrations should be more popular. They aren't just a reason for people to dance in the streets and have a good time. May Day reminds us how important nature is. ^{5}____ And St George's Day reminds the country it can come out on top against problems. St George gave us hope and nature gives us food. Those are important things to remember too.

Writing

9 Write an email inviting a friend to join you and a small group of friends on a day out in the city. Include this information.
- Start your email in a friendly way.
- Invite your friend to join you.
- Explain two or three things you are planning.
- Say that you hope your friend can come.
- End the email in a friendly way.

Grammar Time

1.2
Present tenses

Present Simple and Present Continuous
She often *takes* the bus to school. (routine)
He *lives* in Madrid. (permanent situation)
He*'s talking* to his friends right now. (present action)
She's from Brazil, but she*'s studying* in the UK.
(temporary situation)

State and dynamic verbs
State verbs don't normally have a continuous form. Here are some common state verbs: *be, believe, belong, cost, hate, know, like, love, mean, need, prefer, remember, seem, understand, want, wish.*
Some verbs can be state or dynamic, depending on the meaning.
I *think* he's right. (opinion)
What *is* he *thinking* about? (mental process)
I *see* her – she's round the corner. (sense)
I'm *seeing* Peter a lot these days. (action: meet up with)
I *have* a dog. (possession)
I'm *having* lunch. (action)
The soup *tastes/smells* lovely. (quality)
I'm *tasting/smelling* the soup. (action)
Some verbs work both in the simple and continuous forms, but with no change in meaning.
I *feel* tired./I'm *feeling* tired.

1 Choose the correct option. Which verb can be used in the Present Simple or Present Continuous?

✉

Hi Sara,

How are you? I ¹*enjoy / 'm enjoying* my new school. There are lots of after-school clubs and I ²*belong / 'm belonging* to the Drama Club now. We ³*meet up / 're meeting* up every Friday. At the moment the club ⁴*prepares / is preparing* for a show and they ⁵*want / 're wanting* me to be in it. I ⁶*think / 'm thinking* about it and I ⁷*like / 'm liking* the idea, but I ⁸*feel / 'm feeling* a bit anxious about it. What ⁹*do you think / are you thinking* I should do?

Sam

2 Do you belong to a club or have a hobby? Write a few sentences using the Present Simple and Present Continuous and the phrases below.
- I belong to …
- My hobby is …
- I usually/often/always …
- At the moment I/we …

3 In pairs, share your sentences from Exercise 2. Tell the class about your partner.

1.4
Past Simple, Past Continuous and Present Perfect

Past Simple
She *arrived* yesterday. (finished action)
They *studied* every day. (repeated action)
Watch out for spelling changes in regular verbs:
study – stud*ied*   drop – drop*ped*

Past Continuous
Last night/At six o'clock she *was talking* to her friend. (action in progress)

Past Simple and Past Continuous
I *was climbing* the mountain *when* I *fell*.
While I *was sleeping*, the phone *rang*.
(background action interrupted by another action)

Present Perfect
I*'ve had* lunch. I'm not hungry. (result in the present)
They*'ve* never *been* to India. (experience)
We often use adverbs such as *never, ever, just, yet, recently* and *already* with the Present Perfect.
I*'ve just got* up. I *haven't had* breakfast *yet*.

Present Perfect and Past Simple
I*'ve been* to this theatre before. I *came* here with my parents last year. (experience/recent event and a completed action in the past)

1 Choose the correct option.
1 It *rained / was raining* when I *woke up / was waking up*.
2 While I *swam / was swimming*, I *lost / was losing* my watch.
3 I *jogged / was jogging* in the park when I *met / was meeting* my friend.
4 He *broke / was breaking* his leg while he *learned / was learning* to ski.

2 Make questions. Use the Past Simple, Past Continuous or Present Perfect.
1 you / ever / win / a competition / ?
2 what / you / do / at 8 a.m. this morning / ?
3 where / you / go / yesterday / ?
4 the sun / shine / when you / get up / this morning / ?

3 In pairs, ask and answer the questions in Exercise 2. Tell the class about your partner.

4 Write an email to a friend you haven't seen for at least a month. Tell him/her any interesting things that have happened since you last met.

2.2
Past Perfect

We use the Past Perfect to talk about an action that happened before a particular time in the past. For this reason, we often use it with the Past Simple.
We **had done** our homework.
They **hadn't seen** our house.
Had he **bought** the present? Yes, he **had**./No, he **hadn't**.

8 p.m.	9 p.m.	9.30 p.m.	10 p.m.
	Maria left.	I arrived.	

Maria **had left** the party when I **arrived**.

Time expressions
after, already, before, by the time, just, never, until
We **had finished** our lunch **by the time** they **arrived**.
Before she **watched** the documentary, Sally **hadn't thought** much about pollution.
I **hadn't heard** about Luke's news **until** Kelly **told** me.
He started recycling more **after** he **had learned** where his rubbish **went**.
They **had** never **been** to the café **before**.

1 Complete the text with the Past Perfect or Past Simple form of the verbs in brackets.

> Until last year I ¹*had read* (read) about solar energy only in my school books and I ² _____ (never/see) a solar panel. Then last year my uncle ³ _____ (fill) the fields on his farm with solar panels. Before that, he ⁴ _____ (grow) potatoes in the field. My uncle ⁵ _____ (not think) of doing it before, but another local farmer gave him the idea. ⁶ _____ (I/ever/imagine) that my uncle's fields ⁷ _____ (can) produce renewable energy? No, never!

2 Write a few sentences about things you had and hadn't done by the time you were five. Use the Past Perfect and the Past Simple, and a suitable time expression.

By the time I was five, I had learned to walk and talk. I hadn't learned to ride a bike – I learned that when I was about seven. I had never …

3 Write six true sentences about yourself. Use the Past Perfect and the Past Simple with six different time expressions.

4 In pairs, share your sentences from Exercise 3. Tell the class about your partner.

2.4
Used to and Past Simple

We use *used to* to talk about actions that happened regularly in the past, but that don't happen anymore or about things that were true in the past, but aren't true now.
We **used to stay** with my gran every summer holiday.
She **used to have** long hair.

In the negative and question form, we drop the *-d*:
I **didn't use to** play basketball when I was younger.
Did he **use to** live here? Yes, he **did**./No, he **didn't**.

We can't use *used to* to talk about things that happened once. We use the Past Simple.
~~We used to go on holiday to Brazil last year.~~
We **went** on holiday to Brazil last year.

We can use both the Past Simple and *used to* to describe regular actions in the past.
We **used to go/went** on holiday to Brazil every year.

1 Complete the dialogue with *used to* and the correct form of the verbs in brackets.

Mum: I ¹*used to go* (go) to this school.
Jo: Really? What ² _____ (it/be) like?
Mum: It ³ _____ (be) much smaller. Not so many people ⁴ _____ (live) in the town. We all ⁵ _____ (walk) to school every day. And there ⁶ _____ (not be) so many cars on the roads.

2 Make questions with *used to*.

> **My country thirty years ago**
> 1. many people / recycle / all their plastic and paper?
> 2. the countryside / be / more or less polluted?
> 3. people / waste / less energy?
> 4. people / throw away / more or less rubbish?

3 In pairs, ask and answer the questions in Exercise 2. Tell another pair about your answers.

A: *Did many people use to recycle all their plastic and paper?*
B: *No, I don't think many people used to recycle thirty years ago.*

4 Choose one of the questions from Exercise 2 and write a few sentences about your town. Use *used to* and the Past Simple.

Grammar Time

3.2

Present Perfect Continuous

We use the Present Perfect Continuous for:
- actions that started in the past and continue in the present.
  I*'ve been waiting* for two hours. (I'm still waiting.)
- actions that started in the past and have results in the present.
  She*'s been playing* basketball all morning.
  (She's feeling tired now.)
  Have they *been watching* the fashion show?
  Yes, they *have*./No, they *haven't*.

Time expressions
all day/ night, recently, How long … ?
since last Friday/ October/ Saturday/ I woke up
for two hours/three years/a long time/ages

1 Complete the sentences with the Present Perfect Continuous form of the verbs below.

collect   practise   save   wait   ~~write~~

1 Anna *has been writing* her own fashion blog since January.
2 We _____ for Jack for half an hour – and he's still not ready!
3 My brother _____ baseball caps since he was little. He's got over fifty!
4 They _____ their dance for the show all morning.
5 I _____ my money to buy a jacket.

2 Complete the questions with the Present Perfect Continuous form of the verbs in brackets.

1 There's chocolate all round your mouth! _____ (you/eat) chocolate cake?
2 You've got lots of nice clothes. _____ (you/shop) recently?
3 Your jacket's really wet! _____ (rain)?
4 Your jeans are really dirty. _____ (you/play) outside?

3 Write three sentences about yourself. Use the Present Perfect Continuous and the verbs below.

collect   learn   practise   read   save

I've been reading a really good book about the fashion business.

3.4

Present Perfect Simple and Continuous

Present Perfect Simple
They*'ve sold* a lot of jewellery. (focus on the result)
She *hasn't finished* her homework. (focus on the result)

Present Perfect Continuous
She*'s been making* her own jewellery for ages.
(focus on the duration of the activity)
We*'ve been trying on* lots of clothes today.
(focus on the fact that the activity is unfinished)

We can use *since* and *for* with both tenses.
Don't forget that with state verbs (*have, know, be*, etc.), we use the Present Perfect Simple.
They*'ve been* friends *for* a long time.

1 Complete the sentences with the Present Perfect Simple or Continuous form of the verbs in brackets.
1 I *haven't watched* (not watch) TV since Monday.
2 I _____ (learn) English since I was six.
3 I _____ (never/like) shopping.
4 I _____ (sit) here for half an hour.
5 I _____ (have) my mobile phone for five years.

2 In pairs, say if the sentences in Exercise 1 are true for you.

3 Complete the text with the words below.

been   ~~bought~~   continued   for   have
making   since   wearing

Have you ¹*bought* any jeans recently? Did you know that people have been ² _____ jeans ³ _____ more than 140 years? Over the years. jeans have ⁴ _____ both work clothes and fashion clothing. Their style has changed many times ⁵ _____ the start of their history as young people ⁶ _____ been setting new fashion trends for decades. But the original indigo blue colour has ⁷ _____ to be a favourite over the many years companies have been ⁸ _____ jeans.

4 Write sentences about your style. What have you been wearing recently? What's your favourite item of clothing? How long have you had it?

I've been wearing skinny jeans and large T-shirts a lot recently. My favourite item of clothing is …

4.2

Talking about the future

We use *will* for:
- predictions, what we think will be true in the future.
  I think people will work less in the future.
- decisions made at the moment of speaking.
  I won't have any dessert, thanks.

We use *be going to* for:
- plans and intentions.
  Rachel's going to work in the café.
- predictions based on what we know now.
  I'm not going to have time to go out with my friends.

We use the Present Continuous for arrangements, often with time expressions like *this evening, next week, in the summer, at the weekend, on Wednesday*, etc.
Joe isn't helping at the shop this weekend.

We use the Present Simple for timetables, often with times or dates.
The bus arrives at half past two.

1 Make questions. Use the future form in brackets.
1. you / go out / later / ? (Present Continuous)
   Are you going out later?
2. what / you / do / this evening / ? (Present Continuous)
3. you / buy / anything this weekend / ? (be going to)
4. what / the weather / be / like / tonight / ? (will)
5. when / this lesson / finish / ? (Present Simple)

2 In pairs, ask and answer the questions in Exercise 1.

3 Choose the correct option.
A: Hi, Adam. What ¹*are you doing / will you do* after school?
B: I ²*'m helping / help* my uncle at his café. Maybe you can meet me afterwards.
A: Sounds good! I ³*won't do / 'm not doing* anything after school. I ⁴*'ll meet / 'm going to meet* you there. What time ⁵*will you be / are you being* free?
B: My shift ⁶*is finishing / finishes* at six.

4 You are planning to watch a film at the cinema tonight and want to invite your friend. Write a short email to your friend saying what you are going to see, what time the film starts and why you think your friend will like it.

4.4

Future Continuous

We use the Future Continuous to talk about an action that will be in progress at a certain time in the future.
In the summer Tim will be working on his uncle's farm.
She won't be relaxing on a beach.
Will you be flying over the Atlantic this time tomorrow?
Yes, I will. / No, I won't.
What will you be doing?

Time expressions
- in ten minutes / a week / a month / a year / the future
  In two years, I'll be finishing school.
- at 6.45 this evening / midnight / 10 a.m. tomorrow
  At eleven o'clock tonight I'll be sleeping.
- next spring / month / year
  Next winter I'll be teaching children how to ski.
- soon
  I'll be working on a new project soon!

1 Complete the dialogues with the Future Continuous form of the verbs in brackets.
1. A: *Will you be looking* (you/look) for a full-time job when you leave school?
   B: No, I _____ (start) a beauty therapy course at college.
2. A: _____ (you/work) this summer?
   B: Yes, I will. I _____ (help) my aunt on her farm.
3. A: _____ (you/study) this afternoon?
   B: Yes, I _____ (revise) for a test.

2 Complete the email with the Future Continuous form of the verbs in brackets.

Hi Lily,

I got the summer job at the beach café! So we ¹*'ll be working* (work) together this summer. I can't wait! I'm so pleased I ² _____ (not stay) at home all summer. I hope we ³ _____ (do) the same hours. I ⁴ _____ (start) on 28 July. I ⁵ _____ (just/clean) tables in the beginning. I ⁶ _____ (not take) orders for the first week.

Anyway, speak soon!

Katy

Grammar Time

5.2

Zero, First and Second Conditionals

Zero Conditional
If you freeze water, it expands. (scientific fact)
Sarah starts to sneeze if she smells flowers. (always true)

First Conditional
We'll look at the NASA website later if we have time. (the result of another action)
Unless it's a clear night, we won't see many stars. (possibility in the future)

Second Conditional
If I was/were older, I'd train to be an astronaut. (unreal situation)
If my little sister offered to help me, I'd be amazed. (unlikely situation)

Be careful!
- When the *if* clause is at the beginning of the sentence, we put a comma after it.
- *Unless* means 'if not'.
- In the Second Conditional, we can use *was* or *were* with the first person singular.

1 Make Zero or First Conditional sentences.
1. water / freeze / if / you / cool / it to 0°C
2. you / burn / if / you / stay / in the sun any longer
3. Emma / always / call / when / she / need / help
4. we / get / better pictures for our school project / if / we / use / a drone

2 Complete the Second Conditional questions with the correct form of the verbs in brackets.
1. What <u>would you do</u> (you/do) if you <u>won</u> (win) a competition to go into space?
2. If you _____ (discover) a new planet, what _____ (you/call) it?
3. If you _____ (can) travel anywhere, where _____ (you/go)?
4. _____ (you/do) a bungee jump if your best friend _____ (ask) you to?

3 In pairs, ask and answer the questions in Exercise 2.

4 Write a few sentences to answer each question. Use the Zero, First and Second Conditionals.
1. What do you usually do if you have free time?
2. What will you do this weekend if you and your friends are free?
3. What would you do if you won the lottery?

5.4

Third Conditional

We use the Third Conditional to talk about an action in the past that did *not* happen.
If I had known you were coming, I wouldn't have gone out. (I didn't know you were coming, so I went out.)
You wouldn't have broken the camera if you had been more careful. (You weren't careful, so you broke it.)
Would you have done the parachute jump if it had been less windy? (You didn't do the parachute jump because it was very windy.)

1 Complete the Third Conditional sentences with the correct form of the verbs in brackets.
1. If she <u>hadn't studied</u> (not study) Science, she wouldn't have become an astronaut.
2. They _____ (not do) the mission if they had known about the dangers.
3. If they hadn't filmed the first landing on the moon, no one _____ (believe) it!
4. We _____ (miss) the comet if we had gone outside later.
5. If you _____ (come) to the party, you would have really enjoyed it.
6. Peter would have won if he _____ (answer) all the questions correctly.

2 Make Third Conditional questions.
1. what / you / do / today / if / you / not go / to school / ?
   What would you have done today if you hadn't gone to school?
2. where / you / go / on your last holiday / if / you / win / a lot of money / ?
3. if / you / arrive / late at school this morning / what / happen / ?
4. what / you / wear / today / if / the weather / be / different / ?
5. what / you / do / if / you / find / 1,000 euros in the street / this morning / ?

3 In pairs, ask and answer the questions in Exercise 2.

4 Write a few sentences to answer the question below. Use the Third Conditional.
If you had been born 100 years ago, how would your life have been different?

6.2
Reported statements and questions

Statements
Reported speech tells us what someone said earlier.
We usually use the verbs *said* (*to me*) or *told* (*her*).
The verb tenses change as follows:
'I feel sick.' → He told them (that) he felt sick.
'She's taking her medicine.' → They said (that) she was taking her medicine.
'Tim broke his arm.' → She said (that) Tim had broken his arm.
'They will be tired after school.' → We said (that) they would be tired after school.
'I can't get to sleep.' → She told him (that) she couldn't get to sleep.

Questions
In reported questions, the word order is the same as in statements. When we report a *yes/no* question, we use *if* or *whether*.
'Do you need to sit down?' → She asked me if/whether I needed to sit down.
When we report a *wh-* question, we use the question word. We do not use the auxiliary verb *do/does/did*.
'Where do you live?' → He asked where I lived.

Other changes
We often change pronouns, time and place expressions.
'Annabel is allergic to my cat.' → He told us (that) Annabel was allergic to his cat.
'I'll come back tomorrow.' → She said (that) she would come back the next day.
'You can wait here.' → The nurse said (that) that the girl could wait there.

1 Rewrite the sentences and questions in reported speech.
  1 'You're allergic to cats.'
    The doctor told me that _I was allergic to cats_.
  2 'Where are you going?'
    Jack asked me _____.
  3 'I've lost my appetite.'
    She told me that she _____.
  4 'Are you feeling dizzy, Emily?'
    Mum asked Emily _____.
  5 'I'll get your prescription for you, Tom.'
    She told Tom that she _____.

2 In pairs, take it in turns to ask and answer the questions. Tell another pair about your partner.
  1 What do you usually take for a sore throat?
  2 What can people do to sleep better at night?
  3 Do you ever get travel sick?
  4 Can you give five examples of healthy food?

6.4
Reported commands and requests

Requests
We usually use *ask* (*me/him*/etc.) to report requests (verb + person + *to*-infinitive).
'Can you read the information, please?' →
She asked him to read the information.
In negative requests, we use *not* before the *to*-infinitive.
'Please don't forget your appointment.' →
She asked us not to forget our appointment.

Commands
We usually use *tell* to report commands (verb + person + *to*-infinitive).
'Take the tablets with water.' →
The doctor told her to take the tablets with water.
In negative commands, we use *not* before the *to*-infinitive:
'Don't worry.' → She told us not to worry.

1 Rewrite the sentences in reported speech. Use the verbs in brackets.
  1 'Can you lend me your surfboard?' Adam said to Jenny. (ask)
    Adam asked Jenny to lend him her surfboard.
  2 'Don't use your mobile phone now!' the teacher said to the student. (tell)
  3 'Please help me with the shopping,' the man said to his children. (ask)
  4 'Stand up,' the teacher said to the pupils. (tell)
  5 'Can you follow me?' the nurse said to the visitor. (ask)
  6 'Take a deep breath, please,' the doctor said to his patient. (ask)

2 Complete the reported commands and requests in the email.

✉

Hi Theo,

Guess what I did with Matt last weekend? Bungee jumping! When Matt ¹_____ (ask/go) with him, I was a bit nervous because I'd never done it before. But he ²_____ (tell/not worry). He said I would love it! He was right! I ³_____ (tell/call) me next time he was going. He ⁴_____ (tell/bring) you too next time, and I said that would be great. So what do you think?

Sophie

Grammar Time

7.2

The passive

We use the passive when the person doing the action is not known, not important or obvious.

Present Simple
Facial expressions *are used* to show emotions.

Past Simple
They *weren't told* about the party.
Was the message *sent*?

Present Perfect
The problem *hasn't been discussed* yet.
Has the activity *been explained* to you?

Modal verbs
Drinks *cannot be taken* into the theatre.
Tickets *must be bought* in advance.

If we want to say who did the action, we use *by* + the agent (the person or thing that does the action).
The speech was made *by the head teacher*.
She was contacted *by an environmental organisation*.

1 Make passive sentences. Use the tense in brackets and add *by* if necessary.
1 the letter / write / by you / ? (Past Simple)
 Was the letter written by you?
2 we / not show / the film about communication (Present Perfect)
3 some hand gestures / consider / rude (can)
4 an email / send / after every meeting (Present Simple)
5 the school rules / follow / all students (must)

2 Complete the text with the words below.

| annoyed | are | be | been | bought | is | ~~spent~~ |

Every year more than $500 billion is ¹*spent* on advertising worldwide. Television commercials ² _____ still used by many companies, but the biggest growth has ³ _____ seen in online advertising. This is because an online advert can ⁴ _____ seen by a much larger number of people. Also, much less money ⁵ _____ spent on advertising a product online. You might be ⁶ _____ by pop-up adverts on websites, but they are very effective. The products they advertise are ⁷ _____ by many people!

3 In pairs, ask and answer questions about the text in Exercise 2. Use the passive.
How much money is spent … ?

7.4

The passive with *will*

We use *will* + *be* + past participle to talk about the future using the passive.
The information *will be repeated* later.
You *won't be given* any homework today.
Will the show *be advertised* on TV?

Be careful!
Sometimes you can form two different passive sentences from one active sentence.
Active: They will teach French to students.
Passive: French *will be taught* to students.
 Students *will be taught* French.

1 Rewrite the sentences in the passive.
1 They won't understand his pronunciation.
 His pronunciation *won't be understood*.
2 They will advertise their new product.
 Their new product _____.
3 We won't give out flyers this year.
 Flyers _____.
4 We will discuss good posture in the next lesson.
 Good posture _____.
5 They will build a bridge here.
 A bridge _____.

2 Make questions. Use the passive with *will*.
1 when / the workshop / hold / ?
2 who / it / teach / by / ?
3 which / topics / cover / ?
4 what / each student / give / ?

3 Read the flyer. In pairs, ask and answer the questions in Exercise 2.

FREE WORKSHOP: IMPROVE YOUR BODY LANGUAGE!

Every Tuesday, from 4 to 5 p.m., in the sports hall, with Mr Baker

We will cover topics such as:
- making eye contact.
- improving posture.
- how to make the most of your voice.

We will give each student their own folder with information. A fun and useful workshop for everyone!

8.2

Modal verbs for ability

Present
We *can*/*can't* draw.
Can he sing? Yes, he *can*./No, he *can't*.
He *is able to*/*isn't able to* read books in Russian.
Are they *able to* come? Yes, they *are*./No, they *aren't*.

Past
She *could*/*couldn't* run very fast.
Could she paint? Yes, she *could*./No, she *couldn't*.
They *were*/*weren't able to* finish the book.
Were they *able to* help? Yes, they *were*./
No, they *weren't*.

manage to
We use *manage to* to talk about specific achievements.
We *managed to*/*didn't manage to* go to the party.
Did Ann *manage to* complete her painting?
Yes, she *did*./No, she *didn't*.

Future
They*'ll be*/*won't be able to* come to the meeting.
Will you *be able to* join us? Yes, I *will*./No, I *won't*.

1 Complete the sentences with the words below.

> able   could   ~~couldn't~~   managed   to   will

1 I *couldn't* write my name until I started school.
2 After watching the play, the students were _____ to write about it.
3 Next year we'll be able _____ see the film version of this book.
4 We _____ to get the book we wanted from the library.
5 The teacher _____ be able to help you.
6 He _____ paint very well when he was just five years old.

2 In pairs, ask and answer the questions.
1 What couldn't you do last year that you can do now?
2 Can you paint or draw?
3 Will you be able to meet up with your friends this weekend?
4 Did you manage to finish all your homework last night?

> A: What couldn't you do last year that you can do now?
> B: Last year I couldn't do handstands. Now I can do handstands and cartwheels.

8.4

Modal verbs for obligation and prohibition

Obligation
We use *must* or *have to* to talk about present obligation, but we only use *have to* for past or future obligation.
She *had to*/*will have to* help him.
You *must* be home before nine. / You *have to* be home before nine.

Lack of obligation
We use *not have to* to show lack of obligation in the present, past and future.
We *don't*/*didn't*/*won't have to* read the book.

Prohibition
We use *mustn't*, *can't* or *(not) be allowed to* for something that is prohibited.
We *mustn't*/*aren't allowed to* touch the sculptures.
We can only use *be allowed to* for the past or future and to form questions.
I *wasn't*/*won't be allowed to* touch the sculptures.
Are they *allowed to* touch the sculptures?
Yes, they *are*./No, they *aren't*.

1 Choose the correct option.
1 You *don't have to* / *mustn't* be good at art to enjoy it.
2 We *don't have to* / *aren't allowed to* leave until we have finished.
3 You *don't have to* / *mustn't* be late for class.
4 It was raining, so we *must* / *had to* finish our paintings inside.

2 Read what Ben says. In pairs, ask and answer questions about him.

1 At school we mustn't use mobile phones.
2 At weekends I'm allowed to stay up late.
3 At home I don't have to wash the dishes.
4 When I was younger, I wasn't allowed to play computer games.
5 Next year I'll be able to learn another foreign language.

> A: Is Ben allowed to use a mobile phone at school?
> B: No, he isn't.

3 Write sentences like Ben's that are true for you.

At school we mustn't take food into the classroom.

Grammar Time **133**

Grammar Time

9.2

Defining and non-defining relative clauses

Defining relative clauses
We don't use commas in defining relative clauses.
That's the hotel *where our prom will be held*.
Tom's the boy *whose birthday we're celebrating*.

We can use *that* instead of *which* or *who*.
I'd like to find some shoes *which/that* go with this dress.
These are the boys *who/that* helped me.

When *that*, *which*, *who* or *where* is the object of a defining relative clause, we can leave it out.
I'm wearing the prom dress *that I bought last month*./
I'm wearing the prom dress *I bought last month*.

Non-defining relative clauses
We use commas in non-defining relative clauses.
Lee, *who is my best friend*, is a really good dancer.
Liam, *whose sister is in my class*, is a DJ.
We can't use *that* instead of *which* or *who*.
~~This jacket, that was a present from my mum, is my favourite.~~
This jacket, *which* was a present from my mum, is my favourite.

1 Complete the sentences with *who*, *which*, *whose* or *where*.
1. This is the house <u>where</u> we were living when I was ten.
2. Look at the ring _____ I bought.
3. My brother, _____ wedding was last Saturday, is now in Bali with his wife.
4. These are the earrings _____ I bought my mum for Mother's Day.
5. This is the field _____ they'll let off the fireworks after the show.
6. Amanda, _____ made my costume, is an Art teacher at the local college.

2 Look at the sentences in Exercise 1 again. Which relative clauses are defining and which are non-defining? In which sentences can you leave out the relative pronoun?

3 Write down the name of a person, the name of a place and a possession which are special to you. In pairs, take it in turns to tell your partner why they are so important. Use relative clauses.

She/He is the person who …
This is the place where …
This is the watch/guitar that/which …

9.4

Direct and indirect questions

We often use indirect questions when we want to ask about something more politely. The word order in indirect questions is the same as in statements and we don't use the auxiliary verbs *do*, *does* or *did*.
We use different expressions like *could you tell me*, *I was wondering* and *do you know*.

Wh- questions
Direct: When does the festival take place?
Indirect: *Do you have any idea when* the festival *takes place*?
Direct: Who did you take to the prom?
Indirect: *I was wondering who* you *took* to the prom.

Yes/No questions
Direct: Does the fireworks display start at 9 p.m.?
Indirect: *Do you know if* the fireworks display *starts* at 9 p.m.?

1 Complete the indirect questions.
1. Where's Sam?
   Do you have any idea <u>where Sam is</u>?
2. Did you hear that bang?
   I was wondering _____.
3. What colour is the flag of your country?
   Could you tell me _____?
4. What do I need to wear to the party?
   Do you have any idea _____?
5. Do you believe that black cats bring bad luck?
   I'd like to know _____.

2 In pairs, write one or two indirect questions for each situation.

1. I'm hungry – I hope dinner's soon!

   I was wondering when dinner will be ready.
   Could you tell me what time dinner will be ready, please?

2. I've no idea what this food is!

3. I hope the parade finishes soon – I'm tired!

4. Is it the custom to make a toast? I don't know!

5. I don't know what's for homework.

Irregular Verbs

🔊 10.1

Infinitive	Past Simple	Past Participle
be	was/were	been
beat	beat	beaten
become	became	become
begin	began	begun
bet	bet	bet
bite	bit	bitten
blow	blew	blown
break	broke	broken
bring	brought	brought
build	built	built
burn	burned/burnt	burned/burnt
buy	bought	bought
can	could	been able to
catch	caught	caught
choose	chose	chosen
come	came	come
cost	cost	cost
cut	cut	cut
deal	dealt	dealt
dig	dug	dug
do	did	done
draw	drew	drawn
dream	dreamed/dreamt	dreamed/dreamt
drink	drank	drunk
drive	drove	driven
eat	ate	eaten
fall	fell	fallen
feed	fed	fed
feel	felt	felt
fight	fought	fought
find	found	found
fly	flew	flown
forget	forgot	forgotten
forgive	forgave	forgiven
freeze	froze	frozen
get	got	got
give	gave	given
go	went	gone
grow	grew	grown
hang	hung	hung
have	had	had
hear	heard	heard
hide	hid	hidden
hit	hit	hit
hold	held	held
hurt	hurt	hurt
keep	kept	kept
know	knew	known

Infinitive	Past Simple	Past Participle
lay	laid	laid
lead	lead	lead
learn	learned/learnt	learned/learnt
leave	left	left
lend	lent	lent
let	let	let
lie	lay	lain
lose	lost	lost
make	made	made
mean	meant	meant
meet	met	met
pay	paid	paid
put	put	put
read	read	read
ride	rode	ridden
ring	rang	rung
rise	rose	risen
run	ran	run
say	said	said
see	saw	seen
sell	sold	sold
send	sent	sent
set	set	set
shine	shone	shone
show	showed	shown
shut	shut	shut
sing	sang	sung
sit	sat	sat
sleep	slept	slept
speak	spoke	spoken
spell	spelled/spelt	spelled/spelt
spend	spent	spent
stand	stood	stood
steal	stole	stolen
strike	struck	struck
swear	swore	sworn
sweep	swept	swept
swim	swam	swum
take	took	taken
teach	taught	taught
tell	told	told
think	thought	thought
throw	threw	thrown
understand	understood	understood
wake	woke	woken
wear	wore	worn
win	won	won
write	wrote	written

Grammar Time

Student Activities

Unit 1 — Lesson 1.6 Exercise 7

Student A
1. Ask Student B to help you with your homework.
2. Student B has lost his/her phone. Offer to help find it.

Student B
3. Ask Student A to help you do the dishes.
4. Student A isn't feeling well. Offer to help.

Unit 1 — Revision Exercise 5

Student A

Situation 1
1. You have problems understanding your phone (think of a specific problem). Ask Student B for help.
2. Accept Student B's offer and listen to his/her advice.
3. Thank Student B.

Situation 2
You walk by while Student B is moving some heavy boxes. Offer to help.

Unit 2 — Lesson 2.1 Exercise 7

The environment quiz

Answers
1. The easiest thing to recycle is aluminium cans.
2. It usually takes about eight hours to fully charge an empty battery.
3. Iceland gets ninety percent of its energy from hot water under the ground!
4. An electric shower uses the most energy in five minutes.
5. Trees take in the most carbon dioxide.

Unit 2 — Revision Exercise 8

Student A
1. Say one of these sentences to Student B. He/She will agree, partially agree or disagree. Have a conversation.
   - Zoos are a good way to protect endangered animals.
   - Keeping pets is a great way to learn about animals.
   - It's better not to walk alone in forests because dangerous animals live there.
2. Listen to Student B's sentence and agree, partially agree or disagree.
3. Continue the conversation.

Unit 4 — Lesson 4.7 Exercise 2

A

Summer staff needed at City Souvenirs

We are looking for shop assistants for our busy gift shop. You must be reliable, friendly and enjoy speaking to customers. A second language is preferred as many of our customers are tourists from other countries. The positions are part-time and you will work mostly at weekends. Visit our website for more info.

B

Star summer job!

Little Stars Summer Camp is looking for activity leaders to organise activities for children aged 5–8. You will work as part of a team, and activities will include arts and crafts and sports. Working hours are between 1 p.m. and 5 p.m., Monday to Friday. So, if you love working with children and have lots of energy, please write to: littlestars@pmail.com.uk.

C

Train on the job

Are you organised? Have you got good people skills? The South London Arts Centre is looking for a part-time receptionist for the months of July and August. An interest in art and some experience of working with the public is an advantage. You must be available at weekends. For more information, please email us at info.ccc@qmail.com or call 0786 5542 1342.

Unit 5 — Revision Exercise 6

Student A
1. Give Student B instructions for drinking from a water bottle in zero gravity. Use words/phrases like *first, then, next, after that, you need to, it's important to … , try to*, etc.
   Begin: *I'm going to give you instructions for …*
   Give instructions following the prompts below.
   - hold bottle near face
   - squeeze out small amount of water
   - wait for water to form a ball in the air
   - move head forward, catch water in mouth
   Finish: *OK, now try it!*
2. Now listen to Student B's instructions and respond. Use words/phrases like *Of course., Sure., No worries., Now what?, I hope it works.*

Unit 6 Revision Exercise 5

Student A

1. Ask Student B for advice for each of the problems below.
   - My cat is at the top of a tree and can't come down.
   - I feel sick after eating fish in a restaurant.
   - My back aches when I work on my computer for a long time.
2. Now listen to Student B's problems. Give advice or explain that you cannot give advice.

Unit 7 Revision Exercise 4

coffee

Unit 8 Revision Exercise 6

Discuss the things below. Follow these steps for each one.

1. Compare both options. Use phrases like *on the one hand … , but on the other hand … ; personally, I think … is more … than …*
2. Take turns to give your opinion on each option. Use phrases like *in my opinion, … is …*
3. Together, decide which option is better.

> two classroom decorations: some plants or a wall map of the world

> two paintings for the main school hall: a landscape or a portrait

> two sculptures for the school reception area: a rare animal or an athlete (not a famous one)

> two themes for a school photography exhibition: unusual fashion or wildlife in the city

Unit 9 Lesson 9.6 Exercise 7

In pairs, write a dialogue for one of these situations. Use phrases from the Speaking box on page 118 to help you. Then act out your dialogue to another pair.

1. You meet a celebrity and want to take a selfie with him/her.
2. You tell your head teacher about why you missed an exam.
3. You meet a foreigner and want to find out where he/she is from.
4. On your first day at a new school, you can't find the gym.

Unit 9 Revision Exercise 5

Student A

When you start the conversation:
1. attract the attention of Student B politely.
2. ask (for) something politely. Choose one of these things.
   - You want Student B to pass the water jug.
   - You want to know if there are any games planned.
   - You want to know when guests can ask questions.
   - You are interested in what Student B might like to study at the college.
3. Listen to Student B's answers and thank him/her.

When you answer:
1. listen and respond to Student B's request/question.
2. respond when he/she thanks you for your help.

Student Activities **137**

ENVIRONMENT

CLIL 1

Digital carbon footprints

Every time you send an email, a message, a photograph or post something on social media, you save paper. However, you leave behind a trail of your digital carbon footprint.

Why is this bad?

You may think that the internet has no impact on the physical world, but we store all the information on different websites, apps and social media on computer servers. These are big rooms with different equipment and computers. They all use a lot of electricity. These rooms need to be cool, so we use more equipment and more electricity to keep the temperature low. So electricity makes our lives easier and better, but its production increases our carbon footprint. These emissions heat up our planet.

All information, pictures and music on the internet travel in small packets called data. So when we do an online search, the question we have typed in the computer becomes data. The computer sends this data to the servers. They then process the question and send it back to our computers as data. The faster the search engine works, the bigger the use of electricity. We use the most electricity when we watch a video online. This is because a lot of data travels to and from the server, especially if the video is high resolution.

Different types of technology need different amounts of electricity to work – for example, mobile phones use electromagnetic waves. These waves need more energy to move through buildings, bad weather and even plants, so again, the use of electricity is bigger. Cloud computing also uses a lot of energy because instead of saving your material on a memory stick or on your computer, you store it on the server. So again, more data travels back and forth between the servers and the computers, using large amounts of energy.

What can you do?

One way to stop this waste is to always update your apps or software to make sure they are more efficient. For example, an old word processing tool needs four times more energy to work than a new one. Another way is to think before we click on that button: do you really need to watch that video for the tenth time?

1 Look at the photos. What do they show? What's the connection between them?

2 🔊 10.2 What do you think a digital carbon footprint is? Discuss in pairs. Then read the article and check your ideas.

3 Read the article again and answer the questions.
1. What are servers?
2. Why do servers use a lot of energy?
3. How does information on the internet travel?
4. Why do high resolution videos use more energy?
5. Why do mobile phones do more damage than computers?
6. Why should our apps always be up-to-date?

4 Do you think you will use your computer and mobile phone differently after reading the article? How can you reduce your digital carbon footprint? Discuss in pairs.

5 **GO ONLINE** Use the internet to find out more about digital carbon footprints. Find how big the footprint is for:
- sending and receiving emails.
- using social apps.
- streaming music and videos.
- using search engines.

6 **SHARE IT** Create a short presentation. Write a paragraph about digital carbon footprints and add pictures or graphs and statistics. Share your presentation with the class.

ART AND DESIGN — CLIL 2

Fashion

In historical terms, the idea of fashion design is quite new. Charles Worth, who was from England, is thought to be the first fashion designer. He set up his fashion house in Paris in 1858. Before Worth people usually asked dressmakers to create what they, the client, wanted. Charles Worth did the opposite – he told his customers what to wear! He set trends and established the job of a fashion designer. Design houses like his started to employ artists to sketch pictures of clothes to show their clients, instead of making complete garments, which was very expensive, especially if the client didn't like them! The clients made choices and orders from the drawings. The fashion houses started to earn a lot of money. Today fashion houses and top designers control what we all wear, from hats to shoes and everything in between. There are three types of clothes that designers and manufacturers produce today.

Haute couture
This is also called 'bespoke tailoring' and is the most expensive and exclusive clothing to buy. A garment is made specifically to fit one person only. The fabric that is used is very good quality and the garment is almost completely created and sewn by hand, which takes a long time. Because of the cost of creating the clothes, haute couture doesn't make a big profit, but it is excellent for the reputation of the designer and the fashion house.

Ready-to-wear
Ready-to-wear clothes are not as expensive as haute couture. They are produced using good quality fabrics and they are well-designed and made. However, these clothes are not created for individual people, but for the general public. They are sold in standard sizes, in shops. Usually, there are only a limited number of pieces of the same design, so this means that not everyone is wearing the same dress or jacket. The designers' collections of ready-to-wear clothes are shown during fashion weeks in cities around the world twice a year.

Mass market
Most people buy this type of clothing. After top fashion designers show their collections in fashion weeks, the high street clothing companies wait to see which trends, styles and colours become popular. Then they make their own versions using cheaper materials and methods of production. These clothes don't always last very long and people throw them away regularly and replace them.

---

1 Label the photos (1–6) with the skills a fashion designer needs (a–f).

a sewing
b cutting a pattern
c using a tailor's dummy
d sketching designs
e knowing about textiles
f understanding colour theory

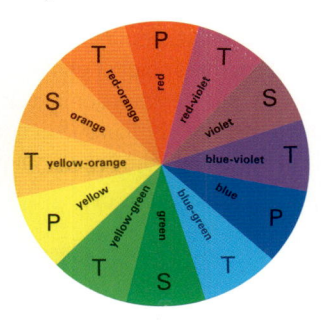

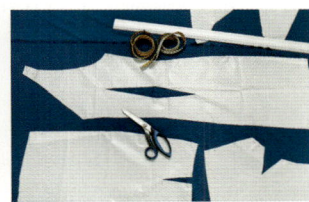

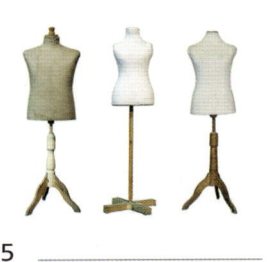

1 _____   2 _____
3 _____   4 _____
5 _____   6 _____

2 🔊 10.3 Read the article and answer the questions.
1 Who was Charles Worth?
2 How did he change the way people ordered clothes?
3 Why is haute couture expensive?
4 Where can people see new ready-to-wear trends?
5 Why can't people buy cheap versions of catwalk fashion soon after the shows?
6 Why might some people throw clothes away quite often?

3 **GO ONLINE** Use the internet to find out about a famous fashion house in your country. Make notes about its most famous designer(s), its history and its recent designs.

4 **SHARE IT** Create a fact file about the fashion house. Add pictures. Share your fact file with the class.

SCIENCE

CLIL 3

HEALTHY BRAINS

1 ____
Our brains are very complicated organs. As they get older, the nerve cells die, connections between nerve cells are lost and the brain gets smaller and lighter. This affects all our brain functions – our memory, our thinking skills and our emotions. However, people's brains age at different speeds. Why is that? And can we protect the brain against ageing?

2 ____
Scientists used to think that the speed of brain ageing was a result of genetics, that it ran in the family, but now they say only twenty-five percent of the differences are a result of genetics. Seventy-five percent are a result of our upbringing and lifestyle. So, it is possible for people to do things to keep their brains young.

3 ____
Exercise plays an important role. Some exercise such as table tennis, which is fast and competitive, and where you have to think very quickly, can improve the connections between nerve cells and affects our ability to solve problems. It can also make us happier and less depressed. Exercise like fast walking can help our memory. This might be because aerobic exercise can create new neurons.

4 ____
Food, of course, is also important. Scientists believe that a particular pigment, a natural plant colouring, helps the brain stay young. It can be found in vegetables and fruit that are blue, purple and red such as purple sweet potatoes, red cabbage, blackcurrants, blueberries and blackberries. It is also believed to help form new nerve connections.

5 ____
Research has also shown that education plays a big part in protecting our brains as we get older. The more new things we learn when we're younger (and throughout our lives), the better for our brains. Some people believe that learning a second language is one of the best ways to keep our brains healthy.

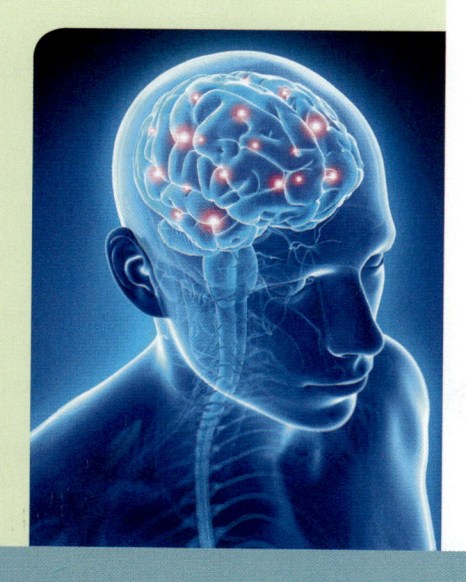

1 In pairs, discuss the questions.
1. How do you think our brains change as we get older?
2. What things can people do to improve their memory as they get older?

2 Read the article quickly and check your ideas from Exercise 1.

3 🔊 10.4 Read the article again and match paragraphs 1–5 with headings a–e. Listen and check.
- a Colours are important
- b In the family?
- c Keep learning
- d Natural changes
- e Challenge is good

4 Write one sentence to summarise each of the paragraphs in the article.

5 (GO ONLINE) Use the internet to find out more about research into brain function. Make notes about:
- what the research/experiment was.
- where it was carried out.
- what the results were.
- how it can help the brain.

6 (SHARE IT) Create a short presentation. Write a paragraph about the research. Add some pictures. Share your presentation with the class.

HISTORY

CLIL 4

Guy Fawkes and the Gunpowder Plot

One of the most well-known national celebrations in the UK is 5 November. It is called Guy Fawkes Night or Bonfire Night. It commemorates an event from 1605, but not an event that happened – an event that didn't happen! If the event had taken place, English history would have been very different.

It was all about religion. At that time in England people were either Roman Catholic or Protestant (Church of England). Elizabeth I, who was a Protestant queen, treated the Catholics badly. When James I became king – although he was also a Protestant – Roman Catholics hoped he would be kinder to them. Unfortunately, this didn't happen and a group of Roman Catholic activists planned to blow up the Palace of Westminster when the King opened Parliament; this plan was called 'the Gunpowder Plot'. The leader of the group was Robert Catesby and he organised the smuggling of thirty-six barrels of gunpowder into the basement of the building. Guy Fawkes, who was the explosives expert, stayed to light the fuse. If all this gunpowder had exploded, it would have destroyed a huge area in the centre of London. Unfortunately for the plotters, Guy Fawkes and the gunpowder were discovered at the last minute and the plan failed. All the members of the gang were eventually found and punished.

After the plot, Parliament passed an act which made 5 November a national day of thanksgiving, and it has been celebrated ever since. On this day people build bonfires and make a type of doll, called the 'guy' which is put on the top of the bonfire to burn. It is a festive evening with lots of fireworks and parades in many towns. The 'guy' represents Guy Fawkes and the fireworks represent the explosion that didn't happen. Traditionally, children used to make the 'guy' and take it round the streets asking people for 'a penny for the guy'. However, this custom has almost disappeared. The celebrations on 5 November happen all round the country. However, there is one place where they don't burn a 'guy': St Peter's school in York, Guy Fawkes' old school.

1 Do you know anything about a national celebration in another country where people celebrate the life of an important person from the past?

2 🔊 10.5 Read the article quickly. How do people celebrate Guy Fawkes Night?

3 Read the article again and say why these names and numbers are important.
1 1605
2 Elizabeth I
3 James I
4 Palace of Westminster
5 Robert Catesby
6 36
7 St Peter's School

4 What new information did you learn from the article? What was the most interesting part? Why? Discuss in pairs.

5 Read two people's comments about Guy Fawkes Night. Which person do you agree with? Why? Discuss in pairs.

1 I think it's important to celebrate things like this. It's great fun to have a bonfire. In some places they make a 'guy' that looks like a politician and burn that! Great fun!

2 In my opinion, it's a horrible tradition! Burning something that represents a person – that's just old-fashioned and scary. Maybe we should just light a bonfire or maybe even forget about this custom altogether.

6 **GO ONLINE** Use the internet to find out more about a national celebration in your country. Make notes about:
- when it takes place.
- what happens.
- the history behind the event.
- how the celebration varies in different parts of the country.
- any other interesting information.

7 **SHARE IT** Create a short presentation. Write a paragraph and add some pictures. Share your presentation with the class.

Student Activities

Unit 1 Revision Exercise 5

Student B

Situation 1

Listen to Student A's problem and offer to help.

Situation 2

1. Student A walks by while you are moving some heavy boxes. Greet him/her.
2. Accept Student A's offer.
3. Thank Student A.

Unit 2 Revision Exercise 8

Student B

1. Listen to Student A's sentence and agree, partially agree or disagree.
2. Continue the conversation.
3. Say one of these sentences to Student A. He/She will agree, partially agree or disagree. Have a conversation.
   - It's a good idea to introduce pet animals to very young children.
   - We can help endangered animals by saving forests.
   - We need more national parks to protect animals.

Unit 5 Revision Exercise 6

Student B

1. Listen to Student A's instructions and respond. Use words/phrases like *Of course., Sure., No worries., Now what?, I hope it works.*
2. Now give Student A instructions for washing your hair on the International Space Station. Use words/phrases like *first, then, next, after that, you need to, it's important to … , try to,* etc.
   Begin: *I'm going to give you instructions for …*
   Give instructions following the prompts below.
   - hold shampoo bottle next to hair (no water)
   - squeeze out small amount
   - rub shampoo all over your hair
   - take a towel and rub your hair dry
   - put wet towel near air flow from air conditioning
   Finish: *OK, now try it!*

Unit 6 Revision Exercise 5

Student B

1. Listen to Student A's problems. Give advice or explain that you cannot give advice.
2. Now ask Student A for advice for each of the problems below.
   - I've dropped my phone in a fish pond and it isn't working.
   - A cute dog follows me home from school every day.
   - I played football a lot yesterday and now my legs ache.

Unit 9 Revision Exercise 5

Student B

When you start the conversation:

1. attract the attention of Student A politely.
2. ask (for) something politely. Choose one of these things.
   - You want Student B to pass a paper plate.
   - You want to know if it is OK to start eating the snacks.
   - You want to know if guests can see the educational facilities.
   - You want to know what entertainment is planned for later.
3. Listen to Student A's responses and thank him/her.

When you answer:

1. listen and respond to Student A's request/question.
2. respond when he/she thanks you for your help.

Unit 3 Lesson 3.6 Exercise 2

Pearson Education Limited
KAO Two
KAO Park
Hockham Way
Harlow, Essex
CM17 9SR
England
and Associated Companies throughout the world.

pearsonenglish.com/widerworld2e

© Pearson Education Limited 2022

All rights reserved; no part of this publication may be reproduced, stored in a retrieval system, or transmitted in any form or by any means, electronic, mechanical, photocopying, recording, or otherwise without the prior written permission of the Publishers

First published 2022

ISBN: 978-1-292-42275-6

Set in Frutiger Next Pro
Printed in Mexico

Acknowledgements

The Publishers would like to thank all the teachers and students around the world who contributed to the development of Wider World Second Edition: Milena Aleksić, Tuğba Arslantaş, Gülşah Aslan, Mahgol Baboorian, Katarzyna Beliniak, Burcu Candan, Seri Diri, Hanna Dudich, Sema Karapinar, Nadiia Kasianchuk, Duygu Kayhan, Iryna Kharchenko, Ana Krstić, Ilknur Manav, Fulya Mertoğlu, Ivana Nikolov, Banu Oflas, Duygu Özer, Jagoda Popović, Marija Šanjević, Karmen Irizar Segurola, Elif Sevinç, Ludmila Shengel, Ayşe Sönmez, Anna Standish, Natalia Tkachenko, Pamela Van Bers, Jelena Vračar, Agnieszka Woźnicka, Münevver Yanık.

The Publishers would like to thank the following people who commented on the Wider World Second Edition content: Milena Aleksić, Mahgol Baboorian, Hanna Dudich, Izabela Kołando, Karmen Irizar Segurola, Joanna Srokosz, Anna Zając.

We would also like to thank the authors of the first edition of Wider World whose work has been the basis for creating this adaptation: Kathryn Alevizos, Carolyn Barraclough, Catherine Bright, Sheila Dignen, Lynda Edwards, Rod Fricker, Suzanne Gaynor, Bob Hastings, Jennifer Heath, Liz Kilbey, Stuart McKinlay, Sarah Thorpe, Tasia Vassilatou, Damian Williams, Sandy Zervas.

Photo Acknowledgements

123RF.com: Algars Reinholds 41, Anna Schram 41, Batuhan Toker 41, Bernd Friedel 84, f8studio 110, famveldman 113, fizkes 34, Galyna Andrushko 32, Jakub Krechowicz 139, Leung Cho Pan 105, mainzahn 115, Maksym Bondarchuk 41, Mark Bowden 59, mihail39 27, olexie 93, pictrough 40, saintantonio21 103, Tamar Dundua 139, tonobalaguer 101, vvoennyy 139, wernerimages 112; **Alamy Stock Photo:** Dave G. Houser 8, Paul Quayle 121; **BBC Studios:** 23, 47, 47, 72, 73, 91, 99, 99, 123, 123; **European Space Agency (ESA):** 72; **Getty Images:** AFP 16, Alexander Medvedev 74, Besjunior 54, Blackout footage 53, Catherine Farrell 39, Charles Gullung 102, Coolpicture 76, CoreyFord 71, Craig Moore 79, Dan Porges 15, Daniel Berehulak 65, David Madison 81, DGLimages 104, Disability Images 84, Emin Kelekci 92, Evgeniia Silankovskaia 98, Fine Art 100, Gilbert Rondilla Photography 95, GlobalStock 22, gremlin 36, Heritage Images 41, 107, ilyast 87, Jonathan Leibson 64, LeoPatrizi 138, Luke Walker 122, Media News Group/The Mercury News via Getty Images 103, Michael Mcgimpsey/EyeEm 105, Mike Harrington 141, MoMo Productions 57, MStudioImages 12, Peter Dazeley 25, Phil Clarke Hill 112, Photoservice 116, Ron Levine 84, rusm 1, Sean Justice 79, Sepia Times 107, serguacom 79, SimonSkafar 50, SOPA Images 17, Stocktrek Images 69, tiero 138, Tim Graham 46, undefined undefined 74, Vifotcorp 110, Vitalii Petrushenko 75, Zolotaosen 40; **Pearson Education Ltd:** 100, Gareth Boden 14, 14, 34, 38, 64, 90, 90, 114, 114, HL Studios 139, Jon Barlow 6, 9, 10, 11, Silversun Media Group 18, 30, 42, 56, 68, 80, 94, 106, 118, 142; **Shutterstock:** 14, 34, 54, A StockStudio 21, Africa Studio 48, 105, Andiano 138, Andrey Armyagov 62, 71, AstroStar 62, Atiwan Janprom 48, Bomshtein 48, Borodin Denis 71, carballo 55, Dahabian 139, Dean Drobot 34, Delpixel 117, Dikushin Dmitry 55, Dragon Images 83, EKramar 139, Elena Schweitzer 119, FocusDzign 34, gabor2100 33, George Dolgikh 41, George Rudy 120, gypsy.aiko 26, Ivonne Wierink 34, James Steidl 71, KK.Kickin 62, Krivosheev Vitaly 110, Lightspring 140, muratart 71, Nightman1965 84, Oleg Krugliak 14, 38, 64, 90, 114, Olesya Kuznetsova 88, Olga Danylenko 110, Pavel_D 41, Pavlo S 2,3, phatymak's studio 112, Photo Volcano 19, Rafa Irusta 48, Robert Nyholm 15, RonaldL 39, Sebastian Kaulitzki 140, Stewie74 79, Sunti 71, Svitlana Hulko 58, sylv1rob1 88, Tanya Keisha 28, Tarzhanova 37, Triff 63, 70, valkoinen 48, Vera Petrunina 52, Viacheslav Nikolaenko 90, Victor Metelskiy 77; ZouZou 34

Illustrated by Gergely Fórizs (Beehive Illustration) 29; Kevin Hopgood (Beehive Illustration) 36; Adam Larkum (IllustrationX) 60,78; Maguma 35,61,85,111 (IllustrationX); Dina Rhuza (IllustrationX) 24; Martin Sanders (Beehive Illustration) 67

Cover photo © *Front:* **Getty Images:** Copyrights by Sigfrid López